Nadja-Christina Schneider / Fritzi-Marie Titzmann (eds.)

Kommunikationswissenschaft, Band 6

Nadja-Christina Schneider/Fritzi-Marie Titzmann (eds.)

Studying Youth, Media and Gender in Post-Liberalisation India

Focus on and beyond the 'Delhi Gang Rape'

Verlag für wissenschaftliche Literatur

Umschlagabbildung unter Verwendung eines Fotos von Gurinder Osan/Hindustan Times (Kerzenmahnwache im Rahmen der Proteste gegen sexuelle Gewalt in Neu-Delhi im Dezember 2012) und eines Standbildes aus dem Film „No One Killed Jessica".

ISBN 978-3-86596-535-6
ISSN 1860-8353

© Frank & Timme GmbH Verlag für wissenschaftliche Literatur
Berlin 2015. Alle Rechte vorbehalten.

Das Werk einschließlich aller Teile ist urheberrechtlich geschützt.
Jede Verwertung außerhalb der engen Grenzen des Urheberrechts-
gesetzes ist ohne Zustimmung des Verlags unzulässig und strafbar.
Das gilt insbesondere für Vervielfältigungen, Übersetzungen,
Mikroverfilmungen und die Einspeicherung und Verarbeitung in
elektronischen Systemen.

Herstellung durch die Frank & Timme GmbH
Wittelsbacherstraße 27a, 10707 Berlin
Printed in Germany.
Gedruckt auf säurefreiem, alterungsbeständigem Papier.

www.frank-timme.de

Acknowledgements

The editors wish to express their gratitude towards the German Research Foundation (DFG) for funding the research network "Medialisation and Social Change outside Europe: South Asia, Southeast Asia and the Arab-Speaking Region" (2011–2014) which provided an excellent framework for the discussion, conceptualization and realization of this volume. They would also like to thank Maruan Mourad at the Institute of Asian and African Studies for his assistance during the editorial process.

Contents

Acknowledgements 5

NADJA-CHRISTINA SCHNEIDER
Introduction 9

PART I
THE 'DELHI GANG RAPE' AS A CRITICAL MEDIA EVENT:
REPRESENTATIONS, NEW PRACTICES OF DEBATE AND
MEDIA SOCIABILITY

MAITRAYEE CHAUDHURI
National and Global Media Discourse after the savage death of 'Nirbhaya':
Instant Access and Unequal Knowledge 19

JESNA JAYACHANDRAN
Outrage, debate or silence:
An analysis of reader comments and online rape news 45

FRITZI-MARIE TITZMANN
"The Voice of the Youth" – Locating a new public sphere
between street protest and digital discussion 79

MAREN WILGER
The Delhi Gang Rape Case – Dynamics of the Online Debate
on the Social News Aggregator reddit.com 113

URMILA GOEL
The Delhi rape case and international attention –
An interview with Urvashi Butalia 133

PART II
LINKING YOUTH, GENDER AND MEDIA STUDIES:
MEDIA PRACTICES, NEW IM/MOBILITIES AND
EVOLVING SEXUAL IDENTITIES

THOMAS K. GUGLER
New Media, Neosexual Activism and Diversifying Sex Worlds
in Post-Liberalization India 143

NADJA-CHRISTINA SCHNEIDER
Filming Urban Spaces and Entangled (Im)mobilities:
Experimental Documentaries by & about Young 'Muslim Women' in Delhi 167

KABITA CHAKRABORTY
Young people's mobile phone cultures in the urban slums of Kolkata 191

List of Authors 215

NADJA-CHRISTINA SCHNEIDER

Introduction

The brutal gang rape and subsequent death of a young woman in Delhi in December 2012 led to an instant and unexpectedly huge media attention in India and almost everywhere in the world. Contrasting the intense 24x7 coverage this case received in the Indian media with the continued indifference to sexual violence against women from lower castes and classes or to rape cases in non-metropolitan regions, many critical observers saw it as yet another evidence for a very close interlocking of the urban middle class and metropolitan media companies in the political center of India. Media attention increased significantly when thousands of peaceful demonstrators endured the winter cold in order to protest against the discrimination and violence against women. Security forces reacted with disproportionate rigour, while some Indian politicians displayed the kind of machismo which made many citizens feel that the gap between the political class and the citizens, especially the younger generation, was widening even further.

Candle-light demonstrations, which had already increased in frequency and scope in India since the mid-2000s, exemplify the aesthetic rapprochement to new global urban protest forms. In addition to that, the clear interrelationship between the new digital spaces (especially the social media networks) and the physical places of protest made them look 'familiar' to media and audiences worldwide, hence the Delhi protests were quickly ranged in the new global wave of urban protests which were often labeled as 'middle class', 'youth' or 'middle class youth protests'. Sociologist Saskia Sassen, for instance, included the protests in Delhi – and in other cities in India – in the winter of 2012 and 2013 in a gradual global process in which the middle classes are increasingly disconnected from the liberal state because they don't feel represented by the state any longer. Even if the trigger and reason for the new kind of urban street protests may be very specific in every case, Sassen argued that it is always also about a larger mix of injustices, not least what she calls the "grand larceny" of tax revenues and state resources which are increasingly fed into the global corporate system:

"I think of it as grand larceny because it goes well beyond the privileges enjoyed by rich firms and rich families in all our countries. This partly explains why middle class people everywhere, from Chile to Egypt to India were taking to the streets to protest this in different ways. [I]n short, something is happening. But we don't have a language that captures this mix of conditions. [O]ne very general reason is that the social contract with the liberal state is not working any more. The elites are not affected and the super poor never got any benefits. It is the middle class which got so many benefits […], now there is a new geography of privilege and disempowerment that cuts across the old divide of rich and poor countries, or North and South. And the ones that are emerging as the contesting actors are young men and women of the middle classes. They are the ones losing the most, who feel the social contract with the state is broken."[1]

However, the widespread notion that it is above all the urban middle class youth which takes to the streets was put into perspective by Sanjay Kumar. He points out that it would be incorrect to assume that the participation in demonstrations and protests is limited only to the middle class and upper crust of society, but that it "cuts across youths with various levels of educational attainment and across economic class, though in varying proportions (Kumar, 2013:40)". Besides the social composition of protest groups another issue which triggered very interesting debates was the question whether this new form of media-cum-urban street protests is a feature of a new kind of politics. Political scientist Zoya Hasan acknowledged in an interview in 2013 that it actually is a new kind of politics and she argued that it is "a reaction to the misdemeanors of politicians and misgovernance. The middle class which dominated these protests has become assertive".[2] But at the same time, she worries that the new urban street protests have a flip side and could turn dangerous too, as this movement "has delineated itself from organized politics. It has no agenda. It is leaderless, chaotic and lacks vision".[3]

Like many other observers, Hasan fears that it could even lead to authoritarian solutions like the protesters demanding the death sentence for rapists in January 2013.[4] Other observers also noticed that the wave of the Delhi protests in the winter of 2012/13 was not led by any political party, leader or individual, which was, for instance, the case during the widely covered anti-corruption protests in 2011 which were led by Anna Hazare and his team. This time, however, the street protests were rather spontaneous and coordinated as well as mobilized largely through social media networks. So while some saw the positive potential in current protests and in the new kind of sociopolitical awareness among youth which "could take democracy to a new level and redefine the role of the people in it"[5], others felt that due to the lack of leadership and a clear ideological background, there is always the danger that the movement could be 'hi-jacked' by actors who have no concern for it.

In the German media, the coverage and discussion about the protests was much less differentiated. The impression one could get from many reports and articles was that India had never before witnessed widespread protests against the continued oppression and violence against women. Quite understandably, many Indian academics who specialize in the history of the Indian women's movement and have themselves actively supported the movement for several decades, were annoyed by the level of ignorance in global news reports and even in many background articles about India. The same applies to the knowledge production in the field of jurisdiction where feminist activists and law experts have, for instance, also laid the groundwork which enabled the Justice Verma Committee to quickly produce a report in January 2013 which provided recommendations for amendments to the Criminal Law which would provide for quicker trial and enhanced punishment of criminals accused of committing sexual assault against women.

A common feature of many critical media events is the partial repetition or 'recycling' of a good deal of the original coverage in order to let audiences 'remember' what happened one, two or ten years ago. In the German media, a question which was typically asked in many headlines one year after the 'Delhi Gang Rape' and subsequent protests was what, if anything at all, had actually changed for women in India since then? Needless to say, many articles and reports found that, although there had been a lot of media coverage and activism in India in the wake of the crime, the situation for women in India had not changed or improved significantly. But can they actually substantiate such an assessment in a large and extremely diverse country like India? How do we define 'change' and is it at all possible to 'measure' it?

From a critical Indian Media Studies perspective, the editors of this volume feel that the emergence and fostering of an issue-based public debate among citizens is a very central precondition and element of any process of sociocultural change, hence a lot more in-depth analysis of the form, content and dynamics of these debates is required in order to develop a more nuanced understanding of the ongoing social processes in India's contemporary and increasingly media saturated society. In this context it is relevant to mention that Delhi may well be said to have become one of the important "nodes" and "switches", to cite two concepts established by Manuel Castells and Andreas Hepp, of the global network society and that without the intensified medialisation and 24x7 coverage of this critical event in India, international media would perhaps hardly have become aware of it. However, this aspect which is significant for the analysis and understanding of media-society dynamics has not really been taken into consideration so far.

This volume aims to look both at as well as *beyond* the 'Delhi Gang Rape' through the lens of Indian Media Studies. While a dominant media framing in the Eurocentric media represented the 'Delhi Gang Rape' as evidence that a highly paternalistic and misogynistic Indian culture and society remained essentially 'unchanged', we consider it a critical event, or rather critical media event, that needs to be contextualized within a rapidly changing, diversifying and globalizing society which is as much confronted with new ruptures, asymmetries and inequalities as it may still be shaped by the old-established structures of a patriarchal social order. Hence the question how the 'Delhi Gang Rape' is framed and represented by the media (in this volume: TV, digital as well as online print media) requires as much attention as the ways in which readers, users and viewers interpret, debate and contextualize it in their everyday lives, which may in turn lead to new social practices. At the same time, we are convinced that the study of this critical event should not be disconnected but rather placed in a growing research area which links the study of youth cultures, gender and media in contemporary Indian society. Accordingly, we have divided the volume in two parts.

PART I focuses on the 'Delhi Gang Rape' as a critical media event. It looks at the representations and framings in national as well as international media (Chap. 1 by MAITRAYEE CHAUDHURI and Chap. 5 by URMILA GOEL) and at the interface of new practices of debate, information sharing and media-specific sociability (Chap. 2 by JESNA JAYACHANDRAN, Chap. 3. by FRITZI-MARIE TITZMANN and Chap. 4. by MAREN WILGER).

MAITRAYEE CHAUDHURI argues that although there is a growing convergence between 'national' and 'global' media discourses, important differences still persist in the content and tenor between the two sets of discourses. She finds that this observation holds true today in most key sites of knowledge production other than the academia, for instance international institutions (IIs), global think tanks, corporate research institutions and non-governmental organizations (NGOs). As CHAUDHURI establishes in her article, they also form key sources of information for contemporary media and for the emerging global public sphere. While the "asymmetry of knowledge" may not be new at all, as she argues, what is new indeed is the "potent convergence of 'ignorance' and 'instant access' that new technologies have made possible". It is within this specific configuration that she analyzes both the content and form of the mediated discourse in the aftermath of the 'Delhi Gang Rape'.

In her contribution, JESNA JAYACHANDRAN draws our attention to the problem that, despite the academic interest in participatory cultures opened up by digital and especially by social media, the study of reader comments in online print media remains an underexplored area. In view of the fact that the Indian newspaper market (online & print) is one of the largest in the world, and that commenting online in newspaper websites provides an "immediate, common mode of participation, interaction and expression of alternative views in degrees of anonymity for readers" in India, more research should be dedicated to this specific area. Based on her analysis of online comments about rape and sexual violence that were published on the *Times of India* website in 2013, JAYACHANDRAN argues that one of the major reasons why gender equality continues to be a challenge precisely lies in the problem that while some selected stories about sexual violence are made visible (and many more are underreported and hence rendered invisible), journalists rarely link them to larger social problems. Reader comments are hence as much reflective of this specific asymmetry of knowledge and information as they give us, according to JAYACHANDRAN, a very clear idea about the current "male moral panics over changing notions of legalities, gender and relationships".

Based on the assumption that the physical places and digital spaces of protest were very closely connected in the context of the 'Delhi Gang Rape', FRITZI-MARIE TITZMANN looks at the web portal *Youth Ki Awaaz* (Voice of the Youth) which has emerged as a major English-language platform for youth-related issues in India over the last couple of years. In contrast to the media-specific sociability and practices of debate (or non-debate) in other online fora, TITZMANN's analysis of posts on *Youth Ki Awaaz* shows that many of the young people who contributed to the debate and emergence of an issue-based public also actively engaged in the mobilization and participation in street protests in the wake of the gang rape case. Contrary to the often-heard perception that especially the urban youth in India is not so interested or engaged in sociopolitical movements, TITZMANN finds that the "emerging discourses around gender, mobility, space, politics, and the media are far from trivial and contain serious critique of the existing system".

Focusing on the role specific media and online communities play in the remediation of critical events, MAREN WILGER in her articles looks at the dynamics of discussions about the 'Delhi Gang Rape' and the media coverage it received on the U.S. based social news aggregator *reddit.com*, a very popular website which serves to collect and structure content that is exclusively uploaded and shared by registered users. Using multiple methods of online ethnography or *netnography*, a term coined by Robert Kozinets, WILGER gives a nuanced insight into what she considers an "ambiguous role" of a specific online community which on the one hand has the capacity to highlight hitherto invisible or neglected issues while it may on the other hand actively reproduce and even reinforce existing culturalist stereotypes and imaginations about India as a "rape culture or country".

The problem of a continued culturalist stereotyping of India and now, more specifically, essentialising of the Indian capital Delhi as a 'rape capital' is also addressed in the interview URMILA GOEL conducted with renowned Indian writer, historian and publisher URVASHI BUTALIA about the 'Gang Rape Case' and the enormous attention it received worldwide. Like many other feminists and scholars of women's studies in India, BUTALIA is very critical of the ignorance displayed in many media reports of the December 2012 protests in Delhi and other Indian cities which led Western audiences to assume that this was the first time in Indian history women and supporters of women's rights stood up and fought for their rights.

PART II introduces three exemplary case studies which serve to illustrate the relevance, interconnectedness and methodological scope of India related Youth, Gender and Media Studies.

Access to new media technologies as well as the general rapid medialisation of society since the mid-1980s was crucial for the development of specific media practices which could spur the communication and recognition of distinct Lesbian, Gay, Trans(gender) and Queer (LGBTQ) sexual identities in India. At the same time, as THOMAS GUGLER argues in his article, the project of sexual liberation is increasingly shaped by the capitalist change, hence active participants in pride parades are, in the eyes of ever growing advertising and pornographic industries, simultaneously becoming potential consumers. Notwithstanding the process of commodification and despite severe backlashs on the legal and on other levels, he thinks that the pluralization and diversification of "sex worlds" in India is "unstoppable".

In her article on two young filmmakers based in Delhi, NADJA-CHRISTINA SCHNEIDER suggests not to look primarily at their documentary films about "young Muslim women in the city" as 'alternative representations' vis-à-vis the dominant stereotypical representations in Indian media. Instead, she uses the lens of entangled im/mobilities (i.e. technical, physical, communicative, emotional, imaginative etc.) in order to contextualize the two filmmakers' exploration and understanding of documentary forms and filmmaking practices in the specific experiences of a generation who was born in the 1980s and 90s and who, besides the dramatic political and socioeconomic changes, has seen an accelerated transformation of many urban localities in Indian cities.

Based on a long-time ethnographic study on the impact of mobile phones on local youth cultures in two *bustees* (urban slums) in Kolkata, KABITA CHAKRABORTY argues in her article that for those young people who have access to this technology, mobile phones have become an ordinary feature of their everyday lives during the last decade, much like in many other parts of the world. Her analysis of emergent mobile phone practices shows how they intersect with gendered social, employment and educational changes and how mobile phone usage is also impacting on the "landscape of romantic relationships" in the two *bustees*. In view of ever decreasing ownership and maintenance costs, Chakraborty predicts a future *bustee* where the mobile or cell phone becomes "an ordinary part of local youth culture".

While employing different angles and approaches, all eight contributions in this volume are driven by the motivation to render visible the interconnectedness of (new) media, gender, youth and its political implications.

As mentioned above, the exceptional densification of communication about the 'Delhi Gang Rape' served as a starting point to explore the diverse landscape of mediated discourses on gender in the contemporary Indian context. But the volume also looks beyond the critical media event and introduces other related thematic areas of this research field. We hope that this compilation contributes in a meaningful way to the growing research of Indian Media Studies.

1   Fernandez, Milena. 2013. "Why the middle class is revolting". Interview with Saskia Sassen. *The Hindu* (12 January 2013) Online available at: http://www.thehindu.com/opinion/interview/why-the-middle-class-is-revolting/article4299097.ece (last checked 31 Aug 2014).
2   Agency Report. 2013. "Politics of street protests; its power, its danger". *Current News* (5 January 2013). Online available at: http://currentnews.emsme.in/2013/01/05/politics-of-street-protests-its-power-dangers/ (last checked 31 August 2014).
3   Ibid.
4   Ibid.
5   Ibid.

PART I
THE 'DELHI GANG RAPE' AS A CRITICAL MEDIA EVENT:
REPRESENTATIONS, NEW PRACTICES OF DEBATE
AND MEDIA SOCIABILITY

Part 1

MAITRAYEE CHAUDHURI

National and Global Media Discourse after the savage death of 'Nirbhaya': Instant Access and Unequal Knowledge

On December 16, 2012, a 23-year-old physiotherapy student was brutally gang-raped and assaulted by 6 people in New Delhi, the capital of India. The victim, who came to be known as 'Nirbhaya' (one without fear) died thirteen days later. The ghastly incident evoked widespread protests. The national and global media covered this extensively. It was the cover story in Indian media for a few weeks and never quite dropped out of national discourse unlike other issues. This was unprecedented. But given that it happened in the Indian capital and Indian media's own past in engaging with women's issues, it is more easily understandable. The widespread coverage of this incident in international media calls for greater explanation given India's traditionally low visibility in it. One possible explanation is that Delhi has emerged as one of the important nodes and switches, in Castell's language of the global network society and that without the massive mediatisation of this critical event in Indian media, western media would hardly have become aware of it (Castells 1990, 2000).

While this is an undeniable fact, I would argue that any attempt to understand this has to also pay careful attention to the historically specific context within which the discourses were played out. The context I argue is new. Both globally and nationally, it is defined by neo-liberal globalization, India's own economic ascendency within it[1], the rise of a host of international organizations fitting norms of global governance; new technology, media convergence and the unprecedented role of a mediatized public discourse. This paper argues that though there is a growing convergence between 'national' and 'global' discourse, important differences still persist in the content and tenor between the two sets of discourses. It is through a comparative study of the two on 'Nirbhaya', that this article seeks to examine how and why they differ.

This paper therefore argues that an imperative need exists to bring in history and political economy to have a better understanding of contexts, commonalities and differences between 'national' and 'global' discourse. Neither the logic of media nor the mandate of proliferating project-based research would explain this. Yet it is evident that India's past bears heavily on the present 'national' discourse. And the history of orientalism cannot be wished away entirely from global discourse. The latter, one can argue stems from 'the inequality of ignorance' that Dipesh Chakbrabarty pointed to many years ago that persist between first word and third world scholars (Chakravarti 1992). Academic centres of global excellence such as Harvard University too are not free of this bane of unequal ignorance' as Prabha Kotiswaran's remarks in the context of 'Nirbhaya' imply. She argues that "circuits of feminist scholarship and activism have become so inter-disciplinary and transnational that maintaining and policing turf is an utterly useless endeavour." The problem however lies in the fact that. "Some Western feminists ... barely care to become familiar with the context in which they are trying to intervene[2]" even as their "particular versions of American legal feminism[3] have been propelled out of their provincial contexts into international law and policy making"[4] (Kotiswaran 2013, 1).

I would like to argue that the above observation holds true today in most key sites of knowledge production other than the academia such as international institutions (IIs), global think tanks, corporate research institutions and non-governmental organizations (NGOs). These institutions hold great influence in the contemporary global order and we shall see how they also form key sources of information for contemporary media and for the emerging global public sphere (Chaudhuri 2010b). While this asymmetry of knowledge perhaps has been long true, what is new is a potent convergence of 'ignorance' and 'instant access' that new technologies have made possible. It is within this configuration that I attempt to analyze both the content and form of the mediated discourse in the aftermath of the gang rape.

This article is based upon a thematic analysis of public discourse in the aftermath of the 'Nirbhaya' rape. I have followed discussions in newspapers, television and Internet on a daily basis in the immediate months after the event and have continued to follow them since. Television channels followed have been primarily English and Hindi, and occasionally Bengali, while my study of the Internet and print media has been in English.

The Argument and Approach

My emphasis on a historical and political economic perspective stem from a certain unease with the manner that media is often seen as a discrete entity that can be analyzed either in terms of its texts/images or their reception and resistance by people who too are treated as bounded empirical beings, rather than an ensemble of social relations. My argument is that it is important to distinguish between the concrete economic and legal structures of the global order from the logic of new media technologies and its almost magical possibilities. I make this claim, fully aware that the latter is played out within the ambit of the former. This section therefore first elaborates how my distinction between 'national' and 'global' discourse rests on a political economic understanding of contemporary capitalism. And second explicates the nature and consequences of new media technologies and the reason for my use of the term mediatization.

The political economic

The transformed relationship between the 'national' and the 'global' I argue has to be seen in the way states and markets have been recast in contemporary capitalism. I am not using 'national' and 'global' to refer to empirical regions or entities alone. But fundamental to this article is the idea that in the current stage of capitalism the state and nation as we have understood since Westphalia has been reconfigured to take on board the play of global capitalism and trans-national capitalists. My argument is that though distinctions between national and international media in the Nirbhaya case are apparent, it is equally true that significant processes of transformation are already underway. Important structural changes mark the relationship between Indian and international media. An example of collaboration between *India Real Time* and *Wall Street Journal* is one example[5].

My contention is that states have been major players in laying the terms of public discourse in modernity. In India, where civil society had not emerged in the way it had in western modernity, the state had an even more important role to set the agenda for public discourse (Kaviraj 1991). The media did play a significant role in the growth of Indian nationalism and later in projecting state policies. A greater role was however played by the engagement of political leaders and organizations with people through direct interaction at different levels. Public meetings held in different corners of India even at a time when travel entailed considerable time, defined the story of India's nation building project. Stories of how news of protests travelled by word of mouth to different parts of India, are also part of this history. In the current context of global capitalism however, the state is no longer the only player. Social movements leverage media and the media itself no longer simply 'represents' but 'sets' agendas. This would be evident in both the national and global discourse, which I examine below. The media does not act alone in this regard but along with a host of national and new transnational players within which the media as an industry is implicated.

In the 'Nirbhaya' case, we see within the national discourse the role of: Indian feminists; civil society organizations; political parties representing different ideological positions; and the Indian state. In the global discourse on 'Nirbhaya' we witness a greater role of: international institutions (IIs); international non-governmental organizations (INGOs); consultancy sectors such as risk assessment organizations; and the tourism industry. The pervasive presence of the global discourse draws its legitimacy from the hegemonic position that IIs occupy in this new order. However, this omnipresence would be impossible without the technology that makes media convergence possible. As stated earlier, this article therefore at once privileges both political economy and media logic. If the former reflects the compulsions of capital, the latter provides information of a "format" of "how material is organized, the style in which it is presented, the focus or emphasis on particular characteristics of behavior, and the grammar of media communication" (Altheide and Snow 1979, 10).

Media logic, new technology and mediatization

This article acknowledges that the extraordinary spread with which 'Nirbhaya's' tragedy travelled would be impossible sans the new configuration of media technology brought about by the digital revolution and the birth of the World Wide Web. This ushered in paradigmatic changes of creating, delivering, and consuming content. The emergence of new media, widespread use of multimedia and an inevitable transformation of traditional media has ushered in a world of instant access to people and institutions across the world. Notwithstanding the magical possibilities of new technology, instant access does not necessarily spell either equal or informed access to content. For content remains constitutive of a host of historical, political, economic, cultural and social forces.

In this regard, I would like to also make a point about media convergence, which is often understood as post-ideological for convergence speaks of a cultural shift where consumers seek out what they want, making discrete connections among the scattered media (Jenkins 2006). The claim is that people are no longer 'passive media spectators' but participate at all three levels of production, selection, and distribution. I disagree for there is a clear ideological content that is emerging from specific sites of knowledge production and decision making in the new global order. This article develops this argument at some length. Jenkins also contends that the digital divide is less about access and more about the "participation gap". I agree with this for even in a country like India where inequality is sharp and the digital divide[6] large, a very large section of people, literate or illiterate, rural or urban do watch, see, listen to the media, and then discuss what they saw and heard. They are not 'passive victims' but the script of their debate is also not entirely theirs.

A key approach that informs this article is the intersection of the political economic and the new multimedia technology. This is most evident in the increasing cross ownership[7] in the media sector and media convergence. Cross-ownership of media has been a matter of some concern as India is one of the few countries where there has still not been any regulation in place, though it is in proposed policy discourse. Strong opinions have emerged in the media industry – both for and against – the Telecom Regulatory Authority of India's (TRAI) initiatives regarding cross-media ownership in the country.[8] It has been defended from associations representing the print media on the grounds of attaining economies of scale for "Cross-media operations can reduce the cost of news gathering, news dissemination, while also providing affordable access to international news" (Kumar 2013).[9] My concern here is not about the need for economy of scale, nor to economy of access but the trend towards less diversity of sources.

It is within this convergence that I seek to capture the themes that emerge in the multiple discourses in the aftermath of the December Rape. The case of 'Nirbhaya' is an early and dramatic instance of 'mediatization' in India where the media appeared to shape and frame the processes and discourses of political communication (Lilleker 2008). Different actors in the event 'adjusted to the demands of the mass media' in the manner that Kent Asp in 1986 described as the 'mediatization of political life' (Asp 1986). I use the term 'mediatized' therefore to enable one to see the media not as an external institution that effects social life but as entangled in almost all spheres of economic, political, social and cultural life.

Key Assumptions

There are a couple of assumptions which flow from my understanding of the political economy of 21st century global capitalism on one hand and media logic on the other The first is that some of the key tropes that define dominant global discourse-governance, development, gender and human rights are broadly crafted by international institutions (IIs) such as the World Bank, World Trade Organization (WTO), the United Nations (UN), and a host of human rights agencies. Crucial in the dissemination of this script have been the large number of international non-governmental organizations (INGOS), new and critical sites of knowledge production, which actively engage with the media. There is a dominant presence of a global human rights discourse in the responses to the 'Nirbhaya' case. Admonishment for India's human rights violation is evident in: travel advisories issued by foreign states; statements by international institutions; commentaries in international media; trans-national feminist academia; sundry blogs; and corporate commentaries.

Second, in the national discourse, there is greater intervention by different sections located within the Indian nation such as social movements, women's organizations, legal fraternity, courts, conservative patriarchal sections of Indian society and the state. Hence my contention is that the 'national' does continue to matter even as 'global' discourses impinge upon the 'national.' It gets transformed but is not entirely subsumed within the global.

Thirdly my use of the term 'national public sphere' is deliberate. I am acutely aware of India's 'internally differentiated publics' in view of language plurality and the manifold asymmetries within the public sphere in India. However empirically, as would be evident from this article, there is a basic difference in the intense and variegated discourse within the country from the reactions of institutions and people located outside India (irrespective of 'national' or 'ethnic' origins) to the case. I would also stand by the term 'national public sphere' to counter theoretically the idea that the 'fragments' of the nation, or in this instance the various 'publics' within the political entity India are discrete, bounded entities that operate independent of each other. This view has widespread academic currency in postcolonial theory but is questionable on grounds that are both theoretical and empirical. Theoretically it looks at the 'publics' as 'bounded' entities, in the manner that traditional western anthropology studied 'native' 'communities' and 'villages' as though untouched by macro processes even of the scale of colonialism. Historically, it belies the fact that politics outside the dominant Indian 'nationalist framework' had to engage to counter and critique the former.

Empirically we know that there has been a long tradition of Indian newspapers being read aloud and discussed in village teashops among people, literate and non-literate. The last quarter century has witnessed the ubiquitous television set in city barbershops, which again is a 'public' and shared site of consumption and discussion. Nothing brings this more to the fore than the General Elections in India 2014[10] where '*chai pe charcha*' (discussion over tea) became a key campaign strategy of the Bharatiya Janata Party (BJP) after its Prime Ministerial candidate Narendra Modi was mocked for his humble beginnings as a tea seller. He won the elections. In other words the idea of a "split public" (Rajagopal 2001) appears to make both the role of the political state and an expanding market in the making of everyday life inconsequential. Significantly the last few years have seen greater expansion of Indian language media than English language ones.[11] More recently we have English language television channels conducting interviews in Indian languages with English subtitles.[12] Further, media logic has increasingly transformed Indian language media on lines that mirror the format and content of English media, once again raising questions whether one can hold on the idea of split publics.

My fourth contention is that the purported boundaries between old and new media seem to collapse as we witness in the multiple discourses a seamless continuity in both content and form. One of the profound ways in which the Internet and new media change the public sphere is through a change in temporality. Highly mediated and highly capitalized forms of circulation are increasingly organized in the 24x7 instant access rather than punctual (Warner 2002). There is, in other words, a dissonance between a content reflecting a deep-seated hierarchy and a form that apparently spells instant uploading and global access. In this regard my fifth contention is that we need to take history into account to appreciate that the women's question has been central in modern Indian public discourse and this past that has been rendered invisible in media gender discourse. A historical perspective therefore is more important than ever before, as we face an increasingly dominant, homogenized and effectively mediatized narrative[13] that can travel instantly and spread everywhere even as 'unequal ignorance' in key sites of knowledge production persists.

The sixth and final contention of this article therefore is that in a mediatized and publicity driven world, we have to recognize that the role of talking, discourse and communication acquire a different order of centrality.[14] As a sociologist, I am aware of the limits of seeking to understand the 'social' through a study of media discourses. However, what I would like to underscore here is that we need to take cognizance of the fact that the 'social' in a fundamental sense has been redefined. The volume of information and images, their scale and reach, speed and persuasive power marks a new era. This redefines the meaning of 'experience' as a commodity form that mediates people's relationship to both their pasts and presents. There are a couple of theoretical and methodological issues that this observation raises with regard to any attempt to study the events pertaining to the case of 'Nirbhaya'.

Can we study this particular event sans its media discourses? How do we look at the matter of commodification of experience in the media? Did the personal 'experience' of the victim or her family or her friend get commoditized in the media? The broader political question that arises thereof is whether this commoditization cancels out the expansive potential of democracy contained in the sheer scale of public protest and the wide-ranging debate on core feminist questions even within mainstream media. A more careful examination of the responses may provide an answer to the limits and possibilities of mediatization for democracy. The structure of this article flows from the argument articulated above. It is broadly divided into two parts: the *national* discourse and the *global* discourse; that there will be inevitable overlapping is part of the story that I seek to tell.

Part A – National Discourse

Bringing in History

Historically, gender issues have often been central to modern India's public discourse and even as gender remained a pivot, it tended to spawn discussions on a whole range of issues that do not directly pertain to gender. My decision to overtly refer to history is to counter the current obsession with the 'contemporary' if not the 'immediate'. That this is widespread in the media with its 24x7 logic and 'breaking news' syndrome few would disagree. I however contend that this focus on the immediate and an orientation towards a checklist of 'problems' and a readier check-list of 'solutions' increasingly inform social science academia too. It is not surprising therefore that there is a widely prevalent view in gender global discourse, now spilling into the 'national', that gender rights in India are a fall-out of the United Nation's Declaration of International Women's Year and Decade in 1975 and the initiatives of IIs and INGOs since.[15] A social science analysis of media discourse therefore has to bring in history, political economy and the minutae of everyday life[16] apart from the specificities of media logic and its form of presentation.

From the early beginnings of modern media in colonial India, various issues pertaining to women have occupied centre stage: sati[17], widow remarriage[18], child marriage[19], age of consent, and education for women (Chaudhuri [1993] 2011). Debates in the then young Indian media (ibid.) and within women's organizations such as in All India Women's Conference (AIWC) (1926), Women's India Association (WIA) (1917) and others have in a fundamental sense been debates on: Indian modernity and its uneasy relationship with tradition; on nationalism and democracy; culture and individual rights, inequality and citizenship; public and private spheres; west and east; gender and sexuality; progress and backwardness. This is how it was during the 19th century and this is how it is in the 21st century.

There was a retreat of the women's question from public discourse after independence in 1947 and resurgence with the Indian women's movement in the 1970s, also termed as the second phase of the Indian women's movement, triggered by the Mathura rape case that led to sustained efforts by the women's movement to change the law.[20] The range of issues raised in the second phase of the Indian women's movement, as in the first, were carried widely by a media, increasingly engaged with questions of women's equal rights as citizens (Kumar 1997, Shah and Gandhi 1992, Sen1990).

The 1980s witnessed the Shah Bano[21] and the Deorala Sati[22] case which once again brought back many of the old contestations such as cultural versus gender rights, community versus state centre stage (Sundar Rajan 2003; Sangari and Vaid 1989; Chaudhuri 1993). The media played an active role raising questions of gender justice with regard to this case (Chaudhuri 2000). However the nature of the media during this entire period was different. It had neither the broader political economy set up by neo-liberalism, nor the technological sophistication of an interactive media, nor a publicity driven culture, which is constitutive of the media today. It is this transformed media that was both an actor and a central site for representing the public outcry against the gruesome case of rape and murder of a young woman in Delhi in December 2012.

Sixty-six years of Indian independence, development, affirmative action by the state, and social movements have all contributed to both a deepening and expansion of democracy. There is an increasing presence of marginalized sections in the public sphere (Rege 2006). In the immediate years preceding Nirbhaya's death, India has seen the rise of a strong anti-corruption movement and a growing presence of what has been termed civil society organizations. This movement has drawn huge support among the urban middle class and it has used the social media extensively. This movement was actually being covered in real time. At its peak it was a media event, drawing more audience than even the most popular soaps.[23]

The anti-corruption movement, drawing heavily from the transparency and governance discourse of the World Bank was primarily directed against the ruling government. The state and not the corporate was the object of critical scrutiny as the media had actively projected since the early 1990s that the 'market' was more accountable and responsive to the 'public' than the 'state' (Chaudhuri 2000, 2001, 2010b). More recently however, in the campaign for the 2014 general elections, the Aam Aadmi (common man) Party (AAP), whose leading members were part of the anti-corruption movement, has been attacking the major political parties for being in cohort with big business houses who now have a major say in state functioning.

It is however with the emergence of new media and media convergence that recent practices of an interactive 'public' became possible. A significant convergence of a political mood of the 'public' and the technological possibility for enhanced public interactivity took place. In the aftermath of the December 2012 rape, the dominant media rhetoric was that the 'public' has risen. The 'public', the media pontificated, will no longer 'take things lying down'. Significantly it was the word 'public' that was increasingly being used even in Indian language media discourse. In everyday parlance it meant the 'everybody'. The spontaneous outburst was triggered by what happened to 'Nirbhaya', but it happened at a point where there was already a growing anger against the government seen as corrupt, as cut off from and unresponsive to the ordinary person, the 'Aam Aadmi'.[24] It is worth mentioning here that it is a common sight in Indian television these days to watch a news broadcaster breaking off in the midst of debating live with a range of people[25] to read from purported SMS, or attend a caller, even as the television screen would have audience responses ticking below[26].

Multiple sites, multiple discourses after the brutal incident

I have already stated in my initial observations that in the national discourse, the central actors are members representing different sections located within the Indian nation such as social movements, women's organizations, legal fraternity, courts, conservative patriarchal sections of Indian society and the Indian state. In my schematic account of the national media discourse on the Nirbhaya case, the role of these actors would become visible. Readers will also notice how the Indian media took on an aggressive position, became a spokesperson of the protests and sought to set the agenda for both public discourse and the state.

In the initial weeks, "Hang the rapists" was the strident cry of the media.[27] Nothing less than capital punishment would assuage the collective grief and anger of the 'public' was dominant discourse. As the crowd surged, demanding justice for 'Nirbhaya', remembering the 'daughter of India', the government appeared unsure about its response. Police attempts to disperse the crowd through water cannons further fuelled public anger. The media was shrill, demanding instant justice. The active intervention of women's organizations and feminist lawyers in media discussions mitigated this stridency.[28] This shift in focus has been described as one from a 'retributive public' where death penalty or castration became a 'vocabulary of protest' to a 'passionate reasoned' public intent on "what the government needs to do to be accountable to rape survivors" (Baxi 2012). The active intervention of women's organizations and feminist scholars appeared to have persuaded the media to change track from hysterical ranting to more reasoned debates (Agnes 2013; Geetha 2013).

However, there did emerge a new "'public in solidarity' which has 'informed, provoked and supported' a 'determined fight' against sexual violence anywhere in the country" (Baxi 2012). Women's groups of diverse ideological persuasions, students' organizations, individuals with no political affiliations, and housewives came together on the streets with a common intent to fight for gender justice. In response to this public demand of Indian citizens, the Indian state set up a committee headed by Justice Jagdish Sharan Verma[29], a retired Chief Justice who passed away in April 2013. Representatives of women's and human rights groups, lawyers and activists from across the country who had for decades fought towards reforms on rape and sexual assault, welcomed several provisions of the Criminal Law (Amendment) Act 2013, Criminal Bill 2013 that was passed by Parliament in response to the Verma Committee recommendations.[30]

If the women's movement alongside many ordinary citizens from diverse walks of life were anguished with the incident, there were others, who raised quite different kinds of questions. Political parties appeared divided. It ranged from dominant liberal views to communist critiques to cultural Hindu nationalist statements. It is pertinent to mention here that for the first four decades after independence, a conglomeration of left of centre liberal ideas defined the dominant discourse. This has been changing over the last two decades with a growing articulation of Hindu nationalist ideas pitted against what they described as pseudo secular politics. It is therefore important to take note of the observations of Mohan Bhagwat, chief of the right-wing Rashtriya Swayamsevak Sangh (RSS)[31] who opined that rapes are an urban crime shaped by westernisation, and is not a matter of concern in rural India where traditional values are upheld. "Mohan Bhagwat doesn't know either India or Bharat," said Brinda Karat, a Communist Party of India (Marxist) CPM politburo member and a leading member of All India Women's Democratic Association (AIDWA) for "the largest number of rapes occurs in rural areas on Dalits, tribals and rural workers (Ghosh 2012). Asaram Bapu[32], a popular Hindu guru, said that the New Delhi rape victim could have saved herself if she had simply "held the hand of one of the men and said, 'I consider you as my brother' (Harris 2013). In yet other sites, debates of a very different order were carried out about Marxism and gender (Chauhan et al June 10, 2013). Yet others commented on the differential response to rape committed against poor Dalit women, which often went unreported and unremarked in the media.[33]

We had a string of administrative measures launched by the government even as parliamentarians during the debate on the anti-rape law made offensive sexist remarks. Sharad Yadav, a legislator of Rashtriya Janata Dal (RJD) justified 'following girls' for 'when you want to talk to a woman…, you have to put in a lot of effort'. Mulayam Singh Yadav, leader of the Samajwadi Party (SP), the ruling party in Uttar Pradesh state wanted to stop co-education while Lalu Prasad Yadav, head of RJD a regional party in Bihar… called on the government to cover up ancient erotic sculptures in Khajuraho and in Konarak – both of which are UNESCO world heritage sites.[34] Sumitra Mahajan, a member of the BJP, criticized Indian reality television for "throwing young boys and girls together […] and […] dancing together to all kinds of love songs" (N.N. October 2013).

Advertisements since Nirbhaya have often addressed questions of gender and sexual harassment.[35] Popular television serials dealt with training women for self-defense[36] even as other TV programmes discussed gender related issues, including glass ceiling for corporate women. In this entire process the news channels in particular took on the role of spokespersons speaking to and behalf of the 'nation'[37] and the public. What however cannot be ignored is that gender justice did become a key issue in public discourse, something that every political party has had to contend with in India's 2014 general elections.

Part B – Global Discourse

Part A provided a glimpse of the diverse discourses that covered an entire range of perspectives – marxist, liberal, Dalit, patriarchal, feminist – in different languages that constitute the national public sphere. I had earlier stated my reservations about the idea of a "split public" and would like to once again suggest that there does appear to be a mutually comprehensible though diverse conversation going on across the nation.[38] In Part B, I look at the global discourse whose focus and tenor do appear to differ. Two significant differences are: one, global media's condemnation of the Indian state's failure to live up to India's global brand image as an economic power expressed variously in a tone of horror, dismay, shock and mockery; two, greater dependence on specific sources for information which I elaborate upon below; three a broad brush treatment of India as one monolithic entity.

A central contention of this article has been that any analysis of the media has to take into account the new structure and functioning of trans-national capitalism. Linked has been my contention that this new economic order is accompanied by the emergence and growing influence of international institutions, global think tanks, corporate research organizations, a new regime of international human rights and women rights laws that inform the practice not just of states but also big business houses that want minimum norms of gender justice, law and governance in place. Likewise we have the rise of the tourism industry as an essential element of the new global architecture. New organizations like global risk assessment firms have emerged to facilitate both global investment and tourist flow. They monitor social risks such as violence against women. A whole corpus of reports has emerged from these sites. They are readily available sources on the web not just for the media but as I have documented at some length elsewhere, also within the practice of social science (Chaudhuri 2010b). As of now international media's dependence on these sources appear to be greater than in the national media in the 'Nirbhaya' case. This as things stand today is bound to grow in the near future cutting across both national and global discourse. These are significant producers and disseminators of 'knowledge' today and it may not be inappropriate to see them as the new ideological apparatus for governance.

Before I go any further, I would like to make a clarification on my take on these new developments towards better global governance. I would like to reiterate that while at one level, international laws on human and gender rights are commendable and enabling; there is a need for caution. I do not wish to engage with the dangers of an II based governance here except to mention two points: one, a point often ignored in the buzz on 'global governance', that they are sites of power and they work in tandem with other centres of strategic power; and two, that while democratic states are accountable to citizens, IIs are not. Its people can vote the government out but not IIs. This was a major point of debate in India when Indian acceded to the WTO regime.

My focus in this article is however on their role as media sources and I return to that here. There are issues with both the content and format of these studies. The content apart from reflecting 'unequal ignorance' also suffers from the logic of writing 'reports' and 'project evaluations' which have a set motif that defines the questions, indicators and mode of data analysis. The rise of global index as a measure typifies this. This trend gets further compounded in the media with the limits of the form of communication that contemporary media practice deploys sensational stories, sound bites, and set-up controversies programmed to convey flattened, easy-to-consume information.

This straitjacketed treatment of social issues mode also gets reflected at the ground level in the everyday functioning of myriad NGOs, with its mechanical dissemination of buzzwords and tropes that fit in with the managerial mode of much of professional grass-root activism. This, in combination with deep-seated ignorance of histories and contexts, I would like to contend cannot further either critical awareness or democratic rights which in a fundamental sense is the task of the media in liberal democracies. But liberal democracies rested on an institutional base of the nation state and national public discourse. How then do we imagine a democratic 'global public sphere'?

International Media

As mentioned earlier, one significant way that the national media discourse differed from the global was the focus on India as an economic power and its poor showing in its social indicators. The *New York Times* observed how *"India is a rising economic power* but the world's largest democracy can never reach its full potential if half its population lives in fear of unspeakable violence" (Ghosh 2012, emphasis mine). Claire O'Sullivan in the *Irish Examiner Reporter* asks *"What is going on in the world's ninth richest economy* that women are now increasingly scared of being brutalised on the streets, that they can't board a bus, stay in a hotel alone, or camp with their husband?" (O'Sullivan 2013, emphasis mine).

A central marker of orientalist discourse has been 'barbaric' treatment of women.[39] A 2013 report on the Global Slavery Index carried in international media and in the Indian newspaper, *Times of India* reveals a convergence of 21st century human rights discourse and 19th century orientalism.

Sixty-six years after independence, India has the dubious distinction of being home to half the number of modern day slaves in the world. The first Global Slavery Index has estimated that 13.3 to 14.7 million people live like slaves in the country [...] The index, published by the Australia-based Walk Free Foundation, ranked 162 countries based on three factors that include estimated prevalence of modern slavery, a measure of child marriage and a measure of human trafficking in and out of a country [...] India has half the world's modern slaves. (N.N. March 2013).

'Nirbhaya's' case was seen as a major dent to India's image in global business circles. A media report on a visit by the then Prime Minister of India Manmohan Singh to Germany after the incident observed, that *"India ... found itself once again in the dock on its high maternal and child mortality rates. The embarrassment happened in full view of the world press*, which had assembled to hear ... the outcomes of the Indo-German Inter-Governmental Consultations" (Subramaniam 2013, emphasis mine). The report saw this as a serious 'human rights violation' as the state could be seen as complicit in 'murdering' its women and children".

I would like to draw attention to the assortment of keywords in the above news report: "Indo-German bilateral ties, Bilateral Investment and India-EU Free Trade Agreement, maternal mortality, child mortality, gender insecurity and crime against women". They indicate how closely matters of trade and commerce have been intertwined with human rights issues[40] in the new global order. While few would have any quarrel with the extension of human rights, the problem has been that this has often been used by IIs and western states selectively.

O'Sullivan's piece in the *Irish Chronicler* show the same media practice of using available statistics (from UN source in this case) and select interviews with NGO personnel. In this instance it was one Paul Healy who was working as Programme Manager to a local partner INGO Trocaire run by 'National Alliance of Women in Odisha' (NAWO). What is discomfiting is that the O'Sullivan's account of women in India virtually rests on this very limited source of information. This actually exemplifies what I mean by the potent convergence of 'instant access' and 'unequal ignorance'. The quotes from the report below may help make my point clear.

Baby girls and young girls are also more at risk in India than anywhere in the world, according to the *United Nations*. *The Indian child rights organisation CRY estimates say that about 12m girls are born in India every year, however, one million of these girls die by the age of one.* [...] Dowries are still engrained in Indian culture. (O'Sullivan 2013, emphasis mine)

The dismal account does not stop here as it recounts horror stories of the rampant practice of dowry without a mention of either the anti-dowry campaign that marked the second phase of the women's movement or the whole gambit of laws that were put in place or any reference to feminist scholarship in the field.

[...] Sometimes what they do is poison her; they can kill her with weapons, throttle her or bride burning — that is common. They pour kerosene and burn her alive. ... Then with one wife killed, they can get another girl and another dowry (ibid.).

In a world of instant access one can assume that older distances, hierarchies and misrepresentations have been done away with. The quote below suggest otherwise.

[...] According to Paul Healy [...] the victim of *the Delhi bus gang rape was savagely killed as she dared to go out with a boy and at 8.30 pm* [....] (O'Sullivan 2013, emphasis mine).

Wall Street Journal posted an article on the website of *India Realtime* (whose tagline is "The daily pulse of the world's largest democracy") on whether it was safe for foreigners to travel in India. Stancati, the author of the piece provides a compilation of information through interviews with foreign tourists, members from Tourist Bureau as well as information gleaned from websites of different states. I present below a longish quote from the piece to highlight the sources that she uses.

[…] There are always bad things happening everywhere. What is happening here is a little bit worrying but when you are travelling, irrespective of where you are travelling, it's important to have your wits in place," said Ms. Beard, who is traveling with a *tour group*.
[…] Delhi representative of the *Travel Agents Association of India*, a lobby group, says that the December rape case has not affected the tourism industry in the country. "In every country of the globe, these kinds of incidents happen from time to time," says Mr. Singh, adding that the industry is now more aware about the need to help prevent sexual crimes against tourists.
[…] director at the Delhi-based *Sadhana Tours*, says he hasn't received any questions from clients on women's safety in recent months. Still, "there are certain rules we follow […]".
Guide books and *foreign governments* have long warned women to be careful when traveling in India.
Tripadvisor, the travel Website, has a whole page on tips for women traveling on their own in Delhi […].
Foreign governments have similar travel advice for their citizens in India. "U.S. citizens, particularly women, are cautioned not to travel alone in India," says a note from the U.S. Department of State […].
If you are a woman traveling in India you should respect local dress codes and customs and avoid isolated areas […] says a notice on the website of the British foreign office (Stancati 2013, emphasis mine).

Before I end, I would like to refer to one particular debate on the Age of Consent that was covered extensively both within the global and national media- old and new. I quote illustratively from this to make the point of unequal levels of ignorance. An intense public debate on the Age of Consent Bill had divided public opinion in the late 19th century.[41] More than a hundred and a quarter years later, the central actors were different. The colonial state had long since gone. It was the Indian state that was being addressed by the women's movement and other groups to bring in a more effective law.[42] Stating that the Bill is a step forward for women's rights in India, activist and lawyer Vrinda Grover said:

[…] this Bill seeks to protect our entire society from the scourge of sexual violence. *This is not a bill against men; it is a Bill against criminals; it is a Bill from which all citizens stand to gain peace of mind against the mindless violence that stalks us* [...] (emphasis mine).

Farah Naqvi, women's rights activist, went on to say that this stand is not a moral endorsement of teenage sexual activity. *We must recognize that 'criminalising as rape' the consensual acts of young adults will make most vulnerable our young men, particularly those from marginalized communities*" (RINA 2013, emphasis mine).

The government's decision to fix the legal age for consensual sex at 18 from an earlier agreement by the Cabinet for 16 was seen by women's organizations and feminist scholars as succumbing to pressures from conservative leaders that the move would encourage young people to experiment with sex. The police felt that the move could make it harder to secure rape convictions in cases where the victim is between 16 and 18, as she would be asked at trial to show she didn't consent. The fault lines of Indian society were clearly in play.

Globally however this dimension did not get reflected. The caption of a report read: "India which has more child brides than any nation in the world" did not sign a United Nations initiative to end child marriage. This report had to be corrected shortly after.

Correction: an earlier version of this story and headline said that India failed to "sign" the resolution. In fact, it chose not to co-sponsor it. The story and headline have been edited to reflect this.
...Syed Akbaruddin, a spokesman for India's foreign ministry spokesperson said that although the government was not a co-sponsor it nonetheless "supported the objectives of the resolution." (Stuart 2013)

But for Avert, a U.K.-based charity group was quick to conclude that, "by raising the age of consent to 18, India last year became one of the most conservative countries in the world, according to data compiled by Avert, a U.K.-based charity." The global average on the legal sex age according to it is 16.[43] This same report refers to the All India Democratic Women's Association (AIDWA) with an organizational presence in 22 states in India, with a current membership of more than 9 million of which several state units came into existence during the 'freedom struggle'[44] as a New Delhi-based 'non-profit organization'. This may appear a trivial point to make. However it demonstrates the ignorance of the history of social movements in India. For in this global discourse all movements for gender justice are seen as off shoots of efforts by well meaning global NGOs, charity groups and IIs.

Conclusion

The questions that I raised at the start of the article were: Does greater visibility in media means greater democratization and gender justice? And did the logic of media practice and commoditization cancel out the expansive potential of democracy evident in public protest and wide-ranging debate on feminist questions after Nirbhaya.

A year and half later after 'Nirbhaya's' death, one can say that the campaign against gender violence and rape have been sustained by the media. News reports, TV serials, blog discussions have all kept the pressure on[45]. But violent incidents of this kind remain and seem to be growing. It is undeniable that the media was critical in drawing attention to violence against women after 'Nirbhaya' and making gender justice a key issue in the General Elections of 2014. But it is also true that the media is not the magic institution that would solve all problems though this is an impression that has been gaining ground. It is only concerted action by social movements, political parties, the state and society at large that would help usher in changes that would not allow such incidents from taking place. Indeed legal changes have taken place. But it is important to recall that India is a country where historically laws have usually been far more democratic than social norms. This gap between the two reflects the fault lines of Indian society. It can be legitimately asked that despite all the movements why is sexual violence becoming a norm, or is it? We as social scientists need to answer that.

But neither the tropes of Global Indexes nor the here and now sensationalism of media logic would be able to understand the complexities involved. This, in combination with 'unequal levels of ignorance of histories and instant access' cannot further either critical awareness or democratic rights which in a fundamental sense is the task of media in liberal democracies. The problem gets compounded when liberal 'global governance' and 'governance feminism' redefine nation-based democracies. How do we then address what ought to be the nature of a democratic 'global public sphere'?

Bibliography

ALTHEIDE, DAVID and ROBERT P. SNOW. *Media Logic*. Beverly Hills: Sage, 1979.
ASP, KENT. *Mäktiga massmedier: Studier i politisk opinionsbildning*. Stockholm: Akademilitteratur, 1986.
BAXI, PRATIKSHA. "We must resist the cunning of judicial reform." *Kafila* (blog), December 29, 2012. Accessed December 30, 2012. http://kafila.org/2012/12/29/we-must-resist-the-cunning-of-judicial-reform-pratiksha-baxi/#more-14996.
BS Reporter. "Ambani's RIL takes control of Network18." *Business Standard*, May 30, 2014. Accessed May 30, 2014. http://www.business-standard.com/article/companies/ril-to-acquire-control-of-network18-114052901661_1.html.
BURKE, JASON. "Delhi rape: how India's other half lives." *The Guardian*, September 10, 2013.
CASTELLS, MANUEL. "Materials for an exploratory theory of the network society." *British Journal of Sociology* 51, no. 1 (January/March 2000): 5–24.
CASTELLS, MANUEL. *The informational city: A framework for social change*. Toronto: University of Toronto, 1990.
CHAKRAVARTI, DIPESH. "Postcoloniality and the Artifice of History: Who Speaks for 'Indian' Pasts?" *Representations* 37 (Winter 1992): 1–26.
CHAUDHURI, MAITRAYEE. *The Indian Women's Movement: Reform and Revival*. Delhi: Radiant, 1993. Reprint, Delhi: Palm Leaf, 2011.
CHAUDHURI, MAITRAYEE. "'Feminism' in Print Media." *Indian Journal of Gender Studies* 7, no.2 (2000): 263–88.
CHAUDHURI, MAITRAYEE. "Gender and Advertisements: The Rhetoric of Globalisation." *Women's Studies International Forum* 24, no.3/4 (2001): 373–85. Reprint in *The Advertising and Consumer Culture Reader*, edited by Joseph Turow and Matthew P. McAllister, 175–92. New York & London: Routledge, 2009.
CHAUDHURI, MAITRAYEE, ed. *Sociology in India: Institutional and Intellectual Practices*. Jaipur: Rawat, 2010a.
CHAUDHURI, MAITRAYEE. "Indian Media and its Transformed Public." *Contributions to Indian Sociology* 44, no.1/2 (2010b): 57–78.
CHAUDHURI, MAITRAYEE. "Feminism in India: The Tale and its Telling 'Féminismes décoloniaux, genre et développement.'" *Revue Tiers Monde* 209 (March 2012): 19–36.
CHAUDHURI, MAITRAYEE. "Gender, Media and Popular Culture in a Global India," In *Routledge Handbook of Gender in South Asia*, edited by Leela Fernandes, 145–59. New York: Routledge, 2014.
CHAUHAN, BHUMIKA et al. "Anti-Rape Movement: A Horizon beyond legalism and sociology." *Radical Notes* (blog). June 10, 2013. Accessed April 22, 2014. http://radicalnotes.com/category/editorials/.
FLAVIA, AGNES. "No Shortcuts to Rape." *Economic & Political Weekly* 48, no.2. (2013): 1–4.
FRIEDMAN, THOMAS. *The World Is Flat: A Brief History of the Twenty-first Century*. New York: Farrar, Straus and Giroux, 2005.

GEETHA, V. "On Impunity." *Economic & Political Weekly* 48, no.2. (2013): 1–3.
GHOSH, PALASH. "Delhi Gang-Rape Victim: Global Reaction." *International Business Times*, December 31, 2012. Accessed April 20, 2014. http://www.ibtimes.com/delhi-gang-rape-victim-global-reaction-983484.
GUPTA, SMITA. "Anti-rape bill diluted, Cabinet approves new version." *The Hindu*, March 19, 2013. Accessed July 31, 2014. http://www.thehindu.com/todays-paper/tp-national/antirape-bill-diluted-cabinet-approves-new-version/article4524019.ece
HARRIS, GARDINER. "India's New Focus on Rape Shows Only the Surface of Women's Perils." *The New York Times*, January 12, 2013. Accessed April 20, 2014. http://www.nytimes.com/2013/01/13/world/asia/in-rapes-aftermath-india-debates-violence-against-women.html.
HASAN, ABID. "Experts divided over TRAI's move on cross media ownership." *exchange4media.com*, July 29, 2013. Accessed October 2, 2013. http://www.exchange4media.com/52126_experts-divided-over-trais-move-on-cross-media-ownership.html.
JAGANNATH, THEJAS. "From Littering to Spitting: Sanitary Problems in India's Public Spaces." *Urban Times*, February 12, 2013. Accessed May 30, 2014. http://urbantimes.co/2013/02/from-littering-to-spitting-sanitary-problems-in-indias-public-spaces/.
JENKINS, HENRY. *Convergence Culture: Where Old and New Media Collide*. New York & London: New York University Press, 2006.
KALRA, HARSIMRAN. "Report Summary: Report of the Committee on Amendments to Criminal Law, 2013." *PRS Legislative Research*, January 25, 2013. Accessed October 9, 2013. http://www.prsindia.org/parliamenttrack/report-summaries/justice-verma-committee-report-summary-2628/.
KAVIRAJ SUDIPTA. "On State, Society and Discourse in India," In *Rethinking Third World Politics*, edited by James Manor, 72–99. London & New York: Longman, 1991.
KOTISWARAN, PRABHA. "Unintended consequences of feminist action: Prabha Kotiswaran." *KAFILA*, February 18, 2013. Accessed July 31, 2014. http://kafila.org/2013/02/18/ unintended-consequences-of-feminist-action-prabha-kotiswaran/
KRISHNA, T.M. "Conversation flows, ideas don´t." *The Hindu*, November 24, 2012. Accessed July 31, 2014. http://www.thehindu.com/opinion/op-ed/conversation-flows-ideas-dont/article4127471.ece
KUMAR, RADHA. *The History of Doing: An Illustrated Account of Movements for Women's Rights and Feminism in India, 1800–1990*. New Delhi: Zubaan, 1997.
KUMAR, TILAK. "INS wants higher FDI ceiling in print media." *Times of India*, October 1, 2013. Accessed October 2, 2013. http://timesofindia.indiatimes.com/business/india-business/INS-wants-higher-FDI-ceiling-in-print-media/articleshow/23327919.cms.
LILLEKER, DARREN. *Key Concepts in Political Communications*. London: Sage, 2008.
MCBRIDE, MEREDITH, researcher. "INDIA: A Heartless Nation for Women." *Asian Human Rights Commission*, April 16, 2013. Accessed April 28, 2013: http://www.humanrights.asia/news/ahrc-news/AHRC-PAP-001-2013.

NDTV. "Badaun Rape Case." *NDTV*, June 2, 2014. Accessed August 8, 2014. http://www.ndtv.com/topic/badaun-rape-case

NELSON, DEAN. "Female tourists shun India after rape attack." *The Telegraph*, March 31, 2013.Accessed March 31, 2013. http://www.telegraph.co.uk/news/worldnews/asia/india/9963608/Female-tourists-shun-India-after-rape-attack.html.

O'SULLIVAN, CLAIRE. "India's Rape Shame." *The Irish Chronicle*, March 23, 2013. Accessed April 20, 2014. http://www.irishexaminer.com/lifestyle/features/indias-rape-shame-226260.html.

PATEL, VIBHUTI. "Women's Liberation in India." *New Left Review* I, no.153 (August 1985): 75–86.

PATEL, VIBHUTI. "Campaign against Rape by Women's Movement in India. Vibhuti Patel, Women's Research and Action Group (WRAG), Mumbai and President, WomenPowerConnect, Delhi." *GandhiTopia*, December 20, 2012. Accessed September 27, 2013. http://www.gandhitopia.org/profiles/blogs/campaign-against-rape-by-women-s-movement-in-india-vibhuti-patel.

RAJAGOPAL, ARVIND. *Politics after Television: Religious Nationalism and the Reshaping of the Indian Public*. Cambridge: Cambridge University Press, 2001.

REGE, SHARMILA. *Writing Caste, Writing Gender: Narrating Dalit Women's Testimonies*. New Delhi: Zubaan, An imprint of Kali for Women, 2006.

RINA. "Women's groups and activists on latest anti-rape Bill." *RINA (Rabita Islamic News Agency)*, March 17, 2013. Accessed November 17, 2013. http://www.rina.in/news/women%E2%80%99s-groups-and-activists-on-latest-anti-rape-bill/.

SANGARI, KUMKUM and SUDESH VAID, ed. *Recasting Women: Essays in Colonial India*. New Delhi: Kali for Women, 1989.

SATYA PRAKASH and HARISH V NAIR. "16/12: A crime that changed rape laws in India" *Hindustan Times*, September 11, 2013. Accessed October 11, 2013. http://www.hindustantimes.com/India-news/DelhiGangrape/16-12-A-crime-that-changed-rape-laws-in-India/Article1-1120370.aspx.

SEN, ILLINA, ed. *A Space within the struggle: women's participation in people's movements*. New Delhi: Kali for women, 1990.

SHAH NANDITA and NANDITA GANDHI. *The Issues at Stake: Theory and Practice in the Contemporary Women's Movement in India*. New Delhi: Kali for women, 1992.

STANCATI, MARGHERITA. "Foreigners Ask: Is India Safe?" *India Real Time* (Posted by *The Wall Street Journal*), March 18, 2013. Accessed June 1, 2014. http://floost.com/wsj-post-foreigners-ask-is-india-safe-3752859.

STUART, HUNTER. "India Refuses To Co-Sponsor UN Resolution To End Child Marriage." *The Huffington Post*, October 16, 2013. Accessed June 2, 2014. http://www.huffingtonpost.com/2013/10/16/india-child-marriage-un-resolution-sponsor_n_4108408.html.

SUBRAMANIAM, VIDYA. "PM Admits to Gender Insecurity." *The Hindu*, April 12, 2013. Accessed November 17, 2013. http://www.thehindu.com/todays-paper/pm-admits-to-gender-insecurity/article4608628.ece.

SUNDER, RAJAN RAJESHWARI. *The Scandal of the State: Women, Law, and Citizenship in Postcolonial India*. Delhi: Permanent Black, 2003.

TELTUMBDE, ANAND. "Delhi Gang Rape Case: Some Uncomfortable Questions." *Economic & Political Weekly* 48, no.6 (February 9, 2013): 10–11.
UDUPA, SAHANA. "Aam Adami: Decoding the Media Logic." *Economic & Political Weekly* 49, no. 7 (2014): 13–15.
WARNER, MICHAEL: "Publics and Counterpublics." *Public Culture* 4, no.1 (Winter 2002): 49–90.
"About India Real Time." *Indiarealtime* (Blog), Accessed June 2, 2014. http://blogs.wsj.com/indiarealtime/
"Age of Sexual Consent." *AVERT*, Accessed October 2, 2013. http://www.avert.org/age-sexual-consent.htm.
"Anti-rape Bill debate in Lok Sabha: Who among us have not followed girls? Sharad Yadav asks." *Times of India*, March 19, 2013. Accessed June 2, 2014. http://timesofindia.indiatimes.com/india/Anti-rape-Bill-debate-in-Lok-Sabha-Who-among-us-have-not-followed-girls-Sharad-Yadav-asks/articleshow/19070842.cms.
"Britain Issues Advisory for Women Travelling to India." *Outlook*, March 18, 2013. Accessed May 30, 2014. http://www.outlookindia.com/news/article/Britain-Issues-Advisory-for-Women-Travelling-to-India/792870.
"India has half the world's modern slaves: Study." *Times of India*, October 18, 2013. Accessed April 20, 2014. http://timesofindia.indiatimes.com/india/India-has-half-the-worlds-modern-slaves-Study/articleshow/24313244.cms.
"India Readership Survey 2008." *publicitas*, April 25, 2008. Accessed July 31, 2014. http://www.publicitas.com/zh/home/media-news-events/news-detail/?newsid=22413&title=india-indian-readership-survey-20081-irs-round-1#.U-C_o2Pc1Kl
"Mother India (book)." *Wikipedia*, Accessed April 25, 2014. http://en.wikipedia.org/wiki/Mother_India_%28book%29.
"One Billion Rising." *Wikipedia*, Accessed September 12 & October 2, 2013. http://en.wikipedia.org/wiki/One_Billion_Rising.
"Roop Kanwar." *Wikipedia*, Accessed October 11, 2013. http://en.wikipedia.org/wiki/Roop_Kanwar.

---

1   This was an oft-repeated theme in global discourse but absent in the national media.
2   Kotiswaran observes that "So it is not surprising that a couple of years ago, Catharine MacKinnon after urging the Indian government to pass a law criminalizing customers of sex workers, was stumped when asked an innocuous question on what she thought about the ban on bar dancing. And lest we forget, this inequality of ignorance matters! Western feminists have access to Indian institutions in a way that Indian feminists do not. Indicative of this is the profuse thanks that the Justice Verma Committee offered to Diane Rosenfeld of Harvard Law School in their mammoth report (Kotiswaran 2013).
3   This approach has been termed 'governance feminism'.
4   See Halley et al. (2006) for more detail. (online available at http://www.law.harvard.edu/students/orgs/jlg/vol292/halley.pdf).
5   I quote: "*Real Time* offers analysis and insights into the broad range of developments in business, markets, the economy, politics, culture, sports, and entertainment that take place every single day

in the world's largest democracy. Regular posts from Wall Street Journal and Dow Jones Newswires reporters around the country provide a unique take on the main stories in the news, shed light on what else mattered and why, and give global readers a snapshot of what Indians have been talking about all week." [INDIAREALTIME – This is a blog operating from India but with some understanding with Wall Street Journal and Dow Jones].

6   There are indeed more mobile phones in India than toilets. (Jagannath 2013)

7   Even as I put the last touches to this paper the decision has been reported in the media that 'industrialist Mukesh Ambani's Reliance Industries Ltd (RIL) is acquiring a majority stake in Raghav Bahl's Networks18 Media and Investments and its subsidiary TV18 Broadcast through Independent Media Trust (IMT) of which RIL is a sole beneficiary. Network18 Media and TV18 control a suite of broadcasting channels like CNBC-TV 18, Viacom18 and CNN-IBN, besides a bevy of e-commerce business and digital Internet sites. (BS Reporter 2014)

8   It may be recalled that TRAI had organised an open house discussion with stakeholders on June 29, 2013 regarding the ratings issue and cross media ownership. "Experts divided over TRAI's move on cross media ownership" (Hasan 2013).

9   Tilak Kumar, President of Indian Newspaper association (INS) pointed out that though print media continued to register growth in the country, advertising was steadily getting directed to electronic media. Recognizing that internet was fast emerging as a potent force in today's multimedia environment, Tilak Kumar said, "Any attempt to bring in restriction on cross-media ownership in India will almost certainly stop any further investments in the print media industry, which currently operates on fragile profit margins. The horizontal cross-media ownership is important to attain economies of scale." (Kumar 2013)

10 This was also an election where the role of social media and new technology such as widespread use of holograph of the BJP Prime Ministerial candidate Narendra Modi was unprecedented.

11 The Indian Readership Survey (IRS) is the largest continuous readership research study in the world with an annual sample size exceeding 2.56 lakh (256,000) respondents. IRS collects a comprehensive range of demographic information and provides extensive coverage of consumer and product categories, including cars, household appliances, household durables, household care and personal care products, food and beverages, finance and holidays. IRS is not restricted to survey of readership alone but is synonymous with both readership & consumption across various FMCG (Fast-Moving Consumer Goods) products throughout India. IRS covers information on over 100 product categories. IRS is conducted by MRUC (Media Research Users Council) and RSCI (Readership Studies Council of India) The two most widely read Hindi newspapers, Dainik Jagran and Dainik Bhaskar, together recorded a total of 89.8 million readers in 2008, while the most read English daily, The Times of India, had 13.3 million readers (Indian Readership Survey). There are in all 622 TV channels either already operating or planning to commence operations in India. (www.Scatmag.com, accessed January 20, 2009)

12 Narendra Modi, the new Prime Minister's public speeches are either in Gujarati in his home state or Hindi elsewhere. His interviews in the English language TV channels such as *Times Now* were conducted in Hindi.

13 Rajya Sabha Television had a discussion on why we need to bring in history in media discussions which are usually obsessed with the immediate. 1st June 2014.

14 Almost every leading newspaper and magazine in India these days seems to think it is necessary to organize an "intellectual" event. They call these events summits, conclaves or conferences. The organizers project these events so as to appear on the side of "thought" or "ideas", as if seeking credibility and justification for their existence. But these gatherings are nowhere close to the brain storming sessions they are cracked up to be. Basically, they are huge "talking" extravaganza in which every participant is a performer before an audience, and like any other performer, craves its approval (Krishna 2012 emphasis mine).

15 PhD thesis on gender for example invariably begins with the WAD, WID and GAD debate.

16 Inhabiting the world you study offers one what anthropologist call a worm's eye view of your object of inquiry.

17 Satiis a custom practiced by some dominant Hindu castes in India in which the widow was burnt to ashes on her dead husband's pyre. The Sati Act was passed in 1829 (Chaudhuri 2011, 20–24).

18 Upper caste Hindu women of some regions were not allowed to marry if widowed. A campaign to

change this was launched. The Act legalizing the marriage of Hindu widows was promulgated in July 1856 (ibid).

19   Age of marriage for girls was of central concern with child marriage being common across many parts of the country. The first Age of Consent Bill was passed in 1860 (Chaudhuri 2011, 72–78).

20   Mathura, a teenage tribal girl was raped by two policemen in the police station in 1972. The legal battle began when a woman lawyer took up her case but the Supreme Court of India held that Mathura had given consent. A nation-wide anti-rape campaign demanded reopening of the Mathura Rape Case and amendments in the Rape Law. Prominent lawyers took up the issue, as did the national and regional language press (See Patel 1985).

21   The Shah Bano case (1985 SCR (3) 844) was a controversial maintenance lawsuit in India (See Sunder Rajan 2003).

22   Roop Kanwar, aged 18 immolated herself on 4th September 1987 in Rajasthan. Several thousand people attended the sati event. The event quickly produced a public outcry in urban centres. The incident led first to state level laws to prevent such incidents, till then under the central government's Commission of sati (Prevention) Act. See: http://en.wikipedia.org/wiki/Roop_Kanwar.

23   See Udupa 2014 for an analysis of Aam Aadmi Party which spearheaded the anti-corruption movement as a media creation.

24   The emergence of the Aam Aadmi Party bears significant resemblance to earlier political events in recent Indian history. An Emergency was declared in 1975 by the then Prime Minister Indira Gandhi. All democratic rights enshrined in the Indian Constitution were suspended. The large coalition of political parties that fought this and finally won the General Elections in 1977 was tellingly christened Janata Party (translating to People's Party). More recently, the anti-corruption movement initiated by Anna Hazare and led by others such as Arvind Kejriwal chose to form a political party titled Aam Aadmi, meaning literally the 'ordinary man'; figuratively the 'everybody'.

25   This usually comprises of various spokespersons of political parties, other veteran journalists, 'experts' and 'celebrities' from various fields.

26   These are the everyday minutiae that I referred to earlier.

27   Le Monde reported: "New Delhi roars of emotion and anger. The crowds are out in the street, candle in hand, to honour the victim or the more virulent call for hanging attackers" (Ghosh 2012).

28   Flavia Agnes welcomed the nationwide protest but hoped that "for the sake of quick and easy solutions," the discourse "will not flatten out the complexities involved in issues concerning violence against women" (Agnes 2013, 14).

29   See: Justice Verma Committee Report Summary. (Kalra 2013).

30   Acting on the recommendations of the Verma committee, the parliament passed the Criminal Law (Amendment) Act 2013, that widened the definition of rape and also provided for death penalty in rape cases that cause death of the victim or leave her in a vegetative state. It also created several new offences such as causing grievous hurt through acid attacks, sexual harassment, use of criminal force on a woman with intent to disrobe, voyeurism and stalking.

31   The RSS is a critical element of the BJP led Indian government, which took over in May end 2014. What the RSS public position will be now is yet to be seen. It is too early to take a final call even as possible changes may be expected. RSS recently agreed to take a fresh look at homosexuality.

32   Asaram Bapu has since been arrested of charges of sexual assault.

33   "...Dalits who suffer alone when their daughters are raped and murdered with impunity are annoyed by this sudden burst of concern for rape victims" (Teltumbde 2013, 10).

34   The RJD and SP fiercely opposed the Women's Reservation Bill. See Chaudhuri 'Preface' [1993] 2011.

35   A ready example is that of a Gillette Advertisement stating that we need soldiers not for warfare but for standing up for women, has been appreciated by some and condemned by others.

36   The long running popular serial *Balika Badhu* on child marriage had the protagonist Anandi run a campaign on sexual harassment and ways to fight it with her screen husband. *Colours* 17th September 2013. In 2014 we saw the same serial depict one of its central protagonists as a rape survivor.

37 Indian television anchors increasingly invoke the 'nation' on a daily basis. Arnab Goswami of *Times Television*, modeled on Fox Television lines, initiated a combative style, appropriating the voice of the nation.

38 Many experts participating in debates move from one TV channel to another, across Hindi and English language channels.

39 Katherine Mayo became notorious for her polemical book Mother India (1927), in which she attacked Hindu society and religion, and the culture of India. The book created an outrage across India, and it was burned along with her effigy. It was criticised by Mahatma Gandhi as a "report of a drain inspector sent out with the one purpose of opening and examining the drains of the country to be reported upon". The book prompted over fifty angry books and pamphlets to be published to highlight See: http://en.wikipedia.org/wiki/Mother_India_%28book%29.

40 Core labour standards are inserted into an article within the WTO Agreements. If a member state violated the social clause, the breach could become subject to WTO scrutiny, through the usual WTO dispute settlement provisions. At the request of the complaining party retaliatory trade measures could be taken against the offending country.

41 While the orthodoxy had criticized this on grounds of religious sanction, a section of nationalists had opposed it on grounds that the British state had no business in interfering in domestic matters of Indians when they had turned a deaf ear to other pressing issues raised by Indians.

42 A Criminal law (amendment) Bill- 2013 was passed and women's groups persisted with their campaign to ensure that the law passed by the Union cabinet was approved in parliament. (*The Hindu* March 17, 2013).

43 See: 'Age of Sexual Consent' on http://www.avert.org/age-sexual-consent.htm.

44 The All India Democratic Women's Association (AIDWA) is an independent left oriented women's organisation committed to achieving democracy, equality and women's emancipation. AIDWA members are from all strata in society, regardless of class, caste and community. ...About two-thirds of the organsation's strength is derived from poor rural and urban women. AIDWA was founded in 1981 as a national level mass organisation of women. However, several state units of the organisation came into existence in the crucible of the freedom struggle, each with a commendable record of anti-imperialist and pro-working class actions. See: http://aidwaonline.org/.

45 Two young cousins were raped and hanged in Badoun, Uttar Pradesh, which once again has become a prime event on national media. Political parties, the National Commission for Women, the media has once again rallied around the case. The United Nation's has issued a condemnation. It may not be easy to ignore this terrible crime any longer as an aberration (NDTV, 2nd June 2014).

JESNA JAYACHANDRAN

Outrage, debate or silence: An analysis of reader comments and online rape news[1]

Introduction

In December 2012, the death of a young woman following a brutal gang rape in Delhi triggered massive coverage and protests unlike any other recent crimes against women.[2] Traditional news media definitely played a critical role in mediating women's issues and rights since this incident. Online and offline gender activism through blogs, Twitter and Facebook too drove opinion and appeared to shape democratic discourses. Together they set new horizons for citizen engagement with news within a broader political struggle for gender rights. However, a narrow focus on participatory cultures opened up by new digital formats like social media overlooks other digital experiences like online news consumption and gender discourses in these spaces. Commenting online in news sites provides an immediate, common mode of user-participation, interaction and expression of alternative views in varying degrees of reader anonymity; even challenging journalistic contents and encouraging journalistic engagement in a format that woos the reader-customer. Known as reader comments they are an expression of reader opinions on news, blogs, and other online sites. Yet, globally it remains an underexplored area (Reich 2011). In India, the world's second largest print newspaper market, online news consumption has seen a slow but steady growth despite shallow internet penetration (ComScore 2013). Research about India's online news has been about growth strategies and audience behaviour and much less about its consumption possibilities. This article explores news interactivity in an online news platform, the conversations it enables with other readers and what user-generated content in response to professional journalistic products mean in an instant access, online, global participative scenario. Most of the emergent literature on reader comments and participative practices comes from the West with only few on gender. There are practically none from the Indian context, where print is flourishing and shallow internet penetration indicates a lot of scope for internet publishing (Schneider 2013, 22). Given the conflicting discourse on violence against women at a specific time, this study of reader comments offers a view into everyday user-generated conversations on women's issues.

This article looks at online reader comments to news about rape[3] after the Delhi gang rape in December 2012. Indian women's issues have historically received sustained interest and been part of a longer history of institutional change, confronting gender power structures, women's rights and public visibilities, issues of minorities, kinship, gender norms, religion, caste and laws (Chaudhuri 2005). A critical engagement against sexual violence is a definite part of institutionalization of a democratic process to transform norms that victimize women. Issues of sexual violence and gender consciousness however have always been seized by connections of caste, class and exclusions borne by privilege and marginalization. Activists have pointed out the paradox in mediated narratives about victims of sexual violence in the public sphere: that only certain cases provoke public reaction, the muteness of public reactions to organized violence against minorities, the involvement of state/police and the failure of media in intervening in such violence; all problematic notions maintained by a majority of the public too. Dalit and tribal women's atrocities as many scholars observe have often been under-reported, with some in the media business who explain it with recourse to business logic that drive constructions of news norms partly in response to the demands and interests of an imagined middle class audience. The 2012 incident, however, expanded public discourse. It renewed visibility to struggles against sexual violence and the ensuing legal reforms brought gender to the top of the public sphere debate. This study is located at a specific time in history, when public interest surged around women's rights, itself highly mediated in a commercial, competitive media environment.

When the internet emerged as a site of news, Indian newspapers aggressively courted online growth, experimented with different modes of engaging with readers, innovated content and digitalization to compete with television and competitor newspapers. Offline too, newspapers are experimenting with localization of content, regional-language editions and marketing campaigns to promote local identity in a big way (Schneider 2013). One concern is that the access to internet is difficult for a vast majority of people in India. The engagement of internet users with online news could therefore arguably be acutely class specific. Still, new media (cheap smart phones, mobile apps and SMS) visibly mediate experiences beyond class to a good extent. Social media too has reconfigured public's engagements with news. All this and the availability of cheap cell phones are reconfiguring rural-urban publics and markets in India (Doron and Jeffrey 2013). Conceding Twitter and Facebook function as a widely visible public sphere, much less is known about people's extended online involvement with news, especially the lesser visible spaces of reader comments in online news sites.[4] Although there are online feminist interventions through blogs, conversations within user communities in what appear to be private but definitely public digital platforms like news sites are hardly interrogated. The way journalists frame rape stories in various contexts and report them as unique incidents or as a larger social issue influences reader interests, reader's reaction to stories and how the seriousness of violence is perceived. In this sense news and reader comments about rape and the interlinked manner in which it is analysed become a useful site to illustrate the ways that media and users deploy gender and violence in some discussions while silencing it in others. It is in these contexts that this article seeks to look at online reader comments to examine the possibilities of socially and democratically experiencing news about gender violence in the Times of India (TOI) Online.

The article discusses two stages of analysis. The first stage relying on content analysis asks what is reported about rape and what gets engaged with by readers. I explore readers' comments to different coverage of rape news – the way news is presented online, geographical coverage, what stories generate more response and how news frames initiate discussions associated with gender violence. Secondly, the first findings help to explore the nature of various schemas drawn by ordinary people to discuss rape. Framed against a discussion of online features that structure commenting and readers' engagement, it analyses the ideological structures that mediate gender in online spaces. This focus of technology, news consumption practices and broader social circumstances explain the production and embeddedness of cultural assumptions about sexual violence.

Reader comments to online news

Although online access has never been universal or equal, research on internet based communication has often celebrated the possibility of extending critical, rational debate and public opinion formation and thereby a deliberative, democratic public sphere (Dahlberg 2011). If 'Letters to editor', subjected to editorial interventions, were a limited avenue for deliberation over news in the print format, online spaces in news websites visibly encourage deeper reader engagements (Boczkowski 2004, Reich 2011). The instant global nature of interaction through online reader comments especially appears to revive the "publicness" of newspapers (Wahl-Jorgensen 2002, 122). Moderation strategies have varied according to political climate and legal and economic consideration of news organizations. Instant access, feedback and engaging in dialogues, however, have advantages and disadvantages. Research on reader comments has been diffused partly because they fit within the 'broader context of user-generated content' and because they have not yet been assigned a common name (McCluskey and Hmielowski 2011, 306). A defining characteristic of online news sites is interactivity. Interactivity enacted through commenting to news outside the gatekeeping associated with print media, discussions of issues anonymously with a wider set of people, arguments, tagging and responding to immediate comments and not directly to news alone – all serve to demonstrate modes of online news consumption, a larger public expression of reader views to stories and a certain manner of making sense of news jointly.

Specifically in addressing interactivity, emergent literature explores dialogical or two way communication patterns facilitated through digital formats that allow readers to participate, select, and transform older journalistic patterns of news production. In this context, one research agenda suggests the social construction of technology perspective: the mutual shaping of technology and journalistic practices, news agenda and newsroom practices based on user and producer feedback (Boczkowski 1999). But there are suggestions otherwise about journalists' appraisal of reader participation. Journalistic norms regarding expertise could prevent engagement with readers and the mutual shaping or technology affecting practice and coverage might not necessarily be true (Nielsen 2013). The anonymity afforded through concealing identities while commenting could result in 'utterly aggressive content' that impede constructive discussions (Boczkowski 1999, 105). Generally, 'writing under pen names lowers both the 'intellectual level' of comments and user responsibility for them' (Reich 2011, 104). Others have looked at opinion expression through comments by bridging offline and online modes of news consumption (McCluskey and Hmielowski 2011). Studies in the West observed that political stories tend to be most commented especially during heightened political activity (Boczkowski and Mitchelstein 2012). Elsewhere, interactivity strategies appropriated by readers in news sites like Al Jazeera show a relation with themes in news coverage (Abdul-Mageed 2008). The general focus in most studies has been on sites and the possibilities of reader interactivity while 'very little has been done scientifically to analyse the actual content of the public's comments on online news stories' (Paskin 2010, 71). Again, while news factors and content influence participation and interactive discussions, 'the quality of the users' discourse in the comments' has not been analysed (Weber 2013, 13). The present study is different in that it takes a specific analytical theme instead of broad coverage and analyses reader comments too. Media coverage of rape draws strong responses as it brings attention to women's socially embedded structural oppression, issues of consent and non-consensual sex as well as legal and cultural discourses. Another striking aspect is that even when online technologies are accessible to a few (mostly male), making it 'exclusive, elitist, and far from ideal' (Papacharissi 2002), studies do not specifically examine gender in relation to online news commenting.[5] Unlike gender, evolving comment moderation policies have addressed racist vitriol in the West. But its regulation requires new methodological innovations in discourse analysis of reader comments as racism continue to appear online in 'white-washed' forms (Hughey and Daniels 2013). However, attempts to counter online sexism in reader comments are rare. Again, online gender harassment has made women journalists wary of engaging with the internet (Roderick 2014) and intimidated women even when they work on non-controversial topics (Padte 2013, Wallace 2014). In this study I pay attention to gender discourses within the comments sections of rape news in a news site where moderation policies partly rely on readers and where reader discourses can be expressed in relative anonymity.

The analytical approach here reflects two of the five listed by Reich (2011) as it focusses on (1) the 'rhetorical aspect', i.e. the way a story is framed in order to look at what evokes more or few comments; and (2) the way gender is mediated in rape discussion indicates a number of political and ethical issues. It relies on a more complex understanding of reader agency as users engaged in multiple roles 'in a media environment where the boundaries between commerce, content and information' are possibly being redrawn in a different sense (van Dijk 2009, 42). This would mean exploring the roles of online features and reader content that shape and guide characteristics of the online reader community. Keeping with recent literature this study pursues an empirical strategy that addresses 'multiple relevant dimensions of the phenomena under study' and relies on 'mixed method designs' (Mitchelstein and Boczkowski 2009, 2).

Why The Times Of India?

Out of the many newspapers online, The Times of India (TOI) topped online news ranking with 12.7 million unique visitors in August 2013. Its share of visitors from abroad stood at 37.8 percent of its total audience (ComScore 2013). TOI online has an 'exhaustive local coverage' of 30 Indian cities with a 'unique' feature of speed news that provides real time news updates by 500 reporters across India. It is also the only online news site in India that is available on five major mobile apps platform[6]. Offline too, according to the Indian Readership Survey (2012), the TOI is the only English daily amongst the top publications in India with a readership base of 7.6 million. Besides, the TOI has a highly commercial model of reader connection interactivity campaigns and online loyalty programs. This has intensified since TOI rode the 1990s liberalization wave, promoting privatization through a transformed market oriented news agenda. All this prompted me to pick the TOI as a site.

The TOI website is a dense one that is crowded with news, entertainment, advertisement and videos from TNN (Times News Network). The site opens to home pages based on readers' preferences and various tools facilitate reader interactivity. Names, location, e-mail or log in through Facebook/Twitter are obligatory to post comments, although readers give pseudonymous location and names. At the time of the Delhi gang rape incident the box had a simple 'Have something to say? Post your comment' instruction. Later on the website included a disclaimer to discourage 'libellous, slanderous or inflammatory' comments with a request to readers to help mark offensive comments and keep the conversation civil. Agree, disagree or recommend provisions also allow others to add to what people have already said without logging in.[7] The site subtly updates its comment moderation strategies from time to time.

There appears to be no closing of comments. The site automatically suggests related stories through pop-ups and hyperlinks (implying some degree of reader surveillance for revenue channelling). Readers can access older news about similar topics. As commenting is open, comments can also be placed anytime[8]. Comments can be seen according to the most agreed, latest and most recommended ones. It is also possible to click on member-readers who leave comments and track their activities or what they have been reading on their wall. News is flagged in the rare instance that a journalist responds to comments. Competitively aggressive, the site courts technically suave readers who are treated as valuable consumers as part of brand loyalty initiatives.

Readers are encouraged to post comments as members to earn badges and points reflect membership status based on their online activities.[9] For instance, members who report inappropriate comments with a high accuracy can earn a Moderator badge that allows them to directly remove offensive comments from the site. Therefore there could be other motivations for news consumption and commenting may not purely be an immediate response to news (although there is no clear way to know it).

Methodological Approach

All published stories were collected from February 16 to August 2, 2013 from the TOI database to yield six months of rape related coverage. This broad time period was taken for two reasons: for a reliable generation of sample considering the non-linearity, multimodality and interactivity of websites and because this period witnessed intense debates on gender issues following the December 2012 incident. The search listed hundreds of stories from Punjab, Maharashtra, and Delhi. Online media permit certain flexibility in publishing news. Sometimes the site uploads a story and then updates the same news. If it appears to not have caught attention, the headlines are changed, content is slightly rewritten and the same news would be reposted the next day. News with similar content but with a different headline and vice versa was identified during the period of collecting data. Within a given day only one such news was saved. Once the news for six months was collected, it was sorted into seven days of the week based on the constructed week method. Constant news updates make it difficult to apply the same methodological strategies as for print media.[10] The constructed week method, however, is by far the best to account for cyclical variation in news coverage and representativeness (Riffe et al. 1993). News and comments for six months were plotted into a table. Days with intense coverage following an incident, international women's day and days with too few news or with missing data were removed.[11] Each day of the week (including Sunday) was thus chosen after cleaning to include at least one day from each month. Considering the immediacy of the internet such a frame was intended to capture all coverage in a given day. There were few methodological considerations that permitted this: the way TOI produces news and my research objectives. TOI updates news throughout the day and has an average of more crime coverage in comparison to other papers with reader responses from across the world.[12] I included articles with few comments too. As the results reveal, not being commented upon also shows how a news article is received in a deeply stratified society like India.

The constructed week generated 143 stories and a total of 5534 comments. Data interpretation relied on a mixed method analysis of content analysis and critical discourse analysis. Content analysis was used to determine news and commenting relationship. This was followed with an analysis of comments. Discourse analysis helped to look at meanings, patterns of expression and its contested nature to understand power and politics at play. It also offers a critique of dominance resulting in social inequality through representation, legitimation, support and opposition by looking at structures and strategies of interaction that reproduces these (van Dijk 1993, 250). I relied on a feminist approach so as to locate issues of gender and power and how discourses reproduce it. It also means acknowledging a certain reflexivity to understand language patterns and subject positions (Hammersley 1992, 193).

Data was sorted into two tables – one that looked at prominence with regards to coverage as national news and state wise. Data collected under different cities were collated to state wise codes. A second code classified stories according to incidents of sexual assault like gang rape, rape of children, teenagers, differently abled, Dalit and minorities, etc. against what was most dominantly reported in the story, e.g. the persons involved, government measures, if the story conveyed information about court proceedings, sentencing, arrests and First Information Report (FIR).[13] This was used as a starting point to understand commenting and the nature of discourse. The two codes were tested with another coder to understand how the other coder made sense of the data. There was full agreement with the first code. In the second set there were issues which were resolved after discussion. For example, what to do with poorly edited stories where rape incidents were reported under a single heading along with other crime stories. If the story was only reported in one or two sentences it was discarded, otherwise retained. One article on gang rape charges against Indian-origin men posted online under Non-Resident Indian (NRI) was assigned to 'India' code, a story of the rape of a very old woman was assigned to 'rape and assault' category instead of creating a new one and the story of the gang rape of a married woman was assigned to gang rape to reflect that news (and reader reactions) slant instead of the category 'married'.

News and reader comments

On an average day there were 20.42 stories on rape and 790.57 comments. Content analysis revealed that online coverage appeared to influence the frequency of comments. Table 1 shows (18.88%) stories with national prominence (posted online under the 'India' label) received an overwhelming (61.74%) comments, followed by Delhi (13% comments), Maharashtra (6.9%), and Uttar Pradesh (6.9%). Stories from the North East and Kashmir are few (considering the negligible coverage from mainstream media) and it is not surprising that they do not figure in the sample.

Comments are high from Friday through Monday, while the rest of the week is slow. To correlate whether multimedia influenced commenting, images and videos accompanying stories were analysed. Most stories were without multimedia (86%) but received 39.7% of the total comments. Stories with pictures (6.9%) and with video (6.29%) received 28.7% and 31.5% of the total comments respectively, perceptively showing that commenting was proportionately more when accompanied by multimedia (Figure 1).

33.3% of total comments were dialogical. To explore the full possible range of user interactivity and social practices Facebook likes, Twitter and Google shares of stories were appraised. Google share was hardly used. Stories that received comments were also the ones circulated through tweets and Facebook likes. Stories were shared more through Facebook likes perhaps amongst known people ($\Sigma=2754$) rather than broadcast on Twitter ($\Sigma=1382$) which possibly reaches a larger group of strangers. Larger issue based discussion through posting comments (user-to-user interactivity) dominated.

The comments ranged from a few words to short sentences and large, rambling paragraphs. The number of comments to news was counted to identify any correlations between the categories of the news stories and comment frequencies. As Table 2 shows, comments varied according to incidences covered. It is the reporting of rape instances – assault, persons involved and arrests that received maximum coverage (44.7% stories) and (48.84%) comments. Stories of gang rape (13.9%) received the next highest number of comments (24.9%), and within it readers mostly commented when frames captured arrests, incidents and assault. (26.5%) stories were about incidents involving children, which received a response of (21.16%). Reports of rape by known persons were more (10.4%) than those committed by strangers (4.8%) but they received comparatively lesser comments (7.9%) than stranger crimes (13.6%). The lone story about a rape of a Dalit woman was hardly commented upon, showing that both journalistic and public interest was lacking in the context of minorities who have historically been targets of violence.

The digital context

To begin with, the context of commenting is itself structured. It is overwhelmingly male with roughly 95.7% comments displaying male names.[14] Only 4.2% of the comments appeared to be females (posted with a female name), out of which some where spam. Not all spam can be culled out unproblematically as often done in studies of reader comments. In discussions on gender issues spams referring to political ideologies or to religion crucially evidence positioning politics and religion in gender and violence norm constructions, as often gender itself is a site of ideological battles in social, cultural, political and democratic experiences.

Readers appear to use the comments page as an open forum sometimes. There is recognition of frequent contributors and readers and friendly personal communication. Members 'follow' each other and appear to recognize political positions and perspectives on gender. Occasionally, accusations of posting comments just to garner Times points and earn badges fly fast and high. As mentioned earlier, user-to-user interactivity is acted out through comments by tagging agreements, disagreements and recommendations that are aggregated into reader ranks and badges. In this sense, the reader comments section mirrors an online community where commerce, information, content, users and technology come together; specifically a TOI consumer community whose readers are assessed not through comments alone, but through user-to-user interactivity and the site's commercial rating that motivates readers to engage with news in more ways than one. Beyond commenting to specific stories, evidence suggests that readers use comment spaces to discuss justice, policing and gender norms. Expectedly, heterosexual norms, gender roles and patriarchal discourses dominate. Expressions of outrage, criticism of the government, a slow judiciary and incompetent police rest uncomfortably alongside sexist jokes, patriarchal views on gender norms, sexuality, politics, religion, culture, and morality which to a certain extent are also swayed by online group behaviour. Links to YouTube videos, Google and other news submitted by readers indicate wider avenues of audience participation beyond online news sites.

Anonymity and profiling the reader

Generally studies of reader comments observe that anonymity dampens (critical) discourse, although conversely it encourages greater participation. Anonymity makes it difficult to identify male and female readers. But pseudonyms do not free readers from social judgement. Female pen names pose challenges too. In TOI, even when anonymous comments are posted, readers construct and stereotype identities of gender, caste and religion through pen names, location information, through familiarity with the commenting history of readers and through 'agree' and 'disagree' tags. This appears to dampen participation. For instance, in a story on a court ruling about a bad affair and rape charges, a reader observed that 'all those who said this judgement is good are men' and asked for the opinion of 'women counterparts'. An observation by a reader with 411 followers and a neutral pseudonym (AAM JANTA DAL ATAL)[15] that the ruling was 'tough' and 'either one crime' of 'Defrauding or raping' ought to have been charged was treated by others as a feminine opinion. Further, female readers tend to receive more disagree tags. A women reader who wrote that 'for years girls took the abuse and it is understandable to see resistance when one gets the taste of one's own medicine' goes on to explain why readers 'want to disagree with everything concerning me' by explicitly stating:

> 'They think I am a feminist which is not exactly true. I am really surprised at their unity and to see how all these men gang up against women to defend even rapists/cheats/criminals. Phew'. (Bharathi 12/7/2014)

Subsequently she agrees to the popular opinion of not entering into a relationship before marriage. Quite unlike male readers, who also use emotional language, female readers (or those who use feminine pen names to express similar emotions) are often offered assurances and 'advice' to put their emotions under check. To a woman who reacted in her anger to the news of a girl set on fire after a gang rape, a male commentator left a response, 'we are used to this news. Please stay calm and do not get disturbed. Please take care of one safety. At least keep chilly spray with you. (Sushil, 12/7/2013)'. Readers are also hyper vigilant about Pakistanis or Sri Lankans 'in disguise'. Some readers do not comment to stories at all but pounce to counter anti-nationalist observations and inflammatory posts that slander India or undermine its achievements. Retaliation often resonates with sexual expletives and further flaming. Readers therefore recreate an online social world. Prior registration and the fact that other readers monitored comments did not appear to deter abusive and libellous comments or to make commenting spaces civil by reporting disruptive posts.

Language and participation

Secondly, there is some sort of democratization in terms of participation as people post comments in Hindi, Hinglish and in broken English. While online posts generally contain poor spellings and grammar, readers also use technical terminologies like 'give data points' or 'India needs to updater herself, abolish these time worn customs against women'. To capture this flavour, I retain the incorrect spellings and grammar in the comments used in this study. The use of mixed language evidences that not all participants are the average, urban English educated ones:

> 'if 1 rapist hangout in public place by the government then another not born' (mehulgalani)

> 'Tu toh bahut cool hai !! Surat mein kahan hangout karte rapist ??Koi toh khaas jagahogi...[16] (dawoodsaitsait)

> 'you meant "hanged out", right?' (Donald Duck replies to mehulgalani 12/7/2013)

Comments could also exclude readers when, for instance, readers post comments in Bengali typed in English to stories from West Bengal. The site permits readers to do so, which along with its extensive coverage of regional news could be a brand extension exercise to encourage readers to transit to the 'English mainstream'[17]. Participation, however, is influenced by a certain history of linguistic differences and identities that mark Indian nationalism, often resulting in online confrontations about 'who' comments in what language and how it is understood.[18] For instance, the comment below in Hindi stating that, 'disaster is certain where women are not respected' is misinterpreted by another reader:

> Pralaya door nahin, jahan naari kaa samman nahin wahan vinaash nishchit hai. (Manish, 29/7 2013)

cannot understand HINGLISH...why you guys use this foul language..when the article is in English... respond in English...if you are still fond of Hindi .. file your comments in some Hindi e newspaper... we in south India hate imposition of Hindi and hinglish (foxysusangopi, 29/7/2013)

Such comments thus detract from addressing the main story. Consistent with the findings of other studies, readers also negotiate 'norms' of commenting like 'pls write in small letters' (Barnacles Poche, 18/3/2013) because 'it's really hard to read when someone is shouting in capital letters' (Julian, 18/3/2013), besides disciplining online name-calling over differences of opinion.

Moderation and participation

Thirdly, the online platform also structures how texts are produced and archived. For instance, there is no way to know 'offensive' comments that have been removed. The site's auto-moderation filters flag comments with certain words as inappropriate regardless of story contexts with an alert that the reader is trying to post an inappropriate comment. This makes posting responses to rape news especially difficult and thereby organizes discourses in a constrained manner:

'I am irresistibly drawn to crime news...some deviancy within me that makes this state of affairs "attractive" or...I am so stunned and fraught with disbelief that... \r#pe and mutilation of a 4 year child actually occurs...poverty wasn't necessarily a reason for beastly behavior...vastly more family-against-family crimes in India,...people...once associated with a collective Gandhiesque quality... Maybe it has always been that way except now technology brings out that characteristics...! Why is this post inappropriate? Because it reflects the truth????????????' (naronss, 29/7/013)

Readers therefore deploy pragmatic constructions to participate in discussions. These include, 'Raape', 'r@pe', ' r@pist', 's e x', 'm o l e s t a t i o n', 'rpe', 'r0pe' , 'mole*sting', 's*e*x*ual', 'ra*p*is*ts', 'rapping', 'rap', ', 'rapexx' , 'R&pe'. There is some angst and discomfort with the media's 'new', obsessive coverage of rape with readers reacting in disbelief. Some argue that they are mere media constructs or attempts to increase Target Rating Points[19]. Others worry about the 'effects' of such exposure on 'society', while yet others read through stories to imply that the woman was somehow at fault:

> 'Stop doing this OR Stop reporting this.' (CitiZen India, 12/7/2013)

> 'Yeh sonhc (hindi for sh*t) pe gayi malila ke saath duskarm wali headline/news kab band hogi. Why no one make toilets at home why gandgi doesn't disturb anyone.' (Kumar s, 12/7/2013)[20]

> '...media is blowing this unfortunate event in a big way. this is a rare event...in south India so many foreign tourists roaming so freely they always feel home.' (Suriya Kumar 18/3/2013)

> 'What is wrong with people around Delhi? The press coverage such crimes get encourages more crimes by giving them ideas.' (Raj Kumar 29/7/2013)

There is speculation if publishing rape stories is 'politically motivated to bring bad name to ruling government' (nideeshm 18/3/2013). As these comments show, there is a sense that readers view such news as just another 'story' which evidences the patriarchal tolerance of violence. These comments are occasionally countered by readers who are convinced about the media's role in exposing crime and paving the way for justice in an otherwise 'corrupt' country. Also, in an attempt to make others understand the issue through personal reflections, readers appeal with personal entreaties, if rape would have been tolerated 'had it happened' to their 'mothers and sisters'.

Religion, politics and discussion structures

Fourthly, the comments section is riddled with battles over religion and politics that also drive the very act of posting comments and consuming news including rape news. For example, in a story about a 75 year old Hindu priest who had been caught molesting young girls, a reader (who was not a registered commentator) frantically interrupted others who were posting competing, caustic comments about rape being pervasive within religious cultures:

> Muslim brother please come and comment in the news section where "'-81 shias killlid in pakistan , " „ 25 moslim brothers dead in Iraq . Many hindoos are their in that news writing wrong about islam .We need you in those news section ,no point beating empty band here. Hindoos are abusing s*unnis and wahabis in those news. (Kamran, 17/2/2013)[1]

Such typical patterns in reader comments lead to distinct discussion structures. These typical religious and political responses also appear to indicate the formation of smaller reader communities based on ideologies within the site's readers community, something that is bolstered through online group commenting and activities.

Comments about victims and perpetrators

Many readers leave sympathetic comments and prayers for victims. Others react with rage calling for the violent mutilation of perpetrators depending on the story. Breaking down the media's popular construction of the 2012 Delhi gang rape victim as 'Nirbhaya' (the Fearless One), a reader observed that "Nirbaya' or 'Nirbagya'[21] injustice is nothing less than the cruel acts of those criminals' (A P Madhusudanan 17/2/2013). Occasionally readers use the digital platform to talk directly with victims (giving support, assurances), criminals, politicians and editors. Loaded with emotional language, such comments are posted in a monological style and evidence direct communication. Elsewhere, there are expressions of anger, hopelessness, despair and pain that convey 'severe disgust against inhuman creatures who commit such crimes' as 'A film like scenes move in front of eyes so horrible that they haunt hours long to forget' (romesh.sharma 29/7/2013). Some readers encourage victims to fight for justice. There are odd references to the 'Nirbhaya case' and how 'her sacrifice' has been in vain while criticizing political parties. However, victims are

---

1 The incorrect punctuation follows the original. Also, the use of small letters without capital letters for country or religion and religious groups conveys the sense of urgency with which the reader typed in his comments.

also called outrageous names from 'dirty sex bomb females' to 'whore/pros'. Often the circumstances in the story are used as references to blame victims, e.g. 'she is ready to lose her modesty just for scholarship' (Murali Dhara 18/3/2013).Victim blaming is sometimes countered by readers:

> 'It's not about FAMILY VALUES... She doesn't have to belong to ANY-ONE, she is an INDIVIDUAL, a human, right GOD has given her, not the people controlling her and not the press who may print to get publicity.' (Niraj 12/7/2013)

Again, there is some awareness that, 'silencing of victims (with blaming, shaming and naming) empowers...criminals' (Bahratiya Grihanee 29/6/2013). However, in many instances, news frames and different contexts of rape influenced how victims were perceived by readers. The use of descriptive details and personal quotes in stories like the rare article about the devastating trauma faced by the highly politicized Suryanelli[22] rape case victim elicited many empathetic reader comments unlike fact-laden stories that were reported as incidents. Even then victim blaming and counter comments collide with political loyalties resulting in abusive rants and personal attacks around rape images (occasionally as attempts to force personal reflection). When a reader who doubted the victim's version was accused of being amongst the '42 to have raped her' (Indian 17/2/2013), he countered it with an enraged 'maybe you need to raped!' (Clan 17/2/2013). The Delhi Nirbhaya is then evoked as a yardstick to frame discourses of the 'innocent victim' who cannot be compared to 'blackmailers/TRP hogs' and 'fake cases'. As Norton and Grant (2008) argue, these comments expose rape stereotypes (rather than rape myths like those framed around cultural notions of women's dressing and male sexuality). They illustrate rape myths in a deeper manner as they reveal more damaging ideologies that mark rape experiences that do not confirm to the myth.

Comments about dressing, sexuality, morality and sexual violence are illustrated with examples of the exploitative, sexualized portrayal of women in the media as an explanation for cultural decay. For instance, to bolster this argument, a reader once drew on an advertisement in TOI, 'See, what they are showing on the right side of this screen a girl with red dress... What is that called? A r@pe or Respect?' (Garbha ya, 12/7/2013). These comments rage into short stereotypical exchanges supported by agree/disagree interactivity and promote gender bias. Such online group behaviour combined with the site's ranking into most agreed, recommended comments, etc. pushes the comment to greater visibility. This particular comment received a resounding agreement by 1021 readers and recommendation by 376 readers:

'They have different mindsets... emotionally different. When a beautiful woman wants...sex...has a greater chance...can trick any guy... No guy complains against...sexual harassment...when a guy wants...sex ...lesser chances... needs to try a lot... women will complain against a guy who asked for sex...woman always prefer skimpy dress... Rapes cases are not individual issues...become a social issue...not only about creating a law and punishing the guilty. It's about changing the mindset of people...Women... should care for knowledge, wealth and power rather than caring about being physically attractive, seductive and sexy.' (Social science, 18/3/2013)

How the 'story' is constructed and the way rape circumstances were plotted in the story also influenced readers' stereotypical constructs of shame. It is not unusual to encounter extremely voyeuristic comments in many articles and sometimes they are not challenged or moderated by other readers. Readers insensitively demanded medical examination of victims in response to stories about allegation and charges. In an instance of a teenager who had been raped after she was 'lured' with a scholarship the discussion revolved around consent and coercion, with most readers blaming the teenager. Victim blaming in news about teenagers[23] and children is not confined to victims alone but attributed to girls' parents too. When minor children are involved, comments are sympathetic and qualified with references to the story being true because by being 'innocent' the victims could only be making truthful claims.

Sometimes readers use jokes and sarcasm that tend to normalize and trivialize violence, for example: 'its jungle out there. Some are hunters and other are hunted.' (Ashutosh, 12/7/2013) or 'New Hobby in UP: RAPING' (Truth Prevails 12/7/2013)'. Sarcasm is often lost to others and enraged reactions are responded to with clarifications and advice to study English. Responding to headlines of a story where rape was used as a metaphor for a man's suffering at being accused of scam, a woman reader observed that 'these fellows use the word 'rape' so commonly that it will lose its seriousness in a country which has already a proven record to not take it seriously' (injertuqurestu kaur 21/5/2013). The 'victim', 'crime', 'women' are all easily stereotyped in a series of interrelated comments rather than one expression. In the same manner lower caste and class is used to shift responsibility for rapes with hardly any discussion on how social relations of caste have been legitimized by force and ideological power:

'Kya ghatiya and ganda dimaag hai yaar logon ka. Ye lower caste k log hi hain jinhone India ka naam kharaab kar rakha hai. Mera Bharat Mahaan 100 mein se 99 beimeen and gawaar.'[24] (Mohit Maini 12/7/2013)

Thus different symbols, silences, tacit approval and meanings through articulation condition one another and are naturalised to become common sense in what is called the 'regime of the "taken-for-granted"' (Hall 1985, 105).

The multifaceted ways of news experience is apparent in the way readers engage with journalistic narratives. This includes re-quoting parts of a story in comments, posting observations from videos, posting feelings and verifying news report like '…how that policewoman is standing shamelessly' or 'I saw the girl in TV Channel…sitting on floor…..She is looking around as she is searching for insaaf[25]…….I cry yaar' (Jawed Ahmed 10/4/2013). The inclusion of drawings of women being terrorized to illustrate rape did not elicit any comments. There is some evidence of questioning journalistic content. For instance, in a story titled 'Brothers rape teen, 1 arrested' a reader complained that the 'way of publishing story is not right' as the headline implies 'that the girl is raped by her own brothers' contrary to 'facts' (Satendra Sharma 21/5/2013).

To stories that were accompanied by photos of the accused, readers often responded by demanding their faces to be shown uncovered and followed it with abuses. The 'accused', as often referred to in journalistic parlance, are discussed as 'culprits', 'devils', 'Shameless Demons in the garb of human beings indulge into Devlish/sinister activities' (DP2 12/7/2013). These responses are usually to stories of violence and where victims have been reported to be traumatised. Often readers abuse the men as individually deviant, and others question why their parents have not died of shame. However, they are often stereotyped on the basis of their religion and their identity as North Indians or South Indians. In story frames that convey an allegation, readers draw the perpetrator in more sympathetic lines as a victim of 'anti-male laws'. Ironically, although stories elicit enraged comments to hang rapists by arguing that only death sentence can deter rape, news about sentencing in convicted cases (4.19%) received only marginal comments (2.3%), as Table 2 shows. The usual celebratory response to sentencing is followed up with calls for media publicity.

Readers' angsts: Gender, politics, religion and dominant narratives

Across stories readers offered various 'solutions' to deal with rape like strengthening judiciary, laws, police, death sentence, changes in media, politics and cinema to 'legalizing prostitution', 'mechanical robots who can provide sexual services to men in the country', 're-moralizing society', encouraging child marriage and also invitations to join religion. As Table 2 shows, news about government initiatives for women's safety (6.2%) received poor comment response (6.2%). Instead, readers suggested extreme modes of violence to deal with perpetrators, some too graphic to be reproduced here. A common reference is 'the threat of the rod' – drawing on the Delhi gang rape imagery –, deployed as a tool to 'shock' dissenting online misogynists and others. Readers also appeared to support rape as an acceptable method of custodial interrogation. Online abuse therefore is not simply limited to women but reverberates across gender categories wrapped in a politically correct rhetoric of justice. As language is never free from the social context in which it is constructed, the discourse appears to reflect cultural and everyday notions of violence that are evidently problematic but commonly acceptable. Although moderation policies of TOI subject content moderation to both, public (readers) and private control (by the site), these comments (problematically) are not marked as offensive.

One predominant sentiment is frustration and intense criticism of police forces. In reports about court proceedings, cases involving politicians and children, readers express sadness, shame and frustration about India. Elsewhere there is also much angst amongst readers (including NRIs) about the 'bad name' brought to India and Indians by such crimes and media exposure. Odd rape reports about Indians abroad are used by readers to trumpet relief that 'genetics is important' to counter the opinion that 'upbring and Socio-Economic background' is 'the Biggest factor when it comes to r@pes committed by us Desi's.' (CM Funk 21/5/2013). Rape here is used to salvage collective masculinities through discourses of honour and shame, regionalism and nationalism. In some stories reader reconstruct India as 'R@pisthan', 'Rapistan', Rapeabad', 'Empire of rapists', 'KRISHNAISTAN', 'Rape-ublic of India', 'india…

a ra pe capital of the world.'[26] These constructions are rarely challenged. It is the more explicit comments about gender violence framed within the culturally imagined nation that are challenged by arraying 'us' and 'them' comments of comparisons with rape in Pakistan, Taliban regimes and western countries. Readers who pitch together crime and India's 'image' like, 'never dream of coming to India…get raped and robbed…worst country' (ALI GHAIS 12/7/2013), are often accused of being a Pakistani or Bangladeshi. The typical, instantaneous response reads like this, 'Paki………very active here with your loud comments!! your failed Pakistan, around 99% of r@pe cases never get reported nor action taken against culprits' (Blackie Paki (BLACKISTAN PAKISTAN) 12/7/2013). All this, including the pseudonyms used, usually prompts a volley of comments filled with nationalist rhetoric.

Again, story frames that relate media coverage of rapes to anxiety amongst foreign tourists are criticized for having stereotyped India, Indian culture, and Indian males. It often provokes a clash of cultures and even blatant sexism:

'this report sounds as if I will stand at the arrival counter at the airport…waiting for Australian girls…Australian girls have a nasty reputation and a huge talent for sin' (New Delhi 12/7/2013).

Such comments, also seen in other stories, are supported by real or imagined references to 'facts', crime statistics, and culture to naturalize gender violence as 'proportionate' to India's population. The debate context then turns to arguments that drawing comparisons with smaller countries is 'futile'.

The same goes for constructing crime ridden states in India. References to the accused's regional identity within the story often launch stereotypical comments that display relief about the accused being or not being from a particular community, wild speculations about ethnicity and religious identities and how the 'other' with his 'different identity' is a 'danger to humanity'. This sort of 'social concern' discourse on gender justice when combined with political discourses results in othering and conceals the taken-for-granted nature of violence, its privileging and victimization. As women's issues intersect with ethnicity, the articulation of identity markers and rights, readers refer to crimes to justify and assert religious and political ideologies (like opposing migration of North Indians into Maharashtra). They tend to reiterate a discourse of difference. For instance, to highlight how this provokes and inhibits commenting, a reader wrote down a list of rape headlines from Maharashtra with Maharashtrian names of criminals and accused the media of highlighting 'cases which matters in TRP race'. He suggested that people verify 'on google, then check comment page' which were 'few' in comparison to 'such incidents in Delhi...tired of people labelling criminals to region or religion' (Joker 21/5/13). His observation did not provoke a discussion.

There are some attempts by readers to address issues unrelated to the original news. Odd interjections to direct discussions to state violence against women are quickly intimidated into silences through recourse to violent political and nationalist rhetoric thereby dampening discourse. As discussed earlier, pseudonyms and location information provided by readers also constitute exclusions from a broader discussion and inhibit participation:

'Indian soldiers fight at the border to r@pe Kashmiri women. Google "KUNAN POSHPORA". (AF (Srinagar))

'You are raping your own...never reported in any media! Should you be...opening your filthy mouth you medieval...? Just get out of Srinagar, cross the border and live with your terrorist...devil brothers where you actually belong and die happily there. Shame on you all evil liars...a disgrace to mankind!'(Daniel C. (United India) 18/3/2013)

Readers also speculate when and why an incident would become a 'political' issue or an important case. There is angst against the political class which is blamed for rising crimes. The politicization of some rape cases like the 'Delhi case' is questioned. Readers also evidence awareness that 'politicians have perfected the art of using sexual violence as a resource for politics' (Baxi 2009, 16). References to the evasion of law by politically powerful rapists, leaders who shield rapists and the attention paid to certain rape cases are discussed against vote bank politics. But meaningful arguments, diverse opinions and raising issues of public concern that broaden public discourse are dampened by problematic comments. Undoubtedly, stories of rape attract certain kinds of spam. Readers' frustrations with incidents of sexual violence are rehashed in the comments section to call for alternative democratic change in view of the forthcoming elections.[27] Such spams often combine crime statistics with rhetorical statements for political change like 'vote NaMo'[28] and oust 'CONgress'. Readers occasionally respond to trolls who draw others into pointless conversations with requests to keep politics out of these debates and ridicule them, e.g. 'shame on people...who take political advantage form every human misery' (Ravi 10/4/2013). Usually, reference to politics derails discussion as readers fail to address the original news and launch political shouting matches about political parties. It is often followed by comment threads about political parties and organized violence to compel attention towards alternate political change like '1984 Sikh Genocide when more than 10,000 patriot sikhs were killed'[29] (Ram kamal Gujral 20/6/2013) and the 2002 Gujarat communal riots.[30] The comment contexts of sexual violence, gender relations, nation and religion become key sites to play out oppositional nationalisms and recreate histories of social differences.

Usually, stories of individual incidents receive invitations to join a religion like 'true wickedness growing...O JESUS (the only way...)' (Vivek 20/6/2013). Readers also reference rape crimes to criticize religions and promote relativist stances on minority reservation and national belonging. This particularly encourages personal attacks and online threats, which is prominent in many comment sections across the world (Paskin 2010, 78). When the religion of the perpetrator is revealed, readers from other religious communities regale in abusing that community. Usually, satirical reconstructions of the perpetrator, like being a 'Krishna Bakht[31] at large' act as flames (Tony 10/04/2013). Sexual assault is then attributed to religious ideologies and socialization into violent male sexualities. Readers construct these evidences from religious books, hearsay and media. Religious rants enact histories in competing discourses to shame the collectivities in question and inevitably construct notions of masculine power. The Hindu male readers' discourse of 'othering' rape as a 'religious' culture in Islam or Christianity is often challenged by Muslim or Christian readers who cite examples of gendered violence as inseparable from Hinduism, Hindu gods and mythologies; while the Christian reader's attribution of rape to particular religions is countered with the annotations of child sexual abuse in Churches, the Vatican and the Spanish Inquisition. Readers then supplement these comments with references to religious identities of people involved in the most recent rape news. Often these comments act as hate speech, 'flame' conversations and degenerate into swearing, insults and sexual expletives (Lee 2005, 385). What is striking is the frequency with which they are deployed individually and collectively to construct sexual assault, victims and perpetrators. Over time some readers deny the story itself as a 'religious' conspiracy. All this points to a complex historical interconnection of gender violence with caste, class and religion, that is recreated online.

Many comments are replete with stark discourses of patriarchy that disconnect rape from a broader struggle for equal rights for women's education, work and public spaces. There are also debates about anti-male laws and vigilance against the feminist movement. There is perceptible intervention by readers who claim to be part of a larger, organized campaign to counter the perceived affront to men and 'organize themselves to destroy feminism before it destroys society':

> 'R@pe is not a violent crime as we understand. Recent data shows that in 98.4% of cases, accuser and accused are well known to each other..... r@pe is about deal gone sour. When two people indulge in s*x and marry- wah wah, else man is a r@pist…blatant feminist trivialization of heinous crime…' (Mens Rights Movement 20/6/13)

The question of consent and violence mentioned in the story is drawn to construct 'genuine victims' (often in reference to Nirbhaya) against those who faced 'less' violence. These discussions attribute the rise in rape crimes to 'false rape' cases, 'male injustice', 'misuse' of '498A, 420'[32] and 'compensation'. The impending rape law is rechristened as the 'new 498A'. Such constructions, as feminists argue, evidence a 'backlash anxiety' against gains made by the women's movement (Gavey and Gow 2001). For instance, a reader wrote:

> 'staring at a woman is r@pe bid, multiple phone calls is harassment, sending multiple sms is stalking, consensual s@x between 17 year olds is r@pe. Everything is r@pe. Genuine cases (Nirbhaya) are highlighted for sensational effect so people will be scared to point out the fraud. Lucrative feminist industry received thousands of crores (of our tax payer money) in budget for anti male propaganda, is artificially hiking statistics and creating massive r@pe hysteria with help of well paid feminist media.' (A new 498a has come 20/6/2013, agreed by 36 people)

Online group behaviour

On rare occasions, a sense of cyber surveillance beyond the site acts as a check on gender biased positions and launches politically correct narratives and clarifications. Importantly, complicity through the action of 'agreeing' (tagging) and not the visibility of comments alone structure online gender discourses to promote gender bias. In the online news site, the ranking of comments and tagging, in collusion with the site's commercial intent of promoting reader traffic to particular news or most commented pages, turns online comments into potent sites that may promote and enhance one-sided opinion to news. Tagging by readers could be a partial response and not necessarily to the comment in its entirety. Together it appears to initiate interactive group behaviour that silences opinion diversity and could be explored to understand how biases play out in online comments. Online discourses and struggles over meanings are not purely internal/text/technology specific. Rather they are widely connected to social structures and practices. Exploring how readers tag in agreement/disagreement to one part of a comment and not to entire expressions requires a scholarly understanding of user-to-user interactivity as enabled by the medium, its interdependences, discussion contexts and broader contextual matters which reproduce real life inequalities. This, I argue, has methodological implications for a gender sensitive reading of online comments.

I quote a conversation within a story about khap panchayats'33 views on age of consent and new rape laws as an attempt to capture how 'agree' and 'disagree' tags are clicked as a partial response to different views within a single comment. As van Dijk (2009) observes, the digital medium allows various levels of engagements. Tagging sometimes turns discussions into short thumping, online competitions. It propels patriarchal scores and top scoring comments into greater visibility. Online features and reader interactions thus also direct actions of readers, news visibilities and shapes the actions of a reader community. This abridged conversation below demonstrates how partial tagging and gender bias played out through collective behavior and also as a face-saving initiative for a reader who came under fire from others for his patriarchal views. As the last comment shows, the context and discussions explains 591 readers agreed to reader Wise's clarification while 288 disagreed for more powerful ant-rape laws:

'Lowering age of consent is ridiculous. Girls can ....any man willingly and can complain as if they were r@ped. If This law is passed, No boy will want to be a girl's friend...If a girl does not want to be watched...dress properly and decently...can not create a law to stop people looking at you.'(Wise (US), (18/3/2013))	Agree (123) Disagree (14) Recommend (75) Offensive
@wise:... 'be really scared at having put on record even if cyberspace such utter crappy nonsense, particularly from US...becoz many employers HR...track such activity and judge their employees...if u are in the US then your Green Card is in doubt of turning pink'(dasanjeev (Kolkata) replies to wise, (18/3/2013))	Agree (2) Disagree (488) Recommend(1) Offensive
'You are definitely not from US...your perverted mindset is exposed...treated women either as a sex object or an instrument of procreation...Kapde nahi, Soch badlo.'34 (Nisha (USA) replies to wise, (18/3/2013))	Agree (14) Disagree (262) Recommend(5) Offensive
'Even if you insulted me with your words, I accept and respect your views...misunderstood me.But, the truth is i am the most modern modern and decent type of guy. I welcome even more powerful antir@pe law wholeheartedly. I do not care what dress a girl wears. Even if a woman walks on the road without any dress, No one has any right to r@pe her...I respect women more than you...'(Wise (US) replies to Nisha, (18/3/2013)	Agree (591) Disagree (288) Recommend(261) Offensive

Conclusion

The attempt in this article was to expose reader discourses to rape news. An analysis of comments itself is rare as discussed early on. This study allowed a better understanding of which stories where visible, about public responses to rape and how interests of readers converge. Readers responded the most to stories that were given national coverage. News framed as specific incidents complete with some facts of assault received maximum coverage and response. As van Dijk (2009, 55) observes, site technologies steer reader agency through moderation policies, comment restriction, length, interactivity and discussion structures that emerge. Interactive interdependence amongst news, technology and readers exposes the cultural frames, rhetorical strategies in rape discourses and the way gender issues are reproduced and contested in offline contexts. But there are possibilities for a critical agenda (van Dijk 1993, 252) as these readers observed:

'Will the lame people grow some bal*'s...demand justice or just keep coming on TOI and posting Govt. is corrupt, Justice is slow, politicians are bought off' (Jonn 12/7/2013)

'Pen is the most powerful weapon. Continuous writing will have effect...' (Vidya 12/7/2013)

The contours of online comments in discourses about rape are shaped as much by visible stories and journalistic norms that do not address rape as a larger social issue besides underreported stories that render rapes invisible. Flaming, gender bias, hate speech and male moral panics over changing notions of legalities, gender and relationships in online comments demonstrate that gender equality continues to be a challenge.

User generated content in online news sites is a trend that newspapers cannot ignore. Moderation, however, continues to be resource heavy and challenging. As in online newspaper commenting elsewhere, reader interactivities and possibilities of public debate rest uneasily besides issues of effective reader and gatekeeping regulations. Reader-authored content raises questions about the need to balance readers' right to comment without moderation and news sites' need to strategize comment management considering legal and ethical issues. Despite its limitations, this research illustrates that gender issues are intimately shaped by gender norms and values embroiled in histories of marginalization. Increased moderation, however, would only hide sexism, repress debates about gender violence and like moderation of racism compel novel expressions of the same (Hugley and Daniels 2013). An intervening approach within digital interactive news spaces could encourage gender debates in a meaningful way.

A few observations of reader comments can be drawn, bearing in mind that limited thematic focus makes generalization difficult. Choosing TOI as a research site, I demonstrated that interactive news consumption platforms (technology) shape online commenting just as much as the nature and content of participation which is embedded in socio-cultural contexts. Though moderation filters reign in expletives prior to posting, site policies and collusive silences amongst readers further ethnicized and gendered othering. As this particular study serves to remind, the access that women have to such public arenas and also their possibility of participation are structurally limited.[33] Gender bias, hate speech and online rape threats indicate the resilience of chauvinism in digital spaces.[34] Technology here, while enabling more public news consumption, might also amplify continuities of inequalities in virtual avenues. This also raises the question of dominant media frames and what reader generated content itself could mean for public opinion. It also raises the important point that different digital interactive news spaces open up very specific modes of participation and reader behaviour. As studies are lacking in the Indian context, there is a need for a better understanding of the multiple ways in which reader expressions and engagements induct itself in the making of news and meanings in public online news sites.

Rape Coverage across states	Number of news	Number of comments	Percentage of news	Percentage of comments
India	27	3417	18.11	61.74
Delhi	25	720	17.48	13.01
Maharashtra	13	387	9.09	6.99
Karnataka	2	3	1.39	0.05
West Bengal	6	53	4.19	0.96
Odisha	4	4	2.79	0.07
Chhatisgarh	1	2	0.69	0.04
Jharkhand	3	7	2.09	0.13
Punjab	8	15	5.59	0.27
Tamil Nadu	4	205	2.79	3.7
Gujrat	6	16	4.19	0.28
Goa	8	31	5.59	0.56
Andhra Pradesh	3	56	2.09	1.01
Rajasthan	6	144	4.19	2.6
U.P.	11	386	7.69	6.97
Bihar	6	5	4.19	0.09
Kerala	1	1	0.69	0.02
Madhya Pradesh	9	82	6.29	1.48
Jammu & Kashmir, North Eastern states & others	0	0	0	0
Total	143	5534		

Table 1: Aggregate national and state wise coverage of rape news and comments received.

Key codes in rape incidents		Gang rape	Minor child	Rape assault	Married	Dalit/tribal	Disabled	Minor teenager	Total
Known person	News	0	6	3	2	0	0	4	15
	Comments	0	301	32	2	0	0	106	144
Unknown person	News	1	2	2	1	0	1	0	7
	Comments	225	309	49	0	0	121	0	731
Court	News	1	2	12	0	0	0	0	15
	Comments	0	340	818	0	0	0	0	1158
Government Measures	News	1	1	7	0	0	0	0	9
	Comments	5	3	340	0	0	0	0	348
Politician/ Personalities	News	0	1	12	0	0	0	0	13
	Comments	0	9	676	0	0	0	0	685
Case related (FIR/Arrest)	News	16	14	21	0	1	1	11	64
	Comments	1122	65	239	0	3	11	36	1476
Protests and debate	News	1	4	5	0	0	0	0	10
	Comments	2	11	372	0	0	0	0	385
Victim	News	0	3	1	0	0	0	0	4
	Comments	0	70	109	0	0	0	0	179
Punishment	News	0	5	1	0	0	0	0	6
	Comments	0	63	68	0	0	0	0	131
Total news		20	38	64	3	1	2	15	143
Total comments		1381	1171	2703	2	3	132	142	5534

Table 2: shows an aggregate of news and comments to two broad codes – incidents of violence and what the story's main frame conveys.

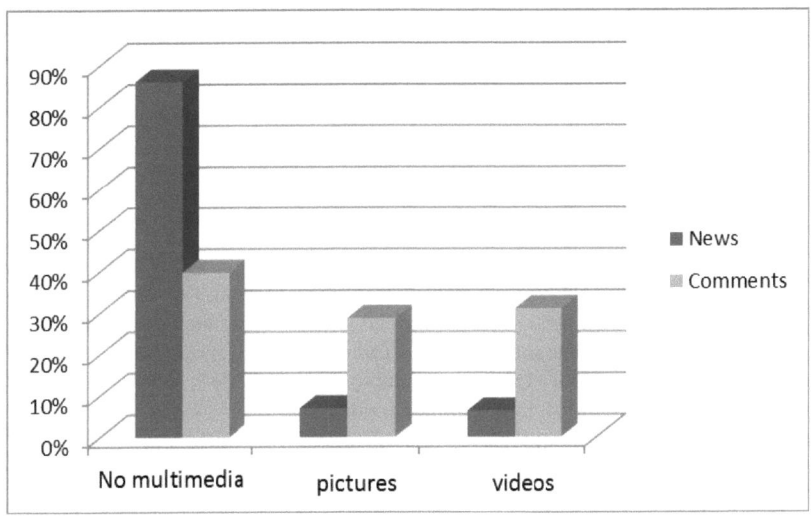

Figure 1: Percentage of comments received against percentages of online news without any picture or video, with pictures or photos and with video.

Bibliography

ABDUL-MAGEED, MUHAMMAD. "Online News Sites and Journalism 2.0: Reader Comments on Al-Jazeera Arabic." *Cognition, Communication, Co-operation*, no.6 (2008): 59–76.

BAXI, PRATIKSHA. "Violence of Political Rhetoric on Rape." *Economic & Political Weekly*, no.320 (2009): 15–16.

BOCZKOWSKI, PABLO J. "Understanding the Development of Online Newspapers: Using Computer-Mediated Communication Theorizing to Study Internet Publishing." *New Media Society*, no.1 (1999): 101–25.

BOCZKOWSKI, PABLO J. 'The processes of adopting multimedia and interactivity in three online newsrooms." *Journal of Communication* 54, no.2 (2004): 197–213.

BOCZKOWSKI, PABLO J. and Eugenia Mitchelstein. "How users take advantage of different forms of interactivity on online news sites: clicking, e-mailing, and commenting." *Human Communication Research* 38, no.1 (2012): 1–22.

CHAUDHURI, MAITRAYEE. *Feminisms in India*. New Delhi: Zed Books, 2005.

COMSCORE. "India's Daily Readership of Online News and Information Jumps 34 Percent in the Past Year." *ComScore*, September 30, 2013. Accessed October 10, 2013. http://www.comscore.com/Insights/Press_Releases/2013/10/Indias_Daily_Readership_of_Online_News_and_Information_Jumps_34_Percent_in_the_Past_Year.

DAHLBERG, LINCOLN. "Re-constructing digital democracy." *New Media & Society* 16, no.6 (2011): 855–72.

DORON, ASSA and ROBIN JEFFERY. *The great Indian phone book: How cheap cell phone changes business, politics and daily life.* Cambridge: Havard University Press, 2013.

GAVEY, NICOLA and VIRGINIA GOW. "'Cry Wolf', Cried the Wolf: Constructing the Issue of False Rape Allegations in New Zealand Media Texts." *Feminism & Psychology* 11 (2001): 341–60.

HALL, STUART. "Signification, representation, ideology: Althusser and the poststructuralist debates." *Critical Studies in Mass Communication* 2, no.2 (1985): 91–114.

HAMMERSLEY, MARTYN. *On Feminist Methodology* 26, no.2 (1992): 187–206.

HUGHEY, M.W and J. DANIELS. "Racist comments at online news sites: a methodological dilemma for discourse analysis." *Media Culture Society* 35, no.3 (2013): 332–347.

Indian Readership Survey 2012 Q4. Topline Findings. Accessed July 3, 2014. http://mruc.net/irs2012q4_topline_findings.pdf.

JHA, P. "In Doordarshan, ratings infuse a lease of energy." *The Hindu*, May 10, 2013. Accessed May 30, 2014. http://www.thehindu.com/news/national/in-doordarshan-ratings-infuse-a-lease-of-energy/article4699885.ece.

LEE, HANGWOO. "Behavioral strategies for dealing with flaming in an online forum." *Sociological Quarterly* 46, no.2 (2005): 385–403.

MCCLUSKEY, MICHAEL and JAY HMIELOWSKI. "Opinion expression during social conflict: Comparing online reader comments and letters to the editor." *Journalism* 13, no.3 (2011): 303–19.

MCMILLAN, SALLY J. 'The microscope and the moving target: The challenge of applying content analysis to the World Wide Web." *Journalism and Mass Communication* 77, no.1 (2000): 80–98.

NIELSEN, CAROLYN E. "Coproduction or cohabitation: Are anonymous online comments on newspaper websites shaping news content?" *New Media Society* (2013): 1–18.

NORTON, RUSSEL and TIM D. GRANT. "Rape myth in true and false rape allegations." *Psychology, crime and law* 14, no.4 (2008): 275–85.

PADTE, RICHA. "Street talking." *The Caravan*, July 1, 2013. Accessed May 29, 2014, http://caravanmagazine.in/print/3782.

PAPACHARISSI, ZIZI. "The Virtual Sphere: The Internet as a Public Sphere." *New Media and Society* 4, no.1 (2002): 9–27.

PASKIN, DANNY. "Say what?" *Journal of International Communication* 16, no.2 (2010): 67–83.

RAJAGOPAL, ARVIND. *The Indian Public Sphere: Readings in Media History.* UK; Oxford University Press, 2009.

REICH, ZVI. "User Comments: The Transformation of Participatory Space". In *Participatory Journalism: Guarding Open Gates at Online Newspapers*, edited by Singer Jane. B. et. al., 96–117. Malden MA: Wiley-Blackwell, 2011.

RIFFE, D., and C.F. AUST, and S.R. LACY. "The effectiveness of random, consecutive day and constructed week sampling in newspaper content analysis." *Journalism Quarterly* 70, no.1 (1993): 133–39.

RODERICK, KEVIN. "Gender and the female journalist who dares read the Internet." *LA Observed,* January 21, 2014. Accessed July 2, 2014. http://www.laobserved.com/archive/2014/01/the_next_civil_rights_iss.php.

SCHNEIDER, NADJA-CHRISTINA. "More than a belated Gutenberg Age: Daily newspapers in India." *Global Media Journal* 3, no.2 (2013): 1–25.

SHARMA, ABHINVA. "Don't let Rajasthan become Rapistan: HC." *The Times of India,* April 3, 2013. Accessed July 3, 2014. http://timesofindia.indiatimes.com/india/Dont-let-Rajasthan-become-Rapistan-HC/articleshow/19353315.cms.

The Hoot. "When rape claims prime time." *The Hoot,* January 18, 2013. Accessed October 20, 2013. http://www.thehoot.org/web/home/story.php?sectionId=9&mod=1&pg=1&valid=true&storyid=6552.

The Times of India. "I feel relieved the Delhi girl died or she'd have faced the same porn-tinted questions." *The Times of India,* February 17, 2013. Accessed May 30, 2014. http://timesofindia.indiatimes.com/home/stoi/deep-focus/I-feel-relieved-the-Delhi-girl-died-or-shed-have-faced-the-same-porn-tinted-questions/articleshow/18538041.cms.

The Times of India Group. *The Times of India Online.* Accessed October 27, 2013. http://www.timesgroup.com/brands/digital/internet/the-times-of-india-online.html.

The Times of India Group. *The Times of India (English).* Accessed October 18, 2013. http://www.timesgroup.com/brands/publishing/newspapers/the-times-of-india.html.

VAN DIJK, TEUN. "Principle of Discourse Analysis." *Discourse and society* 4, no.2 (1993): 249–83.

VAN DIJCK, JOSE. "Users like you? Theorizing agency in user-generated content." *Media, Culture & Society* 31, no.1 (2009): 41–58.

WAHL-JORGENSEN, KARIN. "The Normative-economic Justification for Public Discourse: Letters to the Editor as a Wide Open Forum." *Journalism & Mass Communication Quarterly* 79, no.1 (2002): 121–33.

WALLACE, AMY. "Life as a Female Journalist: Hot or Not?" *The New York Times,* January 19, 2014. Accessed July 2, 2014. http://www.nytimes.com/2014/01/20/opinion/life-as-a-female-journalist-hot-or-not.html?_r=0.

WEBER, PATRICK. "Discussions in the comments section: Factors influencing participation and interactivity in online newspapers' reader comments." *New Media & Society* (July 8, 2013): 1–17.

---

1 The author thanks the editors, Nadja-Christina Schneider and Fritzi-Marie Titzmann, for their detailed comments that helped improve the paper; and Maitryee Chaudhuri for her feedback..

2 According to a study carried out by Centre for Media studies at Delhi, 'almost nothing, in the past or present compares with this media attention, roughly 7,551 minutes or 252 hours of news coverage, special bulletins and talk shows against the 46 minutes devoted to all rape cases in March 2012' (The Hoot 2013). Even the national channel Doordarshan News which claims a policy of, "no screaming, no need to shout patriotic credentials" ethos where, "we do not overplay rape, but the retribution to rape" had devoted almost equal coverage to the Delhi incident just as the private channels (Jha 2013).

3 I refer to rape as in the wider context of crimes of sexual assault to mean the violation of mental and bodily dignity.
4 Some news websites like The Hindu and The Indian Express require registration to post comments. Comments appear online after editing and/or moderation. The TOI provides registration options too. Comments are uploaded instantly when logged in through e-mail or other sites. Site filters handle moderation. When readers report offensive comments they undergo moderation by the editorial team. TOI by far shows heavy commenting in comparison to other online newspapers perhaps because the tactic of reader registration is not followed up with sufficient reader accountability.
5 Using androgynous names or pseudonyms and access to registration information poses a methodological problem.
6 See http://www.timesgroup.com/brands/digital/internet/the-times-of-india-online.html, accessed on October 27 2013.
7 This provision has changed since this study and now requires registration though e-mail or Facebook to do so.
8 The story about the Bandra rape case of a Spanish visitor posted on November 6th 2012 for instance was still receiving comments as late as January 16th 2013 (total comments 760), accessed on October 31st 2013.
9 TOI recently started offering prizes that readers could redeem, based on points collected through reading news, badges and other activities. See http://timesofindia.indiatimes.com/abouttimesrewards.cms, accessed on July 2nd 2014.
10 See for instance McMillan (2000).
11 For example, the story of the rape of a five year old child in Delhi in April 2013 accumulated 7000 plus comments per day, the week had a total of 273 rape stories and roughly 25,187 comments totally.
12 37% of TOI's readers are from abroad (ComScore 2013). Although readers enter anonymous places, location information also suggests a global participation.
13 I came up with this classification as a way to look at how readers responded to 'different' instances of rape news after having noted differences in comments received while collecting data.
14 Androgynous names, pseudonyms and no access to registration information do pose a methodological problem.
15 Roughly translates into 'the ordinary people's party'.
16 Translation reads as, 'you are a cool guy. Where in Surat does rapists hangout? There must be some special place'.
17 Although regional language papers are ahead of English papers in terms of readership TOI identifies itself as the mainstream. See: http://www.timesgroup.com/brands/publishing/newspapers/the-times-of-india.html, accessed on October 18, 2013.
18 For a discussion on history, media, language, nationalism and public sphere see Rajagopal (2009).
19 Target Rating Points (TRPs) are the gross rating points delivered by a media vehicle to a specific target audience.
20 A rough translation reads as follows: 'when will "woman-met-with-a-terrible-fate-because-she-went-to-defecate-in-the-open" type of headlines or news stop?'. 'Gandgi' means litter.
21 Meaning 'The Unfortunate One'.
22 In 1996, a 16 year old girl from Suryanelli, Kerala was enticed into a trap and raped by many men for forty days. See: The Times of India, February 27, 2013.
23 Eighteen is the age of consent. Even if consent has been gained, a person could be legally charged with statutory rape as the consenting individual, when below 18, is considered a juvenile and hence incapable of giving consent.
24 'What a bad and dirty mind people have. It is these lower caste people who have spoiled the name of India. In My India is Great, 99 out of 100 people are cheats and villagers'.
25 Insaaf (Urdui): Mercy.

26 The construction of 'Rapistan', a land of rapes, appears to be a popular but old one. A news article in the TOI on April 3 2013, titled, "Don't let Rajasthan become Rapistan: HC", contains observations by a Rajasthan High court judge on the 'laxity' of police on acting upon gang rape complaints, "when Bhanwari Devi case came to forefront we read someone quoting Rajasthan as Rapisthan we wish that Rajasthan does not get converted actually into Rapis'than" (Sharma 2013).

27 At the time of writing, the Indian general election 2014 was upcoming.

28 Narendra Modi, candidate of the Bharatiya Janata Party (BJP).

29 In 1984 anti-Sikh riots erupted in North India as a response to Prime Minister Indira Gandhi's assassination by her Sikh bodyguard for authorizing military operation against the Sikhs.

30 In 2002, the burning of a train that resulted in deaths of Hindu pilgrims returning from Ayodhya triggered weeks of violent communal riots between Hindu and Muslims in Gujarat resulting in loss of lives, property and organized mob violence against Muslim women.

31 Meaning 'Devotee of Krishna'. In Hinduism, one perspective depicts Lord Krishna as a supreme lover and playful prankster.

32 They refer to anti-dowry laws and domestic violence laws of the Indian Constitution.

33 Women account for less than 40 per cent of all Indian users, a far lower sex ratio than that of other countries. The Hindu (2013), August 14. A recent study observed that extensive online gender based abuse faced by women and gender rights activists is similar to what women encounter in public spaces (Padte 2013)

34 Section 66A of the Indian Information Technology Act, as a legal recourse, prohibits offensive messages through communication devices. But its terminologies have been vague and were misused to further censorship and arrests in many cases.

FRITZI-MARIE TITZMANN

"The Voice of the Youth"[1]
Locating a new public sphere between street protest and digital discussion

> "As a woman, I'm shocked. As an Indian, I'm ashamed.
> And as someone who's recently moved to Delhi, I'm scared."
> (N.N., in a comment posted to Youth Ki Awaaz on December 20, 2012)

Introduction

On 16th December 2012 a 23-year-old paramedical student was gang-raped in a private bus in Delhi. The girl had been out with a male friend to watch a movie and was on her way home. Detailed descriptions of the horrifying brutality and her multiple gruesome injuries that eventually led to her death on 29th December in a hospital in Singapore could be found all over national and international media. Hence I don't want to repeat these accounts. The following article focuses rather on the dynamics that led to the incident sparking off vehement and ongoing online and offline protest and activism. Immediately after the incident on 16th December, college students and thousands of other citizens joined in spontaneous demonstrations in Delhi and elsewhere, "mobilized by a sense of outrage, social media tools and word of mouth" (Sen 2013, 1). The 24-hours television coverage intensified the protests and attracted more participants until the protests reached a peak after the death of the victim. The immediate medial impact was enormous and manifested itself not only in unresting news reporting but posting and interactions on social networking sites unleashed processes that reached unimagined dimensions. For weeks it seemed that India's social media landscape was solely dominated by the case. It triggered long standing anger and frustration, motivated people to speak out and act upon their complaints. Activism formed to a great extent in an emerging digital public sphere: On online discussion forums, blogs and particularly via Twitter and Facebook. Interaction and exchange generated networks and consequently brought many people together in real life, down to the streets, manifested in numerous demonstrations, solemn vigils, and various other protest activities. Nationally prominent hashtags[2] included #DelhiGangRape, #StopThisShame, #DelhiProtests, #Amanat, #Nirbhaya and #Damini[3] (Barn 2013). From the college students who identified with the rape victim to feminist activists who commemorated the evils of Indian patriarchy and celebrities who mourned the decay of India's cosmopolitan image, India's Facebook, Twitter and blog spheres spread news and opinions, as well as calls for demonstrations, castration of rapists and a political revolution. The digital and street turmoil continued well into the new year and was fuelled by the disclosure of the victim's real name[4] by her father and by the following revelations of ever new rape cases. In contrast to the usual scenario, the protests involved no political parties and politicians were conspicuously absent. The virtual and real-life protests vehemently criticized politicians for their failings and their sole concentration on quick solutions to appease the outraged civil society. The state's response to the protests was violent. Protesters received lathi-charges (beatings with sticks) by the police and eminent politicians missed the opportunity to jump on the bandwagon. They instead took to conservative rhetoric, e.g. blaming women for being raped because of their provocative dresses, therewith increasing the public consternation and enhancing the protest. Responses by self-proclaimed holy men on how women are at fault because of their disobedience to religious codes of conduct similarly stirred protest.[5]

Millions of young people in India and worldwide felt affected and personally concerned with what it implies to be young (and female) in India. Personal identification with the fate of the raped student served for many as a starting point of further political reflection. Prachee Sinha (2013) wrote in the Economic and Political Weekly:

> "In a state of shock and grief in the immediate aftermath of the incident, I wrote an emotional piece in the social media casting an anguished and tearful glance from the vantage point of a young woman who commutes to work across Delhi spending two hours in public transport each way."

Despite of a globalizing economy and Indian cities aspiring world class status, particularly the capital is notorious for being an unsafe space for young women. Previous cases like the murder of Jessica Lal are evidence to this image.[6] Sinha was by far not the only commentator pointing to the city's ugly nickname as "rape capital of India". She continues to reflect on the inconsistency of Indian democracy which manifests itself on the one hand in outraged citizens protesting for justice and rights, and on the other hand in corruption and dubious vote bank politics where Sinha sees the "criminal elements" emerge from. Therewith she touches upon another crucial aspect of the discourse that followed the incident: The dimension of class and "why certain cases of rape make headlines while others are lost in the small corners of inside pages" (Sinha 2013). But the resulting media discourse centered around several other key concerns too: The government's omissions and commissions, the state's function with regard to women's safety, as well as the misogynist and patriarchic nature of Indian culture and society.

What struck many observers was that the mass protest was led by the educated urban middle classes who are often deemed as apathetic, hedonistic and apolitical. As Sen (2013, 3) notes, "[h]istorically in India voting has been lowest in rich, urban constituencies as opposed to a much higher turnout during election in poorer, rural areas."

Given the medial and political significance of the case and its related consequences one could explore a wide range of interesting aspects. I will in the following concentrate on two crucial questions.

The first question concerns the nature of the mobilization and its middle class participants. Barn (2013) has understandably posed the question whether the social media mobilization of protest generated by the Delhi rape case can be termed as "the Indian Spring" in the style of the so called "Arab Spring", alternatively also named the first "Twitter revolution", in Tunisia, Egypt and the Middle East. She sees an inherent link between the increasing digital mobilization and the political awakening of the urban, young and middle class elites whose emergence she ascribes to the Mumbai terror attacks. Although partly agreeing with her, Sen terms the protests neither anarchic and only media-driven, nor a "serious challenge to the government and the established political order" (Sen 2013, 2). He locates them as part of a continuum with the Anna Hazare movement against corruption that was similarly characterized by middle class outrage, strong media presence, pyramid mobilization and the excessive use of social networking sites. But Sen (ibid, 2) assesses corruption contrary to rape or gender issues "more amenable to a long-term political mobilization" and identifies a "lack of focal organization or figure in the protests over rape" to be successful.

The second and core concern of my research is the content of the discussions in the much debated social media networks. Since an analysis of India's vast social media landscape would go beyond the scope of an article, I will focus on a selection of blog entries posted in reference to the Delhi gang rape case on the online platform Youth Ki Awaaz. While social networking sites like Facebook and Twitter are preferred as mobilization tools, the online platform mainly serves to voice opinions and generate discussion. But given the increasing tendency towards cross-media strategies, Youth Ki Awaaz features many links to social networking sites by operating Facebook and Twitter groups and accounts and by compiling updates and opinions from these platforms. Hence, I will in a first step explore the nature of the protest movement and its mobilization patterns from a broader and more theoretical angle. In doing so, I locate the activism following the Delhi gang rape case in a broader analytical context of new social movements which are local and global at the same time (PART I). In a second step I will then look into the dominant themes of discussion revolving on Youth Ki Awaaz around the rape case and how they relate to the protests (PART II). I understand the expression of opinion and subsequent discussion as an important aspect of any form of social activism and protest. Building on that, my hypothesis is that debates in social media form an integral part of the dynamic discourse within which the protest movement is situated. Furthermore, as the empirical data in the second part of this article show, many of the young people who contributed their views on Youth Ki Awaaz engaged not only in digital discussion and online mobilization but participated in real-life street protests in the aftermath of the Delhi case. These experiences inform their engagement with social media and vice versa.

I.   Protest Movements and New Media

Before I enter the debate on the impact of social media in protest movements, a clarification of the working terms is required. Kaplan and Heanlein (2010, 61) phrase the following definition:

> "Social Media is a group of Internet-based applications that build on the ideological and technological foundations of Web 2.0, and that allow the creation and exchange of User Generated Content."

They subsequently identify six types of social media. Blogs as the earliest form of social media feature chronological entries by one or several authors and allow interaction with others through comment functions. They further list collaborative projects like Wikipedia, content communities like YouTube, virtual game worlds and virtual social worlds (Kaplan and Haenlein 2007, 60). And last but not least social networking sites, particularly Facebook, are probably the most prominent and widely used type of social media. Boyd and Ellison (2007) define social networking sites as

> "web-based services that allow individuals to (1) construct a public or semi-public profile within a bounded system, (2) articulate a list of other users with whom they share a connection, and (3) view and traverse their list of connections and those made by others within the system."

Facebook and the microblogging service Twitter – that also enables networking amongst users through features like "following" someone, "sharing" posts and tagging topics – feature as the key drivers within the context of cyberactivism and protest movements in the digital age. Social media enthusiasts like Shirky see their immense potential in supporting civil society and the public sphere and state that they will facilitate slow change over longer time (Shirky 2011). Castells (2013, 232) argues that the invention of social networking sites

> "transforms culture by inducing the culture of sharing. SNS [social networking sites] users transcend time and space, yet produce content, set up links and connect practices. There is now a constantly networked world in every dimension of human experience."

Located in a globalized "network society" (Castells 1996), internetworked social movements are hallmarked by fluidity, flat hierarchies, multilocality and most importantly by their inherent network character (Langman 2005). Hence, the term network society as coined by Castells describes different phenomena related to the social, political, economic and cultural changes caused by the spread of networked, digital information and communication technologies. Closely related is the discussion of a virtual transformation of the public sphere. Langman (2005) applies the critical theory approach of the Frankfurt School that considers the role of literacy and media in fostering modernist bourgeois movements. He attempts to frame a critical theory of "internetworked movements" by arguing that in Habermas' conceptualization of the public sphere communication technology like print media have been identified as integral to modern social mobilization (Langman 2005, 43). He further argues that an increased overall mobility leads to virtual and consequently back to physical mobility (ibid, 46). Virtual mobility corresponds in his argument to the defining trait of new social movements. He sees a decentralized communication network resulting in "deterritorialized 'virtual public spheres' – cyber salons, cafés, and meeting places in cyberspaces" (ibid, 55). The network character is further strengthened by the fact that most websites feature linkages to related groups and sites. Youth Ki Awaaz' ramified social media linkage illustrates this aspect. Only a small number of sites are actually dedicated to social and political movements but the medium "has enabled unprecedented numbers to have access to progressive agendas" (ibid, 56).

While enthusiasts like Shirky (2011) and Castells (2012) celebrate the new tools for social movements, critics like Morozov (2011) point to the growing threat of surveillance and censorship on national and global levels. India is one of the best examples of a Janus-faced virtual public sphere.[7] While a national and international press celebrated the political awakening of India's middle class through social media activism, arrests related to posts in social networking sites and blogs are frequent. The arrest of cartoonist Trivedi in 2012 for "mocking the constitution" triggered a debate over free speech and India's press freedom. Further examples include the arrest of two young women after an unfavourable Facebook status update referring to Bal Thackeray's death, and many people making critical comments on politicians online (Krishnan 2012). Even though serious attempts to limit or censor internet access is rather absent compared to countries like China and Pakistan, the Mumbai police inaugurated the country's first 'Social Media Lab' in March 2013 to monitor the happenings on Facebook, Twitter and YouTube. The police highlighted the role of social media in the context of the protests against sexual violence as an eye opener to the urgency to keep online activities under surveillance (The Hindu 2013).

Critics also emphasize the lopsided pro-democratic values inherent in social media usage that allow spreading hateful, intolerant and anti-democratic content too (Joseph 2013, 173). Sceptics like Morozov (2013 and 2011) and Gladwell (2010) doubt that decentralized, leaderless networks are capable of organizing revolutions and argue that cyberactivism does not translate into real movements. With little effort it simply pacifies the social consciousness, hence the term "slacktivism" for low-risk activism by clicking "like", signing petitions and forwarding pictures and articles emerged (Joseph 2012, 150). Sassen notes a "common type of conflation of a technology's capacities with a massive on the ground process which used the technology" (Sassen 2011, 577) and stresses the distinction between technology and users. She emphasizes the "toolness" of Facebook in the context of the Tahrir Square movement in Egypt.

Summing up the ongoing debate over the role and importance of social media for social and political activism remains without a clear-cut conclusion. At the very best, one could argue with Joseph that social media like the internet itself are neutral tools without inherent values, their usage and impact depend on the users. But even this assumption requires critical assessment, considering that "ICT can symbolize and reinforce positions of power, status and situatedness" (Holst 2011, 128). Holst challenges the notion of neutrality and argues from a postcolonial perspective that the impact of new media content and debate rests essentially upon technological structures that are not always adjusted to local environments. Issues of language and script, for example, may provide technological disadvantages for many nations in the Global South. Multilingual India is one of the best examples.

However critically Castells' work has been assessed, he carved out a set of common patterns of networked social movements that provides a useful set of analytical categories for the case of the Indian protest movement against gendered violence. The following paragraph summarizes his key points: (1) Castells refers to the multimodal networking of emerging social movements. They connect online and offline networks, the society with the movements, etc. He describes them as network of already existing networks; hence they can work without a center or hierarchical leadership. (2) This "decentered structure maximizes chances of participation in the movement" and reduces the possibility of repression. (3) Incidents that trigger online outrage usually happen in physical environments, not in virtual space. Hence, the role of the Internet is mainly instrumental and cyberactivism translates only into an influential movement "by occupying the urban space". (4) Castells identifies a space of autonomy which he refers to as the "third space" between communication networks and physical sites of action. (5) On account of mutually taking inspiration from other movements around the world, he states that "movements are local and global at the same time". (6) Incidents that turn into media events and consequentially into the causation of networked social movements are "spontaneous in their origin, usually triggered by a spark of indignation". (7) One of the most striking characteristics is the accelerated pace with which messages, news and images are spread. According to Castells, movements become viral when they generate hope. (8) Multimodal networks create a feeling of "togetherness", not in the classic sense of community because there is no shared set of values but a common purpose. (9) On account of integrating multiple demands and generally lacking a unifying ideology, Castells categorizes networked social movements rarely as "programmatic movements". (Castells 2012, 221–29).

Despite his true observations, he neglects the digital divide and thus excludes theoretically those who do not have access to the networked world due to poverty, illiteracy and general socioeconomic inequalities. In the case of India, the population excluded from digital participation is far bigger than the number of cyberactivists. In 2012, India had an internet penetration of roughly 11 per cent and a Facebook penetration of about five per cent. Nevertheless, even though the numbers seems very little in relation, they still represent roughly 63 Mio subscribers (Internet World Stats 2013). Furthermore, the Internet is rapidly growing. The number of subscribers has increased tenfold within one decade and the number of mobile phone users has reached a density of almost 80 per cent of whom many access the internet through their mobile phones.[8]

Returning to the conceptualization of an emerging digital public sphere, this article is mainly concerned with the connection between digital discussion and real-life protests. Sassen's theory of "The Global Street" seems helpful to understand the importance of the urban street as public space. Street protests are part of a modern global experience. From the uprisings in the Arab world to the anti-gentrification struggles in the West, she identifies an "epochal quality to the current wave of street protests" (Sassen 2011, 574). "The Street can, thus, be conceived as a space where new forms of the social and the political can be made" (ibid, 574). Sassen further stresses that certain local issues recur across the globe and can "engender a kind of globality that does not depend on the *communicating*" (ibid, 578). And yet, social media can play a crucial role in spreading the word, mobilize activists, or enable discussion in a networked public sphere. While incidents happen outside of the digital space and consequentially trigger online outrage, debates and mobilization, they are in the course of a protest movement brought back to the streets. The Egyptian artist-activist Bahia Shehab talks about a "full circle" of mobilization in the case of Egypt's revolution in 2011. She refers to medial mobilization inspired by real-life events that lead to street protests and their return into social media through documentation in form of recordings, images and reports that again incite mobilization. She further notes that this "cyberspace-street-dialogue" contains numerous cross-references and is marked by a high degree of intermediality (Shehab 2013).

India's young social media activism: Who and why?

As already noted, the mobilization around the Delhi gang rape case was variably interpreted as a mass protest led by the educated, urban and middle classes, as an elite phenomenon or as the general political awakening of India's citizenry. Bélair-Gagnon et al. (2013) conclude in their analysis of social media used by Indian and foreign correspondents that the democratizing aspects of social media take on a different dimension in India[9], given the low internet penetration and the high density of mobile phone subscriptions. In the Indian context the digital divide is fundamentally a sociocultural divide with the "affluent, educated, English-speaking youth of India's major cities" (Bélair-Gagnon et al. 2013) still forming the biggest social media user segment. Nevertheless, the interviews analyzed by the research team indicate that following the Anna Hazare movement and the Delhi gang rape case, social media began to achieve a critical mass.

"To a greater extent than in previous protests, social media helped journalists keep a finger on the pulse of middle class India and get their immediate feedback on important issues" (Bélair-Gagnon et al. 2013).

Barn (2013) ascribes the political awakening of the young urban middle class to the Mumbai terror attacks, while others see Anna Hazare as a catalyst of politicizing a middle class that traditionally played a marginal role in Indian politics (Sen 2013). Whatever the reasons may be, online social and political activism is, as Castells has rightly argued, always linked to real-life events that trigger outrage and/or hope.

A very small incident that occurred in December 2010 at an independent music festival in Pune illustrates the possibilities of social media within a social context of people who are not necessarily prone to political involvement. During that time, public discussion in India centered on the so called 2G spectrum scam, also known as the Radia tapes controversy.[10] The biggest corruption scandal of India's telecom sector was initially hardly covered by the press and relevant information, rumors and new disclosures were disseminated mainly via Twitter which led to an increasing pressure on mainstream media to report about it. The NH7 Weekender, sponsored by a prominent beverage brand, celebrated its first edition as India's independent music festival in the posh area of Koregaon Park in Pune. It hosted gigs by popular Indian rock, heavy metal, pop and hip hop artists as well as some international acts. Tickets were priced at several thousand rupees. The relatively high entry fees together with the musical content and the sponsored alcoholic beverages accounted for a middle to upper class audience of young urban Indians interested in non-Bollywood music and partying. The crowd cannot be described as one that is particularly concerned with politics, consisting rather of so called "Globo-Indians" (Munshi 2001, 80) who are less concerned with national politics and are significantly underrepresented as voters (Sen 2013, 3). Nevertheless, the gig of the famous Indian electro rock band Pentagram was opened with a political statement by the lead singer against corruption in political and media circles and a call to the audience to get involved in circulating news about the 2G spectrum scam. Even more interestingly, he referred to the Twitter account of a music reporter friend who had compiled a plain summary of the scandal to be distributed via microblogging. After the incident the reporter's number of Twitter followers skyrocketed.

One may now understandably ask for the link to the Delhi gang rape case. The link lies in the nature of political mobilization of the young urban middle class. The combination of word of mouth, social media communication, and the inherent networking results in growing movements consisting of very individualistic participants. In the case of the 2G spectrum scam the aim was to uncover entanglements of media and "dirty" politics, i.e. to raise awareness. A couple of months later, in April 2011, Anna Hazare started his hunger strike against corruption and ignited what has become known as the Indian anti-corruption movement or the Lokpal bill movement (Banerjee 2011, Sitapati 2011). Some of the people, who attended the NH7 Weekender festival and re-tweeted the summary of the 2G spectrum scam, now demonstrated support for Anna Hazare on their Facebook profiles and in their Twitter accounts. One and a half years later, they showed concern and solidarity for the rape victim and signed on to anti-rape Facebook groups called "Stop Rape Now" or "Nirbhaya" (named after the initial pseudonym for the rape victim of the Delhi case). Many of the people who expressed their outrage over corruption, injustice and violence against women in discussions related to the 2G spectrum scam, Anna Hazare and the Delhi gang rape case are college students, young professionals and people working in the media, software and call center industries. Their affinity towards social networking sites goes hand in hand with an interest in lifestyle and pop culture issues. Many claim something one could term as common sense and a basic moral conscience, their education and global exposure implies a certain level of sensibility towards issues of injustice. Thus, cases like the three mentioned ones that generate a lot of publicity and media uproar, so called media events (Dayan and Katz 1992, Lenger and Nünning 2008), are likely to politicize those engaged in social networking to a certain extent.

The nature of the protest movement and its mobilization

Leaving attempts to measure the impact of social media mobilization aside, the Delhi case resembles Castells' (2012) common patterns of networked social movements in many ways.

According to Castells' first point of multimodal networking, the Delhi gang rape case facilitated a coalition between long-standing activist movements, regular citizens, celebrities and global supporters. The emerging pyramid mobilization of protest crowds via online and offline channels further linked the cyberspace to real-life street protests and bridged the dichotomy of virtual and "real" spaces.

The multilocality and decentralized nature of the protests corresponds to Castells' second point. Although Delhi was and continued to be the central site, the protests spread beyond the city's boundaries and despite of lacking identifiable leadership mobilized many people beyond the core of student protesters. Sen also mentions the "lack of focal organization or figure in the protests over the rape" (Sen 2013, 2) as a crucial difference to the Anna Hazare movement. Similar to Shehab's "full circle" or Castells' point of events happening in physical environments triggering online outrage, the real event of a brutal rape triggered immediate media reaction and lead to an ongoing (social) media discourse that brought people nationwide out on the streets and their documentation back into cyberspace. The "space of autonomy" (Castells 2012, 222) that emerges between communication networks and physical sites of action thus facilitated discourse across media formats and the online/offline divide.

It is striking that a local event served as a catalyst for nationwide and increasingly globalized social mobilization against gendered violence and rape. It did not only drive up international news reporting about gender issues in India but also propelled national awareness, hence proving Castells' point of the simultaneousness of local and global movements right. The amounting protest against gendered violence in India facilitated integration into global movements such as the "One Billion Rising" on International Women's Day. The event encouraged women to organize demonstrations and other creative forms of protesting rising violence against women. Many YouTube videos circulated encouraging women (and men) to participate. Media reports showed India trending at the forefront of the global campaign (GlobalVoices 2013).

Castells describes indignation or outrage as the main trigger for the spontaneous formation of networked social movements. This is more than obvious for the case at hand. The most important factor was probably a widely-felt identification with the victim and a feeling of embarrassment and frustration over the state of gender relations in India. There are many reasons why this story caught fire in the public imagination more than any other rape in recent Indian history.

> "There was, most of all, the unfathomably brutal violence involved. But many other things coalesced: the location of the crime, in upper-class South Delhi; the impunity of the attack; the fact that it was early evening; that she was accompanied by a male friend; that there were no complex caste or feudal hierarchies at play; that this was just random urban crime. That she was an average 'wholesome' girl making her way in the world. Women across the country felt, 'but for the grace of God, that could have been me.' She was Everywoman." (Chaudhury 2013a)

In another article, Chaudhury (2013b) asks why hundreds of other stories of rape not sufficed to prick the Indian conscience. "Why does gang rape horrify us more than mere rape? Why do rapes of Dalit or tribal or Northeastern women not shock the nation into saying 'enough is enough'?" Her answer lies in the deeply rooted socioeconomic hierarchies and a patriarchal cultural mindset.

The Delhi gang rape case went viral and thus confirms another one of Castells' set of common patterns. Numerous Facebook groups were created after the incident with up to several thousands of members. Individuals expressed their opinion, joined groups, passed on petitions, information, and audiovisual material, made and responded to calls for demonstrations, etc. Twitter linked and disseminated information. And deeper analysis as well as background discussion took place in forums, blogs, at the dinner table and in mainstream media. Intermediality in form of links between media formats further facilitated the spread of content as well as strengthened the network character.

Castells' last two points could be merged into one as well: A feeling of "togetherness" without a shared set of values but united by a common purpose correlates to a lacking ideology behind the movement. While indignation and the will for change may create a feeling of "togetherness", the protestors form despite their middle-classness a highly heterogeneous group. Adding to the aspect of identification with the victim, Chaudhury allocates a strong symbolism to the figure of Nirbhaya (one of the pseudonyms given to the victim before her identity was revealed):

> "In a sense, Nirbhaya embodied a new India no one has a full measure of yet. India's cities and small towns are full of young men and women like her: restless and on the move; hungry for an education, for jobs, for English, for social mobility, for belonging. They're an Internet generation; they know there's a wider world out there. They're reinventing themselves with energy, dissolving—or at least challenging—centuries-old boundaries of caste and station and wealth. They love their families with a grave sense of duty, but they long to leave the old ways behind. If it's to be a toss of coin, they'd rather look good than eat, rather have a TV set than a bed. They've sloughed off old skins, but not quite acquired the new. Just one chromosome binds them all: aspiration. They are the neo-middle class." (Chaudhury 2013a)

After having outlined the main agents of the networked social movement following the Delhi gang rape case and having identified some key components of the nature of the protests and its mobilization, I focus in the next section on the expressions of self-reflexivity of young Indians' own position, experience and opinion in form of blog posts on the youth portal Youth Ki Awaaz.

II. Debating on Social Media – An analysis of Youth Ki Awaaz posts

Youth Ki Awaaz is promoted as "India's largest online, collaborative, UN awarded platform for young people to express themselves on issues of importance" (www.youthkiawaaz.com). The platform allows users to blog on topics and entertains an extensive cross-media network including a Facebook site featuring more than 45.000 "likes" and a Twitter account with over 3000 followers (December 2013). An anonymous post from 27th December 2012 presented a collection of comments from the Youth Ki Awaaz Facebook page, stating "Every youth in the nation has an opinion about every aspect related to the Delhi rape incident. Be it the government's reaction or the steps taken for the victim's recovery, we have our voices and we MUST speak" (N.N., in a comment posted to Youth Ki Awaaz on December 27, 2012). In the following I present the analysis of 21 posts[11] made in reference to the Delhi gang rape case between 16th December 2012 and 25th April 2013 on Youth Ki Awaaz and relate the findings to the above discussed arguments on networked social movements and the nature of the protests.

Given the context of an online forum, the analyzed posts were contributed by young people who are literate and have Internet access. Few give away detailed information about their personal background but one can assume that the site attracts mainly urban middle-class users whom I see as part of the heterogeneous group taking interest in social media activism and online discussion. Many Youth Ki Awaaz contributors had been participating in their respective cities in the protests and later on reported or reflected on their experience in an online public sphere. The anonymous post quoted at the beginning of this article sums up the overall feeling of shock, shame and fear that is the "spark of indignation" according to the patterns identified by Castells' (2012) triggering outrage. The same author confirms what Chaudhury (2013a) has described as the strong symbolism of the case referring to its potential for identifying with the victim: "Maybe it's because it could happen to any one of us" (N.N., in a comment posted to Youth Ki Awaaz on December 20, 2012). Apart from an obvious personal identification and an overall expression of shock and anger, six dominant themes emerged, namely gender, mobility, space, class, India's image and policy/protests.[12] While all six categories stand for certain thematic clusters, the last one combines the critique of political reaction and police intervention with the evaluation of the nature of the protests.

The category gender refers to arguments made in reference to gender-based discrimination, the women's movement, the role and responsibilities of men and a critique of the status quo of gender relations in contemporary India. Each of the 21 analyzed posts contained references to gender, hence it represents the strongest of all the six generated themes. Key issues are the lacking respect and protection for women and deeply rooted patriarchy. Neelima Ravindran argues that the answer lies within the families and the society that plants the idea of male dominance in the minds of people from their childhood onwards. In an interesting comment, a male reader agrees and takes up the invitation for introspective but cannot find "a trace of sexism" within him. While mostly proving the essayist right, he suggests that women should empower themselves by training physical strength to defend themselves (Ravindran, in a comment posted to Youth Ki Awaaz on December 19, 2012).

The question whether men are responsible for empowering women by allowing them to move freely in public space is treated controversially. Many agree but some disagree and see the responsibility with women, and others express simply fear and a general suspicion of all men: "Every nameless man out there on the streets seems like a violation of my perception of safety" (N.N., in a comment posted to Youth Ki Awaaz on December 20, 2012). The motif of blaming women for inviting rape is dealt with in several texts. Two very similar posts contain compilations of outrageous comments by eminent politicians and religious leaders on rape and women's role in it. Although Sumedha Bharpilana's post is more satirical, both posts provide a deeper understanding of prevailing stereotypes and deconstruct the remarks. Referring to comments that criticize women's dressing, wrong behavior and mindset, Nidhi Sinha (in a comment posted to Youth Ki Awaaz on February 20, 2013) states that misogyny prevails and the common thread that binds all these beliefs is the blame laid upon women for inviting sexual violence and harassment. Bharpilana (in a comment posted to Youth Ki Awaaz on January 14, 2013) satirically refers to the recommendation of modest clothing and make up and to the assumption that women in "Bharat"[13] are treated like goddesses as long as they behave properly. This statement also bears reference to RSS chief Mohan Bhagwat's remark that "rapes happen in India, not Bharat".

Many claim that the question of women's safety is only the starting point for an encompassing revolution in India (Balachandran, in a comment posted to Youth Ki Awaaz on January 1, 2013). There are several suggestions how to tackle the issue. First, there are calls for changes in law towards more gender-justice (N.N., in a comment posted to Youth Ki Awaaz on December 27, 2012). Secondly there is the demand for education. Compulsory sex education involving child psychologists had been among the recommendations of the Justice Verma Commission report.[14] Charumati Haran (in a comment posted to Youth Ki Awaaz on January 30, 2013) welcomes this in her post as a progressive step towards changing attitudes from a young age onwards. Another post refers to the call for educating people to prevent rape and remarks that the protesters at the India Gate in Delhi were mostly educated students. Nevertheless, deeply entrenched patriarchal structures are not so easily dismissed and he links the responsibility of one's own behavior to the question of good citizenship:

"Travesty lies in the fact that these so called educated, knowledgeable civilized, advanced and well cultured people are themselves involved in making women an object of desire. [...]Truly, we need to introspect, all of us, on how we are contributing to the objectification of women. What kind of citizens we are trying to become." (Rawat, in a comment posted to Youth Ki Awaaz on April 24, 2013)

Further noteworthy is the reassessment of feminism in online discourses. While cyberfeminism or online women's activism is definitely on the rise (Gajjala 2004; Gajjala and Oh 2012), the Youth Ki Awaaz bloggers did not overtly embrace feminism as an alternative to the patriarchal structures they are criticizing.

"I am disgusted with every person (irrespective of who they are and what their gender is) who tag me a feminist whenever I try to voice my opinions on the inadequacy of our government to ensure protection to us, our clan!" (Mallick, in a comment posted to Youth Ki Awaaz on April 25, 2013).

A rather strong dissociation from feminism as an ideological movement stands in this remark against an identification with other or all women as "our clan". Uberoi (2001) has analyzed romantic short stories that were published in the Indian English-language women's magazine Woman's Era between 1994 and 1996. Her observations from 20 years ago interestingly reveal a strong parallel to the attitude towards feminism prevalent in the Youth Ki Awaaz posts. Woman's Era's romantic stories, despite of promoting love marriage or independent female role models, were permeated by a conservative, pseudo-nationalistic rejection of the women's movement, "deeming 'women's lib', so-called, a dangerous and foreign-inspired fad that will surely corrupt Indian womanhood and cut at the heart of Indian family life" (Uberoi, 2001, 169). Apparently, 'good' Indianness and feminism are perceived as insuperable antagonism. It is questionable whether Panchali Mallick, who posted on Youth Ki Awaaz, has a deeper understanding of the term 'feminism' but the label itself seems deterrent or even insulting. In this way the young bloggers of Youth Ki Awaaz consciously distance themselves from earlier social movements. But it is not clear whether they do it out of ignorance or with the intention to mark the beginning of a new era.

Many (female) contributors described their limited mobility in public and the social rules that curtail their freedom. "After this episode, a steep decline was seen in the number of women going out freely on the streets, not only in Delhi, but also in other states. Families built up stringent rules for their daughters, wives and teenage girls" (Shetty, in a comment posted to Youth Ki Awaaz on March 13, 2013). While some bemoan their betrayed hopes of increased mobility when moving from small towns to the capital[15], Siddharta Roy (in a comment posted to Youth Ki Awaaz on December 31, 2012) expresses his intention to "fight against every mentality that says woman should be locked up in houses to be safe."

In reference to mobility, Bharpilana writes in her satirical "Here Are Ten Commandments for 'Bharatiya' Women":

"Thou shall not move out of your place of dwelling that is situated in Bharat, after 8 pm in the evening. [...] Thou shall stay away from mobile phones as much as you can. You see, when these contraptions come in contact with the delicate skin of a female, they tend to emanate signals that force the invincible male to believe that the girl is asking for it and it is his duty to satisfy her carnal desires" (Bharpilana, in a comment posted to Youth Ki Awaaz on January 14, 2013*).*

In a more sober style, Nidhi Sinha (in a comment posted to Youth Ki Awaaz on January 20, 2013) quotes Kailash Vijayavargiya, Cabinet Minister in Madhya Pradesh, citing Sita's story from the Ramayana as a warning that women should stay in the space ascribes to them (by men). Clearly, the discussion about rape emanating from the Delhi case has ignited criticism going beyond the sheer condemnation of violence and extends to gendered conceptions of mobility and freedom. Panchali Mallick writes in her post titled "Breaking Free To Reclaim My Freedom: I, The Woman of My Country!":

"All I need is the liberty the freedom of movement and life that I deserve. I feel sorry for myself because I have been forced to demand what is birth right. [sic!]" (Mallick, in a comment posted to Youth Ki Awaaz on April 25, 2013).

Closely related to questions of mobility are issues of space and specific localities. In the discourse Delhi emerged as the "rape capital", a reference that can be found repeatedly within the analyzed posts too (Roy, in a comment posted to Youth Ki Awaaz on December 31, 2012; Mallick, in a comment posted to

Youth Ki Awaaz on April 25, 2013). But the discussion of space extends to an urban/rural divide as well as to particular complaints about public transport or certain streets. Hence, physical space is on many levels inherently linked to freedom or limitations of mobility and, as the next category shows, to social class as well.

Delhi was trending on Twitter as a dangerous and backward locality. A post by Shivani Singh compiles several tweets:

> @RooneyKhosla- "I feel violated. In my own city. Each time I read this kind of news. Everyday when we're harassed on the roads. Are u hearin our voice? #delhi"
>
> @KadambariM- "Problem really, is that #Delhi, like parts of UP & Haryana, has a culture of disrespecting women, a chauvinism scarier bcoz it is so casual." (Singh, in a comment posted to Youth Ki Awaaz on December 19, 2012)

Another text challenges the emphasis on Delhi being highlighted all the time as unsafe for women:

> "What about smaller cities where women are made to feel the violation even much after the incident itself? Most would even perhaps whisk it under the carpet and pass it off in silence, both as an individual and as a community. Instead of screaming around songs of Delhi being unsafe, do look into where it's coming from, what it is returning to and how many cases do you really come to know of from outside Delhi." (Singh, in a comment posted to Youth Ki Awaaz on December 21, 2012)

Although the writer puts Delhi as a specific locality into perspective by confessing a feeling of relative safety produced by cameras, police checks and other surveillance mechanisms, she conforms to the perception of the small town as a conservative and repressive space. Ojaswini Srivastava confirms the underlying notion of Delhi as an aspirational place:

> "I am not a Delhi girl. I am from a small town, but I live here, and there are hundreds others like me. I, we, we all want to be bolder, freer, and more confident than we are at our hometowns, because we are in Del-

hi." (Srivastava, in a comment posted to Youth Ki Awaaz on December 27, 2012)

The motif of Delhi extends even further and the city also features as a beloved space that has been taken over by crime and brutality and needs to be reclaimed (Kumar, in a comment posted to Youth Ki Awaaz on April 21, 2013). The discussion of space is but not limited to Delhi as a locality. Nidhi Sinha (in a comment posted to Youth Ki Awaaz on January 20, 2013) also takes on Bhagwat's already mentioned remark that "rapes happen in India, not Bharat". She interprets it as a condemnation of metropolitan Indian culture and points out the stark Hindu nationalist concept that links a (religiously defined) imaginary space and morality.

The class dimension is one of the most controversial issues. As already mentioned, it features very strongly in the discourse about the Delhi rape case, in the mainstream media as well as in social networking sites. Sinha (2013) puts forward that women, historically as well as today, are seen as the 'Other' and in times of war or conflict are often treated as loot. Women, according to this argument, are not only constructed as opposite to men but are also the "women of the multiple 'Others' created by manifold boundaries of caste, community, religion and nation. It is a long standing tradition of our culture (as well as of many others) that we punish and humiliate our 'Others' by punishing and humiliating their women. […] I suspect, in a peculiarly psycho-demonic way, this tradition was practiced in that white bus on December 16" (Sinha 2013). Hence, referring to the Delhi case, the girl was not only the 'Other' in terms of being female, she was also the 'Other' in terms of class and sociocultural background: "she appeared to be educated, had the guts to fight back and was out with a man late in the evening" (ibid.).

Sinha suggests that educated people of higher classes should know better. The same assumption pervades the Youth Ki Awaaz posts. Shivangi Singh (in a comment posted to Youth Ki Awaaz on December 19, 2012) collects "Twitter Reactions for Rapists, Delhi and The Governance" in her post and quotes a tweet by Preeti Shenoy that conforms to this discourse: "The worst thing about rapes is even educated men ask 'what was she wearing' and 'why was she out so late' Deplorable. #delhi #rape". Other contributions contain references to the class-based mindset of small town inhabitants as more dangerous. The fact that the rape victim hailed from a respectable middle class background was debated vigorously in the media. Many accounted it for the overwhelming media attention and rightly claimed that rapes of women from marginalized social groups are hardly even reported. By asking "Why do rapes of Dalit or tribal or Northeastern women not shock the nation into saying 'enough is enough'?", Chaudhury (2013b) reminds us in her Tehelka article of deeply-rooted social hierarchies.

The category that I have titled 'India's Image' is somewhat related to notions of space and territory but extends further into hurt feelings of national and/or cultural pride, embarrassment over the country's representation and demands for social change in Indian society. India's image appeared as a strong motif. Firstly, the feeling of national shame prevails throughout the 21 analyzed posts. The case is interpreted as the violation of a nation's spirit. Rape statistics and India's prominent position on place three worldwide in numbers of rape are combined with a feeling of inferiority (Roy, in a comment posted to Youth Ki Awaaz on December 31, 2012; Singh, in a comment posted to Youth Ki Awaaz on December 19, 2012). Amongst the compilation of comments on social media is one particular Facebook posts that indicates embarrassment over the fact that the victim had to be flown to a Singapore hospital and couldn't receive appropriate treatment in India (N.N., in a comment posted to Youth Ki Awaaz on December 27, 2012). Many equated the case with the overall struggle for social change in India. In linking so called Indian culture, political shortcomings and the prevailing problem of gendered violence and rape, Upasana Sharma writes:

> "We find faults in the system but do not do what we can on a personal level. We need to build a nation with an awake conscious. Not someone who nods and follows along. Following the modus operandi, I have a name to suggest for her. Till we don't bring about change and develop a conscience, let's call every rape victim, India." (Sharma, in a comment posted to Youth Ki Awaaz on April 21, 2013)

In a similar spirit, Tanaya Singh writes on account of the victim's demise:

> "This is one of the saddest days in the history of India. […] As a citizen of India, the same country she was born in, the same country that helped her dream and the same country that killed her, let us pledge to make this day the beginning of the change that the nation has been

fighting for." (Singh, in a comment posted to Youth Ki Awaaz on December 29, 2012)

Attempts to explain this 'shameful' side of India often lead to arguments linking 'the evil' to culturally sanctioned patriarchy and the upbringing of male children (Ravindran, in a comment posted to Youth Ki Awaaz on December 19, 2012). Lacking respect for women is often cited as the core problem of Indian society. A sense of nationalism, in the form of professed love for the country, produces very emotional and outraged reactions. Bloggers write: "I feel frustrated on being a woman in my country, whom I love unfathomably" (Mallick, in a comment posted to Youth Ki Awaaz on April 25, 2013) or "I feel like running away from this country" (Dahiya/Chaturvedi/Haroon/Shashank, in a comment posted to Youth Ki Awaaz on April 21, 2013). They link their emotions to an overall critique of Indian culture and mentality. A young male blogger claims that India was a country "which was once counted as a topmost nation in the virtue of respect towards the female gender" (Kumar, in a comment posted to Youth Ki Awaaz on April 21, 2013) but with the recent rape cases this "honor" is not considered suitable anymore. Although his statement is historically rather questionable, others contrast India's image as a spiritual and religious nation with the social reality. In these interpretations, the holy place of the mother at the heart of the traditional Indian social system and the worshipping of female goddesses (Poggendorf-Kakar 2003) conflict strongly with the existing gender inequality. "Why do you call her *laxmi,* when you have to rape her?", asks Ojaswini Srivastava in her post (in a comment posted to Youth Ki Awaaz on December 27, 2012). Some go far beyond criticizing gender relations and argue that questions of women's safety are only the starting point for the required encompassing revolution.

> "The Delhi incident has triggered a wave of protests relating to safety of women and the solutions thereof. But these solutions cannot be made or implemented unless we question how India's public offices & institutions function, how our executive, legislature and judiciary work currently and do they really serve the masses and how young Indians expect/want them to work. In short, we need to fundamentally redefine how India works." (Balachandran, in a comment posted to Youth Ki Awaaz on January 1, 2013)

The wave of protest mentioned in the above quote was the ultimate political outcome of the case and is hence seen as a form of political awakening. Although the protests are interpreted by all contributors on Youth Ki Awaaz as a step in the right direction to change India's social and political landscape, the last analytical category reveals conflicting notions of the nature of the protests and the required political action. Predominant themes throughout the texts were the outrage at police brutality, the government's inaction, and inappropriate comments by politicians and religious spokespeople. Further discussed were necessary changes in law and adequate methods of punishing the perpetrators. According to these narratives, the struggle needs to continue because the government does not take appropriate measures. It takes too long to pass new laws and implementation is urgently needed. (Kumar, in a comment posted to Youth Ki Awaaz on April 21, 2013; Garg, in a comment posted to Youth Ki Awaaz on March 1, 2013)

> "The system – whose police and politicians make archaic and wretched quotes on why the girls 'deserve' to be raped or why it was their fault. These primitive brains clearly hold the reins to a country and we, the young, are appalled by our leaders and protectors." (Roy, in a comment posted to Youth Ki Awaaz on December 31, 2012)

Apart from the already mentioned satirical dealings with the outrageous comments and suggestions by Indian politicians and religious leaders, even their expressions of sadness and regret are deemed as disappointing, empty statements (Sinha, Youth Ki Awaaz, 20.01.2013; Shetty, in a comment posted to Youth Ki Awaaz on March 13, 2013). The social media discourse on these outrageous comments and the practice of 'victim blaming' continued well into 2013. A YouTube video released by the Delhi-based comedy collective All India Bakchod titled "It's my fault" went viral in September and October 2013 and caused uproar throughout national and global media (Brindaalakshmi 2013). Gursimran Khamba, a co-founder of All India Bakchod, told Al Jazeera:

> "The notion behind this video was pretty simple. We wanted to attack patriarchy as it exists in India. It sort of comes out every time there is a sexual assault case or a rape case. The first thing that happens, instead of focusing on the crime and looking at the perpetrator, the default for some reason is that the burden is always put on the woman." (McGlensey 2013)

In mid-November 2013 the video had close to 3 million views, 30,000 likes and more than 12,000 comments on YouTube. Critique of politicians and religious leaders is complemented by complaints about the exorbitant police violence against protesters in Delhi (N.N., in a comment posted to Youth Ki Awaaz on December 22, 2012; N.N., in a comment posted to Youth Ki Awaaz on December 27, 2012). Certain instances were highlighted to illustrate the system's failings: e.g. when police forces publicly hit female protesters, when the police tried to bribe the father of a missing child, and when the National Commission for Women chief Mamata Sharma refused to see the parents of the sexually abused child after its retrieval because it was a holiday (Kumar, in a comment posted to Youth Ki Awaaz on April 21, 2013). Other posts warn that "[b]laming government, police, etc. will also not help either of us" (Chaturvedi in Dahiya/Chaturvedi/Haroon/Shashank, in a comment posted to Youth Ki Awaaz on April 21, 2013) and call for introspection instead of pointing fingers at "everyone but ourselves" (Ravindran, in a comment posted to Youth Ki Awaaz on December 19, 2012). The critique of political reactions to the Delhi rape case, the debate around the nature of the protests and the expressed urge for changes in Indian society and mentality are all combined and interlinked in the statements.

Apart from these overall themes, the very concrete question of how rapists should be punished pervades many posts. Common to all is the call for severe punishment and Neelima Ravindran recounts how "the social media has demanded every possible punishment from castration to death by stoning". The death penalty appears even as the lightest version (Singh, in a comment posted to Youth Ki Awaaz on December 21, 2012; Singh, in a comment posted to Youth Ki Awaaz on December 19, 2012; Ravindran, in a comment posted to Youth Ki Awaaz on December 19, 2012).

Some bloggers take up the task of analyzing the nature of the protests beyond criticizing police brutality and the state's incapability. In many ways the posts correspond with Castells' patterns. Definitely, the events following the Delhi gang rape case and the related discourse were triggered by a "spark of indignation" (Castells 2012). The strong identification with the victim and a feeling of national shame that pervade the online discourse on Youth Ki Awaaz testify this assumption. By calling for ongoing protests, compulsory sex education, and social change bloggers connect not only online and offline worlds but also general social issues with a particular movement. An interesting post compares the reaction and consequences following the Delhi gang rape case to the outbreak of the Arab Spring after the self-immolation of a Tunisian fruit seller. He traces the inspiration for the Indian anti-corruption movement to the same incident in Tunisia (Balachandran, in a comment posted to Youth Ki Awaaz on January 1, 2013). He thus links his own experience and the Indian discourse to a global media sphere as well as to social movements around the world. One post features a virtual discussion on the pro and contras of central leadership for the protest organization. The statements were collected from members' Facebook posts and assembled according to overarching questions, e.g. on the survivor being flown to Singapore for further treatment, on the need for central leadership in the rape protest movement, on the attack of Delhi police on protestors, on the protest against Rapes (N.N., in a comment posted to Youth Ki Awaaz on December 27, 2012). Castells' identifies decentral and non-hierarchical leadership as symptomatic and effective for networked social movements (2012). Many collected opinions correspond with his assumption by writing: "This is not any leader's movement, this is a cause of everyone" (ibid.). Yeshu Aggarwal but disagrees and holds India's diversity and lacking unison responsible:

> "It reminds me of India's 1857 War of Independence. According to the History I learned in school, India lost that war because of division across India. Only if we had a leader for a movement. And no I don't intend it to be a political leader. Someone like Kiran Bedi for e.g. would have been suitable." (ibid.)

Interestingly, Aggarwal suggests Kiran Bedi[16] as a political leader who played a prominent role in the anti-corruption movement led by Anna Hazare. Although Castells' argument of decentered structures applies to the organization of protests, the Indian context demonstrates the need for a symbolic lead figure such as the recent Anna Hazare movement illustrates. Similarly debatable is the question of a unifying ideology. Castells argues that networked social movements can rarely be categorized as programmatic. In her post, a young woman agrees with his argument by stating, "[t]he protest is a peaceful 'people's protest', with no political agenda and hence there is no central leadership" (Sundharam, in a comment posted to Youth Ki Awaaz on December 28, 2012). In spite of her statement, she lists the demands of the protesters below. Evidently she analyzes the political agenda behind the protest without categorizing it as such. Apparently, having a political agenda is equated with following a certain party's ideology. One can assume that the fear of parties jumping on the bandwagon and usurping the protests for their own purposes is present here. This critique is clearly expressed and extended to the media in a later post referring to the case of the rape of a five-year-old girl:

> "I also request the AAP or any other political party to stop manipulating the genuine anger of the youth for vested interests. Let us not give the sly media and the administration any opportunities to discredit the protests [...]."(Kumar, in a comment posted to Youth Ki Awaaz on April 21, 2013)

Conclusion

As the above analyzed postings on Youth Ki Awaaz have shown, India's youth does embrace online tools to express their opinions and enable political and social discussion. Through hyperlinks the analyzed platform is connected to a larger network of social media and social networking sites, such as Facebook and Twitter. Given the fact that English as a language prevails and the participating bloggers do have access to the Internet, it is probably justified to speak of a broadly middle class user profile. Nevertheless, it would be misleading to reduce the role of social networking sites and microblogging to a middle class lifestyle phenomenon. As the immense media mobilization related to the Delhi gang rape case demonstrates, there are various other influential agents involved in transforming a media event into a social movement. India has a long lasting tradition of a very active women's movement (see Chaudhuri in this volume) that used the high publicity case both as a point for their existing agenda as well as a cause to criticize the focus on this singular case while neglecting thousands of previous and simultaneous rape cases involving women of lower status. A heterogeneous conglomerate of feminist and social activists equally utilizes the Internet's potential for networking and mobilization.[17] While the analyzed blog posts echo criticisms of highlighting one single event while thousand others go unnoticed, a clear demarcation from feminism as an ideology is present as well. Despite these differences between young college students on Youth Ki Awaaz and ingrained gender activists, the tools which were employed were the same. Neither can one deny the presence of thousands of young Indians demonstrating across the country against gendered violence and rape. As it is evident from their narratives, many Youth Ki Awaaz contributors had been participating in their respective cities in the protests and later on reported and reflected on their experience in an online public sphere.

With this background it is difficult to assess Sen's assumption that "social media warfare" and street protest do not translate into "actual" politics which he measures mainly in the voter representation during elections (Sen 2013). On the other hand, the kind of middle class cyberactivism and online discourse described above could have easily remained what Morozov (2013, 2011) and Gladwell (2010) have criticized as "slacktivism", the easy clicking for a peaceful social consciousness. But the so called "political awakening" of the Indian middle class did against all prognoses not peter out. Mobilization continued with several key events that highlighted new aspects of India's prevalent patriarchal culture and were seen as parts of a continuum: the rape of a Swiss tourists cycling through Madhya Pradesh in January 2013, and the already mentioned rape of a five-year-old girl in Delhi in April 2013. The latter case became infamous when news spread that the police tried to bribe the raped girl's father to keep quiet. While the case of the Swiss woman directed discussion towards safety for tourists and female travellers in general, the second case revealed once more the unbounded absurdity of blaming raped women for inviting rape through their behavior or clothing. The above discussed YouTube video "It's My Fault" by the comedy collective All India Bakchod uses extreme sarcasm to counter this line of argumentation and to reveal the hypocrisy behind it. It is not surprising that particularly the case of the raped child sparked off a new wave of social media campaigning and petitioning. Again, medial mobilization inspired by real-life events leads to actual protests whose documentation finds its way back into the media and completes, what Egyptian artist-activist Bahia Shehab has called the "full circle" or the "cyber-space-street-dialogue" (Shehab 2013).

Hence, the question remains whether one could speak of an emerging digital public sphere revolving around the event? In spite of the accounts of protest movements and online mobilization, an over-enthusiastic positive assertion of the Internet is not quite appropriate. Yes, new media have the ability to link people to each other and to events but their usage do not imply activism. Castells' patterns, as I have argued with respect to the Youth Ki Awaaz posts and other recent examples, apply to the case but are not sufficient to explain the dynamics at work. An increasingly networked world allows participation in a (virtual) public sphere that continues to be dominated by patriarchal structures. Participation is equally structured along existing offline hierarchies such as class and gender and consequently excludes already marginalized groups. These observations are opposed to earlier influential predictions that future technologies may flatten hierarchies (McLuhan 1962). Castells (2012) did not bear in mind that despite of all its benefits, an increasingly important digital public sphere on the other hand deepens the digital divide and favors an elitist discussion. Very important and unfortunately beyond the scope of this article is the fact that a digital public sphere cannot exist entirely separate from other media discourses and is necessarily intermedially linked to news reporting, discussions and debates in the print media, on television channels, and in various other offline spheres. Media discourses inform each other and as much as online and offline experiences are connected, the Delhi gang rape case occurred in a time of intensified medialization in which the Youth Ki Awaaz contributors live and make sense of social realities.

In terms of access, social media do not transcend unequal opportunities but those who had access to online discourses and social networking sites were enabled to express their opinion, anger, hopes and frustration in an unprecedented way and engage in discussion with young people nationwide and even globally. The exemplary analysis of 21 posts on Youth Ki Awaaz shows that the emerging discourses around gender, mobility, space, politics, and the media are far from trivial and contain serious critique of the existing system.

Bibliography

Youth Ki Awaaz Posts

BALACHANDRAN, SURENDRAN, January 1, 2013, "Has India Begun 2013 On A 'Revolutionary' Note?," *Youth Ki Awaaz*, November 4, 2013, http://www.youthkiawaaz.com/2013/01/india-2013/.

BHARPILANA, SUMEDHA, January 14, 2013, "Here Are Ten Commandments for 'Bharatiya' Women." *Youth Ki Awaaz*, January 14, 2013, http://www.youthkiawaaz.com/2013/01/here-are-10-commandments-for-bharatiya-women/.

DAHIYA, VISHAKHA et al., April 21, 2013, "'Our Present Mentality Is The Worst Culture In The World': Delhi Rape Quick Views," *Youth Ki Awaaz*, http://www.youthkiawaaz.com/2013/04/our-present-mentality-is-the-worst-culture-in-the-world-delhi-rape-quick-views/.

GARG, UDITA, March 1, 2013, "Internalizing The Revolution And Battling Personal Hypocrisies," *Youth Ki Awaaz*, http://www.youthkiawaaz.com/2013/03/internalizing-the-revolution-and-battling-personal-hypocrisies/.

HARAN, CHARUMATI, January 30, 2013, "Why Sex Education Is A Very Progressive Point Of Justice Verma's Report," *Youth Ki Awaaz*, November 4, 2013, http://www.youthkiawaaz.com/2013/01/why-sex-education-is-a-very-progressive-point-of-justice-vermas-report/.

KUMAR, AKHIL, April 21, 2013, "The Rape Of A 5 Year Old And The Heartless Police: It's Time To Be Very Very Angry!," *Youth Ki Awaaz*, November 4, 2013, http://www.youthkiawaaz.com/2013/04/the-rape-of-a-5-year-old-and-the-heartless-police-its-time-to-be-very-very-angry/ (Access: 04.11.2013).

MALLICK, PANCHALI, April 25, 2013, "Breaking Free To Reclaim My Freedom: I, The Woman Of My Country!," *Youth Ki Awaaz*, November 4, 2013, http://www.youthkiawaaz.com/2013/04/breaking-free-to-reclaim-my-freedom-i-the-woman-of-my-country/.

N.N., December 20, 2012, "I've Never Been More Terrified In My Life: Shock, Anger, And Terror," *Youth Ki Awaaz*, November 4, 2013, http://www.youthkiawaaz.com/2012/12/ive-never-been-more-terrified-in-my-life-shock-anger-and-terror/.

N.N., December 27, 2012, "India's Fight Against Rape: 20 Youth Tell Us Their Views," *Youth Ki Awaaz*, November 4, 2013, http://www.youthkiawaaz.com/2012/12/indias-fight-against-rape-20-youth-tell-us-their-views/.

N.N., December 22, 2012, "Its Unbelievable How The Indian Police Behaved," *Youth Ki Awaaz*, November 4, 2013, http://www.youthkiawaaz.com/2012/12/its-unbelievable-how-the-indian-police-behaved/.

RAVINDRAN, NEELIMA, December 19, 2012, "While Discussing Rapes In India, Did You Look Within "You?," *Youth Ki Awaaz*, November 4, 2013, http://www.youthkiawaaz.com/2012/12/while-discussing-rapes-in-india-did-you-look-within-you/.

RAWAT, TANUJ, April 24, 2013, "The Hypocrisy Of The Protesters: Abhi Ye Sab Nahi Karange To Kab?," *Youth Ki Awaaz*, November 4, 2013, http://www.youthkiawaaz.com/2013/04/the-hypocrisy-of-the-protesters-abhi-ye-sab-nahi-karange-to-kab/.

ROY, SIDDHARTHA, December 31, 2012, "A Nobody's Perception: Why 'Never Again To Rape' Means So Much?," *Youth Ki Awaaz*, November 4, 2013, http://www.youthkiawaaz.com/2012/12/a-nobodys-perception-why-never-again-to-rape-means-so-much/.

SHARMA, UPASANA, April 24, 2013, "Angry Yet Helpless: Till We Don't Develop A Conscience Let's Call Every Rape Victim, India!," *Youth Ki Awaaz*, November 15, 2013, http://www.youthkiawaaz.com/2013/04/angry-yet-helpless-till-we-dont-develop-a-conscience-lets-call-every-rape-victim-india/.

SHETTY, NEHA, March 13, 2013, "Why A 'Happy Women's Day' When For The Rest 364 Days We Are Terribly Unsafe?," *Youth Ki Awaaz*, November 4, 2013, http://www.youthkiawaaz.com/2013/03/why-a-happy-womens-day-when-for-the-rest-364-days-we-are-terribly-unsafe/.

SINGH, REETI, December 21, 2012, "You Do Not Have To Travel All The Way To Delhi To Get Raped," *Youth Ki Awaaz*, November 4, 2013, http://www.youthkiawaaz.com/2012/12/you-do-not-have-to-travel-all-the-way-to-delhi-to-get-raped/.

SINGH, SHIVANGI, December 19, 2012, "#StopThisShame, #Delhi: Twitter Reactions For Rapists, Delhi And The Governance," *Youth Ki Awaaz*, November 4, 2013, http://www.youthkiawaaz.com/2012/12/stopthisshame-delhi-twitter-reactions-for-rapists-delhi-and-the-governance/.

SINGH, TANAYA, December 29, 2012, "Delhi Gang Rape Victim No More, The 'Cause' Still Survives," *Youth Ki Awaaz*, November 15, 2013, http://www.youthkiawaaz.com/2012/12/delhi-gangrape-victim-no-more-the-cause-still-survives/.

SINHA, NIDHI, January 20, 2013, "They Said It: 'Eminent' Indians And Their Comments," *Youth Ki Awaaz*, November 4, 2013, http://www.youthkiawaaz.com/2013/01/they-said-it-eminent-indians-and-their-comments/.

SRIVASTAVA, OJASWINI, December 27, 2012, "I Am From A Small Town, I Live In Delhi, I Am Scared And I Have Questions," *Youth Ki Awaaz*, November 4, 2013, http://www.youthkiawaaz.com/2012/12/i-am-from-a-small-town-i-live-in-delhi-i-am-scared-and-i-have-questions/.

SUNDHARAM, JOANNA SHRUTI, December 28, 2012, "What EXACTLY Are We Fighting For?," *Youth Ki Awaaz*, November 4, 2013, http://www.youthkiawaaz.com/2012/12/what-exactly-are-we-fighting-for/.

Literature

BANERJEE, SUMANTA. "Anna Hazare, Civil Society and the State." *Economic & Political Weekly* 46, no.36, September 3, 2011.

BARN, RAVINDER. "Social Media and Protest – The Indian Spring?," The Huffington Post, January 9, 2013, Huffpost Tech United Kingdom, accessed January 9, 2013, http://www.huffingtonpost.co.uk/professor-ravinder-barn/india-social-media-and-protest_b_2430194.html.

BÉLAIR-GAGNON, VALÉRIE et al. "Emerging spaces for storytelling: Journalistic lessons from social media in the Delhi gang rape case." *Nieman Journalism Lab*, April 8, 2013. Accessed April 8, 2013, http://www.niemanlab.org/2013/04/emerging-spaces-for-storytelling-journalistic-lessons-from-social-media-in-the-delhi-gang-rape-case/.

BOYD, DANAH M. and NICOLE B. ELLISON. "Social network sites: Definition, history, and scholarship." *Journal of Computer-Mediated Communication* 13, no.1 (2007): 210-30. http://onlinelibrary.wiley.com/doi/10.1111/j.1083-6101.2007.00393.x/full.

BRINDAALAKSHMI, K. "What All India Bakchod Did Right With 'It's Your Fault'." *Medianama, News & Analysis of Digital Media in India*, September 25, 2013. Accessed November 15, 2013, http://www.medianama.com/2013/09/223-its-your-fault-video-all-india-bakchod.

CASTELLS, MANUEL. *The rise of the network society*. Malden, Mass: Blackwell Publishers, 1996.

CASTELLS, MANUEL. *Networks of outrage and hope: social movements in the Internet age.* Cambridge: Polity Press, 2012.
CASTELLS, MANUEL. *Communication power.* Oxford: Oxford University Press, 2013.
CHAUDHURY, SHOMA. "The Girl Who Fired an Outcry in India." *The Daily Beast,* April 03, 2013. Accessed April 5, 2013, http://www.thedailybeast.com/newsweek/2013/04/01/nirbhaya-the-woman-who-ignited-a-fire-in-india.html. [2013a]
CHAUDHURY, SHOMA. "Why did it need an incident so unspeakably brutal to trigger our outrage?" *Tehelka* 9, no.52, January 9, 2013. Accessed October 18, 2013, http://www.tehelka.com/why-did-it-need-an-incident-so-unspeakably-brutal-to-trigger-our-outrage/. [2013b]
DAYAN, DANIEL and ELIHU KATZ. *Media Events. The Live Broadcasting of History.* Cambridge, Mass.: Harvard University Press, 1992.
DESAI, GAURAV, ed. *The Virtual Transformation of the Public Sphere.* London: Routledge, 2012.
LANGMAN, LAUREN. "From Virtual Public Spheres to Global Justice: A Critical Theory of Internetworked Social Movements." *Sociological Theory* 23, no.1 (2005): 42–74.
FUCHS, CHRISTIAN. "Some Reflections on Manuel Castells' Book Networks of Outrage and Hope. Social Movements in the Internet Age." *tripleC: communication, capitalism & critique* 10, no.2 (2012): 775–97.
GAJJALA, RADHIKA. *Cyber selves: feminist ethnographies of South Asian women.* Walnut Creek, CA: AltaMira Press, 2004.
GAJJALA, RADHIKA and YEON JU OH, eds. *Cyberfeminism 2.0.* New York: Peter Lang Pub., 2012.
GLADWELL, MALCOLM. "Small Change. Why the revolution will not be tweeted." *The New Yorker,* October 04, 2010.
GLASER, BARNEY G. and ANSELM L. STRAUSS (1967). *The discovery of grounded theory: Strategies for qualitative research.* Chicago: Aldine Pub. Co., 1967.
"India at the Forefront of one Billion Rising." *GlobalVoices,* February 20, 2013. Accessed October 18, 2013, http://globalvoicesonline.org/2013/02/20/india-at-the-forefront-of-one-billion-rising/.
HOLST, FREDERIK. "Challenging the Notion of Neutrality – Postcolonial Perspectives on Information- and Communication Technologies." In *Social Dynamics 2.0: Researching Change in Times of Media Convergence,* edited by Nadja-Christina Schneider and Bettina Gräf, 127–44. Berlin: Frank & Timme, 2011.
Internet World Stats. "Usage and population statistics: India." *Internet World Stats* 2013, Accessed May 5, 2013, http://www.internetworldstats.com/asia.htm#in.
Internet World Stats. "India: Usage Stats and Telecommunications Market Report." *Internet World Stats* 2014, Accessed April 28, 2014, http://www.internetworldstats.com/asia/in.htm.
JOSEPH, SARAH. "Social Media, Political Change, and Human Rights." *Boston College International and Comparative Law Review* 35, no.1 (2012): 145–88.
KAPLAN, ANDREAS and MICHAEL HAENLEIN. "Users of the world unite! The challenges and opportunities of Social Media." *Business Horizons* 53, (2010): 59–68.

KRISHNAN, MURALI. "Indian Internet users fear trend to oppression." *Deutsche Welle*, November 27, 2012. Accessed October 18, 2013. http://www.dw.de/indian-internet-users-fear-trend-to-oppression/a-16408683.

LENGER, FRIEDRICH, and ANSGAR NÜNNING, eds. *Medienereignisse der Moderne*. Darmstadt: Wissenschaftliche Buchgesellschaft, 2008.

MCGLENSEY, MELISSA. „Rape: It's your fault!" *Ms.blog*, September 9, 2013. Accessed November 15, 2013, http://msmagazine.com/blog/2013/09/26/rape-its-your-fault/.

MCLUHAN, MARSHALL, ed. *The Gutenberg Galaxy*. London: Routledge & Kegan Paul, 1962.

MOROZOV, EVGENY. *The net delusion: the dark side of Internet freedom*. New York: PublicAffairs, 2011.

MUNSHI, SHOMA. "Marvellous Me: The Beauty Industry and the Construction of the 'Modern' Indian Woman". In Images of the 'modern woman' in Asia: global media, local meanings, edited by Shoma Munshi, 78–93 .Richmond: Curzon. 2001.

MOROZOV, EVGENY. *To save everything, click here: the folly of technological solutionism*. New York: PublicAffairs, 2013.

POGGENDORF-KAKAR, KATHARINA. "Virtuous Mother, Virile Hero and Warrior Queen: The Conception of Gender and Family in Hindutva." In *Family and gender. Changing values in Germany and India*, edited by Margrit Pernau et al., 179–95. New Delhi: Sage Publ., 2003.

SASSEN, SASKIA. "The Global Street: Making the Political." *Globalizations* 8, no.5 (2011): 573–79.

SCHNEIDER, NADJA-CHRISTINA. "Medialised Delhi: Youth, Protest, and an Emerging Genre of Urban Films." *South Asia Chronicle* 3, (2013): 86–110.

SEN, RONOJOY. "The Delhi rape protests. Observations on middle class activism in India." *ISAS Brief* 266, (2013), edited by Institute of South Asian Studies. National-University of Singapore. Accessed February 9, 2014, http://www.isas.nus.edu.sg/Attachments/PublisherAttachment/ISAS_Brief_266_-_The_Delhi_Rape_Protests_24012013172633.pdf.

SHEHAB, BAHIA. "Full Circle". Lecture at the conference *Reclaiming Public Space. Culture between Public and Digital Spheres*, April 22–23, 2013 in Berlin, organized by Goethe Institut.

SHIRKY, CLAY. "The political power of social media: technology, the public sphere, and political change." *Foreign Affairs* 90, no.28 (2011): 1–12.

SINHA, PRACHEE. "Run with Gender, Hunt with Class. Curious Ways of Indian Democracy from India Gate to the Slum Habitat." *Economic & Political Weekly* 48, no.4 (2013).

SITAPATI, VINAY. "What Anna Hazare's Movement and India's New Middle Classes Say about Each Other." *Economic & Political Weekly* 46, no.30 (July 23, 2011).

SWAMY, SUBRAMANIAN. *2G spectrum scam*. New Delhi: Har-Anand Publications, 2011. "Mumbai gets country's first 'Social Media Lab." *The Hindu*, March 17, 2013. Accessed September 10, 2013. http://www.thehindu.com/news/national/mumbai-gets-countrys-first-social-media-lab/article4516705.ece.

UBEROI, PATRICIA. "A Suitable Romance? Trajectories of Courtship in Indian Popular Fiction." In *Images of the 'modern woman' in Asia. Global media, local meanings*, edited by Shoma Munshi, 169–85. Richmond: Curzon, 2001.

1   The title refers to the popular Indian online platform *Youth Ki Awaaz*. In a mix of Hindi and English the name literally means "voice of the youth" or "mouthpiece of the youth" as the website itself translates it.
2   A hashtag is a word or a phrase prefixed with the symbol #. It is used to indicate themes or categories in the microblogging service Twitter.
3   Amanat ("treasure"), Nirbhaya ("fearless one") and Damini ("lightning") were Hindi pseudonyms for the rape victim initially given by various media houses prior to the disclosure of her real name. The pseudonym Damini refers to a film by Rajkumar Santoshi (1993) with the same title. The film's theme centres around a woman's fight against society for justice.
4   Section 228A of the Indian Penal Code prohibits the disclosure of the identity of a rape victim.
5   The protest resulted finally in the government's promise to adjust the laws to protect women and prosecute rapists as well as to improve the entire judicial process. The case itself has been moved to a fast-track court.
6   The model and barmaid Jessica Lal was shot dead in a Delhi night club in 1999. The initial acquittal of her murderer, the son of a wealthy Congress politician, was followed by a public outcry. The incident brought to light the long-lasting frustration of the middle class with corruption. There were numerous protest campaigns, including ones involving SMS and email. Rallies and marches took place, as well as candlelit vigils. The protest and supporting media campaigns enforced an appeal and consequently Lal's murderer was sentenced to life imprisonment. The Indian movie "No One Killed Jessica" (2011), starring the popular actresses Rani Mukherjee and Vidya Balan, is based on the media coverage of the case. Schneider (2013, 99–103) analyses the movie within the context of the multi-dimensional interrelation of real-life (youth) protests and the emerging genre of urban protest films in Hindi cinema.
7   For discussion on the virtual transformation of the public sphere see: Gaurav Desai, *The Virtual Transformation of the Public Sphere* (London: Routledge, 2012); Lauren Langman, "From Virtual Public Spheres to Global Justice: A Critical Theory of Internetworked Social Movements," *Sociological Theory* 23, no.1 (2005): 42–74.
8   The mobile sector has grown from around 10 million subscribers in 2002 to pass the 900 million mark in early 2012 (Internet World Stats 2014).
9   The authors' basic assumption of social media as a democratizing force is debatable. The article remains unclear about the question whether the assumption is a flattening of hierarchies in information production and distribution or a democratization of the society through social media. Although social media do increase participation, Joseph (2012, 174) questions that greater participation leads to democracy and pluralism.
10 The 2G spectrum scam was revealed in 2010. It involved politicians and government officials in India illegally undercharging mobile telephony companies for frequency allocation licenses, which they would then use to create 2G subscriptions for cell phones. Media sources such as OPEN and Outlook reported that the two senior journalists Barkha Dutt (group editor of NDTV) and Vir Sanghvi (editorial director of Hindustan Times) knew that corporate lobbyist Nira Radia was influencing the decisions of appointment of telecom minister. The two magazines made public the telephone conversations between Nira Radia, Barkha Dutt and Vir Sanghvi. Critics allege that Barkha Dutt and Vir Sanghvi knew about the nexus between the government and the media industry but still they supported this corrupt activity and suppressed news reporting. See: Swamy (2011).
11 A keyword search on Youth Ki Awaaz for "Delhi rape" resulted in 21 relevant entries that were posted between the day of the incident (16th December 2012) until the close of my data collection (25th April 2013). Posts on other rape cases were not included in the analysis.
12 I have employed the method of grounded theory (Strauss and Glaser 1967) and generated relevant categories through coding the texts.

13 Bharat is the Hindi name for India and carries in the above mentioned context a hindunationalist connotation.
14 The committee under former chief justive J.S. Verma was appointed in the aftermath of the Delhi case in order to review anti-rape law and suggest reforms. The comprehensive report deals with sexual crimes at all levels and with the measures needed for prevention as well as punishment of all offences with sexual overtones. It eventually led to the passing of the Criminal Law (Amendment) Act, 2013. The full report is available under http://www.prsindia.org/uploads/media/Justice%20verma%20committee/js%20verma%20committe%20report.pdf, accessed April 28, 2014).
15 "We can never be free. We hardly wear anything different than what we can wear at our small conservative place. We can hardly enjoy roaming around after dark, we can hardly move about freely everywhere" (Srivastava, in a comment posted to Youth Ki Awaaz on December 27, 2012).
16 Kiran Bedi joined the Indian Police Service (IPS) in 1972 and was the first woman officer. She retired in 2007 from IPS. She served tough assignments and influenced important decisions and reforms, particularly in the areas of narcotics control and prison management. Bedi is a notable social activist. She founded two NGOs and joined the anti-corruption movement in 2010. She did not join the Aam Aadmi Party that resulted from the movement but declared her support for Narendra Modi (BJP) during the election 2014.
17 See Gajjala (2004) and Gajjala and Oh (2012) on South Asian and global cyberfeminism.

Maren Wilger

The Delhi Gang Rape Case – Dynamics of the Online Debate on the Social News Aggregator reddit.com

A brutal rape incident took place at the end of 2012 in the southern part of New Delhi which became publically known as the "Delhi gang rape". All the events connected to the case, starting from the woman's hospitalization until her death on 29th December 2012 were meticulously covered in the national and international media. Following the events, further discussions and protests arose, especially regarding sexual violence and the role of women in Indian society. The proceedings against the six suspects were closely observed by the (international) public. Many voices portrayed Delhi as the "rape capital" and made loud demands for changes in the laws to introduce the death penalty. The media named the victim by several pseudonyms such as *Amanat* ("treasure"), *Nirbhaya* ("fearless one"), *Jyoti* ("flame"), or *Damini* ("lightning"[1]) as well as *Delhi braveheart*, because Indian law forbids the release of victims' real names.

The permanent reporting on the condition of the victim and the surrounding output had strong traits of a disruptive media event: The rape case and its consequences were reported on a wide range of Indian and international channels. As a result, a huge audience came into contact with the subject. Mourning-, commemoration- and protest marches were held and broadcasted; reference to previous input was continuously given, as well as embedded in a broader context.[2]

Based on preliminary observations on the social news aggregator reddit.com and Emer O'Tool's commentary on theguardian.com (O'Toole 2013) which dealt with the neocolonial flavor of the reports on the case, my initial assumption was that Western media coverage on this particular case had a primary Eurocentric and neocolonial bias. One particularly striking example for this biased view was the article "Gang-rape shame could drag India into 21st century" by Libby Purves for the Times (Purves 2013).

Objectives

This article aims to show the dynamics of online discussions on the gang rape case by using methods of so-called netnography (see Kozinets 2010), an approach which relocates the ethnographic field from a physical space to a digital one. The online fieldwork was conducted on the U.S.-based social news aggregator reddit.com[3], a website that collects and structures content (such as articles, pictures, web links) which are uploaded and shared by registered users. The aim was to highlight, how users of a particular online community discussed the case and its media coverage. Since reddit.com is predominantly used by an English speaking community[4], the language of communication is English. Alexa.com, a Web Information Company, states that users are primarily from the Western hemisphere. They are followed by Indian visitors who constitute the second largest group represented on reddit.com. This fact made me curious and was the reason why I wanted to conduct research on the online community of reddit.com. A predominantly Western user group is commenting on international news with a Western bias[5]. However, there is a large Indian group, comparable in size, which also uses the platform of reddit.com. Based on newspaper articles and discussions posted on reddit.com, I assumed that the Western media and the individuals discussing the Delhi gang rape case adopt a Eurocentric view on issues related to the case, as well as in the general perception of India and especially Delhi. The question is, to what extend are the ongoing Western media coverage and its possible views discussed, reproduced or possibly deconstructed. Thus the main interest of this article is to show how users of reddit.com discussed the media coverage of the case by using various modified ethnographic methods in the digital space, such as participant observation, surveys and group discussions for example.

Methodology

Between mid-December 2012 and mid-January 2013, I followed and observed the discussion on the Delhi gang rape case on reddit.com in order to generate insights into how the media and its consumers discussed the case and its media coverage. I decided to focus mainly on the subreddits r/india and r/worldnews[6]. Both will be presented in detail in the paragraph on identifying the community of reddit.com. The methods used in this article are well known in academia, but require adjustments to be applicable to the virtual space. For this reason, I will briefly present the methods I employed and elaborate on the additional factors that an online context requires.

Participant observation happens at another level if there is no direct face-to-face communication. 'Participating' and 'observing' are structured differently in virtual spaces. There is always a medium between sender and receiver. The absence of face-to-face communication in the netnography approach is often criticized. However, the lack of gestures and facial expressions in online communication is replaced by 'emoticons' and so-called 'rage faces'[7] which imitate real life expressions. Nevertheless, this ethnographic approach was adapted for netnography – ethnographic fieldwork in the virtual space, which I used as data source. As is the case with classical participant observation, the researcher needs to get access to the community to collect data. There are several kinds of netnographic data that can be found in online communities. Valuable data could be drawn from discussion boards or by questioning and interacting with the community (Kozinets 2010, 19).

While extensive participant observation can provide the fundament for understanding structure and intentions of online communities, surveys are useful to highlight the (current) opinions of community members. Within this framework, I used an online survey tool to collect opinions regarding the ongoing discussion within reddit.com. This was to make sure that members who wouldn't contribute to the forum discussion per se are still able to share their views on the ongoing discussion outside of reddit.com. Online surveys are inexpensive, quick to administer and a good way to reach a wide online audience since both quantitative and qualitative data can be generated without the need to meet every recipient in person (Kozinets 2010, 43–45). Another feasible method is the online group discussion with a focus group. Even though the personal attributes of each recipient have a great influence on the outcome – an overly dominant or shy user could be counterproductive – focus groups could potentially yield more detailed results than a survey. For this analysis I decided to work asynchronously, instead of having a discussion simultaneously, because of to the members' location across various time zones. Either way, asynchronous discussions are typically used in many online forums. Thus this type of communication is a good way to pose several questions to community members which could be answered later on. The only disadvantage of this kind of online group discussion is that it requires and reaches only online- and writing- savvy members of the community, while others stay silent (Kozinets

2010, 48). Although data from a group discussion is not as abundant as data from observations, it still contributes to the research.

Ultimately, the combination of methods should give insights into the discussion on the gang rape case in an online community. But before introducing reddit.com in detail, I will specify my theoretical assumptions on important concepts and my essential position regarding those assumptions.

Conceptual Assumptions on Online Communities, the Internet and Media Landscapes

All of the concepts presented here are closely linked and intertwined as well as fluid. Online communities for example are fluid virtual groups of users who communicate with one another and are not bound to a specific time or space as physical communities. Within the framework of this article, I understand an "online community" as an internet based group of individuals, connected and founded on the basis of common interests. The individual members of a community do not need to be connected by physical location or their social environment. The formation of and/or being part of an online community occurs on the basis of a variety of factors such as political attitudes, ethnic identity or national origin, religious beliefs or simply common interests and hobbies (Wilson/Peterson 2002, 450). Communities could be built on the basis of national or ethnic identities, for example, but the individuals mostly don't transfer their offline interactions precisely to their online activity and vice versa. Each individual can decide to what extent he or she contributes to which community and may freely take part in and contribute to various communities at the same time. Yet a completely isolated or closed community is unlikely to exist because communities – online or offline – are always in exchange and overlapping with other communities, societies and cultures. A dynamic that is further fuelled by globalization (Wilson/Peterson 2002, 455).

There are different ways to participate in an online community. Kozinets (2010, 31) describes in "Netnography" four types of participating in an online community based on a study conducted by Shelley Corell (1995) on a lesbian online community. Correll identifies the members as "regulars, newbies, lurkers and bashers". Before members become newbies, who start to contribute content to the community, they "lurk" unseen in the forums and simply observe the discussions, instead of contributing to them. These lurkers are an internet-wide phenomenon and represent the majority of users in many online communities. There is a progressive development from each membership stage: From lurker to newbie to regular. The "bashers" are those individuals outside of the community who decide to harass members of the community (Kozinets 2010, 31). Even though Corell's study was conducted at an early stage in the internet development regarding the Web 2.0 shift[8], it still contains valuable concepts. The categories observed by Corell are transferable to the reddit.com online community, but I would rather swap the category of the "basher" with another category: The so-called "trolls". Trolls have become a well-known entity in several online forums and represent individuals who creep into conversations to attract attention through extreme comments, points of view, incorrect advice, or by harassing other users – simply for the purpose of provocation under the disguise of anonymity (Donath 1998, 14). Other than the external position of bashers, trolls often inhabit the position of lurkers within the community until they decide to "troll" other users.

Apart from membership categories, Kozinets defines four types of online communities: (1) *Cruising communities* that involve rather weak social relationships focus mainly on entertainment and exchange (chat rooms or game spaces, video-websites); (2) *Bonding communities* that promote long-lasting and intense relationships (social networks like Facebook or social forums on specific topics); (3) *Geeking communities* which serve to share information, news, stories and techniques in the absence of any profound communalities of individual members (newsgroups, social content sites and blogs); and (4) *Building communities* which combine Bonding- with Geeking communities, by offering both a strong sense of community and detailed information on a particular unifying interest (like interest groups on social network sites or wikis) (Kozinets 2010, 35–36). Interestingly, all these types of online communities are based on shared information, discussions or relations. The higher the value of the information or the discussion is for the users, the more intensely they will engage with it. Moreover, the more engaged the users are with others in the community, the more content and discussions will emerge (Kozinets 2010, 32).

There is an ongoing scholarly discussion as to whether online communities should be seen as 'real' or 'imagined' communities. It is said that online communities are too short-lived to be regarded as classical 'real life' communities. However, a community, as Benedict Anderson already emphasized in his work on imagined communities (1983), does not necessarily need face-to-face interaction to be 'real'. A community can – as an *imagined* community – reach beyond the borders of the local environment of one individual. There is no need to know every single member of a community or be connected via direct communication to create a feeling of belonging and unity (Wilson/Peterson 2002, 456). This seems to suggest an egalitarian virtual space where each individual has the same voice without differences. However, what becomes apparent is that online communities are still subject to mainstream interests and hegemonic structures.

When talking about online communities there is further a need to talk about the virtual infrastructure they are situated in: The internet is the virtual space where online communities meet. In its physical form the internet is a network of servers and computers. In terms of its use, it constitutes the World Wide Web, which is graphic- and text-based and can be accessed via Internet browsers. It is a digital medium categorized as distinct from the 'classical media' such as print media or television (Wilson/Peterson 2002, 452). Within the digital space, more and more social networks and online communities have emerged and are constantly visited by users. All computer-based social networks essentially operate via text-based interaction which is entered at each individual computer[9]. Wilson and Peterson summarize the basic categories of Internet based communication as follows:

Regardless of the particular media, interface, or application — which will continue to change in the coming years — general categories of communication will persist, including one-person-to-one (as in sending an email message), one-to-many (as in publishing a Web page), and many-to-many (participating in a discussion forum). These categories of communication require us to pay attention to the nature of communicative practices and online interactions (Wilson/Peterson 2002, 453).

In this article, I will primarily focus on the second ("one-to-many") and third category ("many-to-many"). The above mentioned forms of online communication have become a daily practice for internet users. The digital natives[10] of the internet lurk and/or contribute to several different online communities every day and navigate the WWW confidently as if they were in physical space. My understanding of space and media landscapes is in line with Arjun Appadurais concept of mediascapes (1990). Appadurai states that there is no global order of dependencies from a center to its periphery or Western to non-Western space (Hepp 2006, 50). The assumption of the West as a superior and imperial culture is challenged by Appadurai's "global cultural flows" which are fluid, multidirectional and which cross local as well as global boundaries. Mediascapes correspond to a space that is not necessarily physically located at one spot. That means that print- and digital media have the power to create medial representations of reality via mediascapes (Wilson/Peterson 2002, 455). The multidirectional flows and the existing multidimensional connectivity of the world are characterized by the concept of globalization. An increasing global connectivity ensures transregional and trans-cultural communication. For this reason, Appadurai advocates the need for "transnational cultural studies" and a "cosmopolitan ethnography" (Hepp 2006, 44–46).

Based on Manuel Castells' (2001) definition of a network, Andreas Hepp suggests that cultural flows and connectivities are structurally linked by nodes which create an ever expanding network. These inter-connecting nodes may be individuals, organizations, groups or geographically anchored places which create the center of the digital networks. Therefore nodes can assume different forms and meanings. Another structural aspect of connectivity is the switch, which is a specific kind of node. Certain nodes that connect different networks can have the special function of translating a prevailing code from one network to the codes of another. This task of translation and transfer — to switch from one code to another — can be performed by global (media) cities where various media, news, cultures and flows meet (Hepp 2006, 47–48).

Cultural flows and globalization are catalysts for "media events". Dayan and Katz coined the term in their 1992 book "Media Events: The live broadcasting of history"[11] and since then it has been continuously reconsidered. The basic indicators for a media event were generally seen as being too narrow for definition. Different scenarios of media events were significantly more diverse than initially presented by Dayan and Katz, so that the previous concept was expanded (Hepp/Krotz 2008, 266–267). Hepp and Krotz define a media event as follows:

A first step might be to understand media events as certain "thickened" performances of media communication that are focused on a specific thematic core, transgressing different media products and formats and reaching a multiplicity of audiences in their diversity. This thematic core can be variable, ranging from war and terror to sport contests and popular games in the media. The geographical extension of a media event can vary extensively, from regional to national and possibly to global media events. At the same time, it should be noted that media events are intended as certain performances by the media or by other social actors who have an interest in constructing reality in specific and perhaps conflicting ways, [...] (Hepp/Krotz 2008, 267).

That means that media events are incidents of any kind that are distributed via different media formats and global actors on a large scale leading to a large audience being reached across various boundaries. Traits of a media event are evident in the media coverage of the Delhi gang rape case in December 2012.

Community Identification: Reddit.com – the Front Page of the Internet

Reddit.com is an interpersonal communication medium which can be categorized as a "Geeking community" according to Kozinets because it provides detailed information and discussion on various topics and there are generally no intense personal bonds between users. It is a social news-aggregator and depends on the upload and sharing of various types of content (pictures, articles, videos, forum comments/questions/discussions, etc.) in thematic sub-forums ("subreddits"). Each content-post can be up- or down voted by the community. The sum of the votes generates a chronology of the posts listed in the subreddits. The best voted entries of each subreddit are documented on the main page: "the front page of the Internet", which has the most traffic. If the posted content is upvoted by users, the original poster (OP) gains reputation-points which are referred to as "karma"[12]. The more upvotes a certain post gets, the higher it is ranked, and therefore the more frequently it is seen and discussed.

The self-portrayal of reddit.com shows an intent to position the website outside of the press- or media apparatus: One of reddit's 2009 merchandise was a T-Shirt entitled "Freedom from the Press – reddit"[13], alluding to "Freedom *of* the Press" in order to present reddit as independent from the press itself. The website and its promoters emphasize that headlines are created and chosen by users, not by editors[14]. Reddit.com had 5,487 active subreddits[15] in June 2013 on diverse topics. This makes it difficult for researchers to map the whole structure and especially the content. For this reason, I will restrict my focus to two subreddits where the Delhi gang rape case was discussed with particular intensity. My main focus is on the subreddit /r/india, the largest India-related subreddit on reddit.com which is frequented by approximately 14,038 users.[16]

Most of the users seem to subscribe to the subreddit because of their common interest in news and topics related to India. After browsing the subreddit for the first time it became obvious that a large section of the users apparently come from or live in India. Many are Indian expatriates. /r/india offers its own wiki with guidelines of behavior ("Redditquett") and directions on how to upload a post. Users are allowed to use any language within this subreddit as long as they attach an English translation where possible (/r/india-wiki 2013). The wiki further mentions that questions about travelling in India and travel suggestions should be made at other recommended subreddits in order to keep the focus on non-tourism related topics. Another important aspect of /r/india etiquette is that (news) articles should be titled with the official headline or a quote directly from the original article. Specific opinions can be highlighted in the comments on this contribution but should not be used as the title of the submission (/r/india-wiki 2013).

In addition to the content on /r/india, I will also focus on discussions which have been made on the /r/worldnews subreddit. This is set as a default subreddit when people register at reddit.com as a member. /r/worldnews defines itself as a platform for "[…] major news from around the world except US-internal news/US politics". Due to the default settings this subreddit was subscribed to by 3,087,391 users in 2013 (/r/worldnews 2013) and deals primarily with news articles.

Data collection and analysis

Gaining access to reddit.com required a two-step procedure: A user account can be created by simply choosing a username and a password. There is no need for validation via email[17]. The account need for validation via email. An account had several advantages for the research: Subscribing to /r/worldnews and /r/india and saving content with the account made it easy to follow the ongoing discussions on the gang rape case. I followed various discussion threads on the case between December 2012 and January 2013 as a "lurker". Due to the high volume of data, I focused on two similar newspaper articles, originally posted on BBC, to exemplify the discussions on media products from a Western background in the two subreddits. I observed the discussion on an article entitled "BBC News – Delhi gang-rape victim dies in hospital in Singapore" on /r/worldnews (/r/worldnews discussion. 2012) as well as the discussion of the article "Delhi gang rape victim has died" (/r/india discussion. 2012). The discussion section under each linked article already revealed a stronger Western bias in the 'international' /r/worldnews than in /r/india. Various stereotypes on India could be found in /r/worldnews immediately after the article concerning the death of the young woman was posted. One user commented: "[...] Something really needs to be done to empower these women to defend themselves against the MONSTERS that inhabit that country. [...]"[18] Other statements contained advice for Indian women who would do well to leave India immediately to protect themselves from *these* rapists. Those opinions are of course not the only ones, yet the notion of the 'Indian male monster' as well as the 'weak woman as prey of the rapists' often reoccurred within this discussion thread and seemed to be the predominant view on the situation in India. The users that opposed these stereotypical views were mainly Indians (and had to identify themselves as such) when they asked for less generalizations of 'Indian men or the Indian culture'. Some supporters underlined the problem by emphasizing that rape happens worldwide and is not directly connected to the culture, society or community in which it happens in (/r/worldnews discussion 2012). What became apparent is that stereotypes came up time and time again in the discussions but were partly discussed and attempts were made to deconstruct them.

The reactions to the article "Delhi gang rape victim has died" on /r/india on the other hand were quite different: A large proportion of the discussion revolved around 'national pride'. Users expressed their shame and the shame for India as a whole nation repeatedly (/r/india discussion 2012). Furthermore, the comments were primarily condolences for the family, as well as highlighting their shock at the victim's death. Most of the reactions were less 'aggressive' compared to those on /r/worldnews. Since the Indian press discussed extensively the naming of the victim, the discussion on /r/india evolved around the importance of naming her to make her death "unforgettable" – despite existing laws (/r/india discussion 2012). An ongoing writing of history (embedding and referencing to the case in a broader context) as well as the iconization of the victim could be observed within this discussion thread.

Further observation of both subreddits revealed that the previously mentioned provocative article by Libby Purves (2013) could be found on both subreddits, while Emer O'Tooles thoughtful comment (O'Toole 2013) criticizing Purves' neocolonial view, as well as the Western bias of the media coverage in general, was only posted on /r/india[19]. A /r/india follower summarized his observations of reactions on reddit.com concerning the gang rape case precisely and formed four categories:

> 4 categories of redditors: a) Indians who know the whys and hows [sic] and are genuinely hurt. b) Westerners who don't know the first thing about India other than castes, cows, farmers & snakecharmers. c) ABCDs and their brethren in India who can't wait to highlight how white their thinking is even though they are brown; d) Some of our friendly neighbours [sic] who are enjoying the turn of events (this is completely my speculation) (/r/india self-post 2013).

Another user added more categories:

> e) Those who are desperate to stop talking about it and go back their [sic] lives. f) those who want to use this as an opportunity to provoke social change. g) those who want to use this to tell us more about how traditional values will prevent rapes and violence, and bring in peace and harmony. h) keyboard warriors who want to talk about this on twitter and facebook cos [sic] it's a popular topic [...] (/r/india self-post 2013).

In identifying the various types of reactions to the case and its coverage, both users emphasized important aspects of the dynamics surrounding the case: Firstly, the /r/india followers felt confronted with prejudices and discrimination, especially by other users on reddit.com. Secondly, it stresses that the incident was reframed for political, social and media agendas. In the end, the media coverage on the incident was the foundation for an expanding debate and discourse on rape and gender within the Indian context. In the discussions on reddit.com, many users addressed the defamation by other users, although the Western bias of the international media coverage was not discussed in detail. On the matter of media perceptions, the researcher was better able to collect statements by conducting a survey.

The survey was conducted on a small scale using the online software of surveymonkey.com. It was posted in the /r/india subreddit as a so-called self-post[20] containing the linked survey as well as a brief explanation of my background and my assumption that Western media as well as reddit.com users reproduce the idea of India as simply 'underdeveloped' and in 'need of modernization' without questioning it (Wilger 2013a). The survey contained five open questions, so that users were motivated to join and were at the same time given the opportunity to contradict my assumption and/or specify additional remarks.[21] The key question was how (Western) reporting on the incident was experienced by the followers of /r/india and how they perceived the discussions on /r/worldnews and /r/india.

Since only a total of 14 /r/india users replied to the survey, the following results can only highlight some aspects of the dynamics surrounding the discussions on reddit.com. The participants were on average 26 years old and were predominantly Indian (12 of 14 respondents). Striking was that only two of the participants were female.[22] Half of the participants lived outside of India. This may be an indication of the fact that many Indians who live abroad use the subreddit to stay up to date with what is happening in India. What became apparent was that most of the respondents kept informed about the incident through the channels of various online media, especially via "The Times of India", Twitter and Facebook. Reddit.com was not listed as primary source.

Experiences in the reddit.com discussions

In summary, the respondents stressed ideas similar to the results from the observation: They criticized that the focus of discussion rested upon sensationalist articles and comments on /r/worldnews.

The sensationalist articles received many upvotes and differentiated discussion was lacking. Moreover, the respondents noted the sudden appearance of self-proclaimed experts who make statements about India and its 'rape culture'. These statements are accompanied by generalizations about 'the prototypical Indian' and the 'Indian man' as 'oriental patriarch driven by desires'. Whilst the case made several other rape cases more visible and discussable in public, the whole debate also fuelled stereotypes. Within a short length of time, other news on rape incidents in India popped up in the international newsfeeds. Respondent 3[23] described the situation as follows: "/r/worldnews was not the place to be if you were an Indian. All the rape cases that were being reported in the regional newspapers too [sic] made the front page of /r/worldnews."

Compared to the situation on /r/worldnews, the respondents experienced the /r/india subreddit as more differentiated and liberal in many instances. The respondents explained that they felt more comfortable because /r/india users were seen as more familiar with several factors that need to be considered when talking about this particular and other rape cases in India. The size of the country and its population as well as further related issues need to be included in the discussions. Many respondents felt forced to become defensive because they identified themselves as Indian. After having identified as Indians, most respondents felt obligated to defend their background. This rather defensive attitude was criticised by a London-based 31 year old Indian (respondent 2): "As Indians we automatically become defensive when someone criticises the country, but criticism about the poor law and order situation and crimes against women is accurate."

Biased tendencies in the ongoing discussions were recognized, but at the same time it was also acknowledged that systematic change has to happen in order to improve womens' rights. That is why many respondents admitted to the 'certain truth' or 'validity' of the biased arguments.

"In the beginning it was just news, then it became 'The News'" (Respondent 3)

But how did the respondents feel about the Western media coverage in general? Three respondents (3, 5 and 11) mentioned that they were wondering why this case in particular was discussed extensively on a global level. A 38-year-old Indian noted the "switch function" of Delhi, which he felt was responsible for the wide international media coverage:

> A horrible story that happened in a city with thousands of reporters and international bureaus was bound to get such coverage. Similar or worse cases in cities with no international bureaus or local bureaus only get a passing mention, if any. (Respondent 5)

Two respondents (respondent 2 and 12) felt that the Western media reports were quite balanced but said that this depended on the source; all others described the reports as judgmental. Respondent 9 addressed the issue of "escalating sexual violence in India" but at the same time the Western media presented the issue as an exclusively Indian one.

Comparisons to the "Ohio-rape-case"[24] in North America were drawn by two respondents (respondent 8 and 11). It was noted that the Ohio-case received far less attention compared to the Delhi case. In summary, all the respondents had to deal with confrontations based on stereotypical remarks.

When questioned further in the form of a later submitted selfpost, users supported the results of the questionnaire by pointing out that there was a differentiation of the 'West' in contrast to India. However, at the same time it was added that many /r/india users distinguished between 'India' and 'Delhi'. That means there are two layers of Othering: The majority of reddit.com presented India as a 'backward rape culture' – Stereotypes of Indian rapists were made on /r/worldnews and sensationalist reports were collected to support this claim. On the other hand, users on /r/india presented the incident as a typically and exclusively Delhi phenomenon. User 'safaraaz' summarized: "You might also want to look into how /r/india discussed [sic] Delhi Gangrape Case. Most were only concerned about Reddit using the word 'India', and not 'Delhi'" (Wilger 2013b).

Conclusion

In the aftermath of the gang rape incident, an article about the rape of a 14-year-old in a bus in Glasgow was posted on /r/worldnews[25]. The discussion shifted quickly to the question of whether "such content belongs on /r/worldnews" because it constitutes only "a fate of a single person" while not touching upon or effecting global events. Such issues were not discussed in relation to the Delhi gang rape on /r/worldnews, which led to users of /r/india to question the behavior of /r/worldnews users[26]. This clearly shows the double standard of users on /r/worldnews. They judged incidents happening in the Western hemisphere differently to those happening elsewhere. In response to the discussion, one user summed up this double standard as follows: "Anything bad happened/happening in Asia is a 'culture' and anything bad happened/happening in the west is a 'tragedy.'" (Wilger 2013a).

Now, about one year after the wide media coverage of the incident, India and the world continue to engage in a public discourse about incidents of rape in India. The arrests of the suspects happened only 24 hours after the incident with the help of the media. The whole trial received wide media attention and the case resulted in changes being made to Indian law on sexual offences in February 2013. On the basis of the new sections which were added to the Indian Penal

Code, rape cases that leave the victim in a vegetative state or cause death are punishable by a minimum of 20 years in prison or the death penalty (Section 367 A).

Other offences which were added to criminal law included sexual harassment, voyeurism and stalking, as well as injuring a victim with acid attacks[27]. On 13th September 2013, the day when judgment was passed on the offenders, reddit.com's highest ranked entry on the front page was a BBC article about the death sentence for four of the rapists[28]. It was originally posted in /r/worldnews and nobody questioned if this article belonged in /r/worldnews or not.

What becomes obvious is that reddit.com, as well as other media distributors, connect the keywords "India" and "rape" nowadays more often in their imaginary: Searching for the keyword "India" on r/worldnews in 2014, reveals that 21 of 100 posted headlines are related to rapes in the list of the most relevant posts of all time. Compared to this, typing "China", "Indonesia" or "USA" (which are comparable in terms of the number of inhabitants) in the search box for the most relevant posts of all time produces only two headlines for the USA and Indonesia.[29] There are various reasons for these perpetuated stereotypes. Due to India's flourishing English press and its function as a switch between international networks, information could be translated and broadcast almost simultaneously, which enables international discussion of events. The international media was and still is 'sensitized' to incidents of rape in India. Even though the data collected for this article can only cover some views and observations concerning the dynamics of the discussion on reddit.com, it nevertheless shows trends on the disruptive media event surrounding the Delhi gang rape case. Given that reporting on the case gained a large audience, it was covered by the media in the most sensationalist manner possible in order to attract the most consumers in the competition for media attention. Whilst this had the advantage of bringing the issues of womens' rights and rape to the center of public Indian discourse, it also triggered the imagination of India as a 'rape country' throughout the world. This was followed by rapidly increasing coverage of other Indian rape cases in the media, whilst comparable cases in other countries did not receive the same attention.

So why was it important to show the dynamics of discussion concerning the gang rape case? It was one way to highlight that online discussions, fuelled by the existing media bias, can perpetuate existing imaginaries of 'the Indians' and 'their culture'. Whilst both subreddits – /r/worldnews and /r/india – posted similar content relating to the case, it was still discussed in different ways. Indian users were put under pressure and felt forced to differentiate between 'India' and 'Delhi' while discussing the event at the local and international level. It is important to keep in mind that media and online communities can play such ambiguous roles in remediating a critical media event. On the one hand, they can drag taboo topics into the public discourse, on the other hand, they support further stereotyping by media and individuals.

Bibliography

ANG, IEN. "Globalisierung der Medien, kultureller Imperialismus und der Aufstieg Asiens." In *Grundlagentexte zur transkultrellen Kommunikation*, edited by Andreas Hepp and Martin Löffelholz, 561–585. UVK-UTB: Konstanz, 2002.
BURKE, JASON. "Rape protests spread beyond India." *The Guardian*. January 4, 2013. http://www.guardian.co.uk/world/2013/jan/04/rape-protests-spread-beyond-india, accessed March 20, 2013.
BUCHER, HANS JÜRGEN. "Internet und globale Kommunikation. Ansätze eines Strukturwandels der Öffentlichkeit?" In *Grundlagentexte zur transkultrellen Kommunikation*, edited by Andreas Hepp and Martin Löffelholz, 500–533. UVK-UTB: Konstanz, 2002.
DHAWAN, HIMANSHI. "Shashi Tharoor bats for making public identity of Delhi gangrape victim, sparks row." *The Times of India*, January 2, 2013. http://articles.timesofindia.indiatimes.com/2013-01-02/india/36111238_1_shashi-tharoor-section-228-a-victim, accessed March 25, 2013.
DAYAN, DANIEL and ELIHU KATZ. *Media Events: The live broadcasting of history*. Cambridge, Mass.: Harvard University Press, 1992.
DONATH, JUDITH S. "Identity and deception in the virtual community." In *Communities in Cyberspace*, edited by P. Kollock and M. Smith, 27–51. London: Routledge, 1998.
ENTMAN, ROBERT M. "Framing Bias: Media in the Distribution of Power." *Journal of Communication* 57, no.1 (2007): 163–137.
HEPP, ANDREAS and FRIEDRICH KROTZ. "Media events, globalization and cultural change: An introduction to the special issue." *Communications* 33 (2008): 256–272.
HEPP, ANDREAS. "Translokale Medienkulturen: Netzwerke der Medien und Globalisierung." In *Konnektivität, Netzwerk und Fluss*, edited by Andreas Hepp, Friedrich Krotz et al., 43–68. VS-Wiesbaden: Verlag für Sozialwissenschaften, 2006.
KOZINETS, ROBERT V. *Netnography. Doing Ethnographic Research Online*. Los Angeles: Sage Publications, 2010.
KUMAR, VINAY. "Anti-rape Bill makes stalking, acid attacks punishable." *The Hindu*, March 13, 2013. http://www.thehindu.com/news/national/antirape-bill-makes-stalking-acid-attacks-punishable/article4525991.ece, accessed March 20, 2013.
MANDHANA, NIHARIKA and ANJANI TRIVEDI. "Indians Outraged Over Rape on Moving Bus in New Delhi." *The New York Times*, December 18, 2012. http://india.blogs.nytimes.com/2012/12/18/outrage-in-delhi-after-latest-gang-rape-case/, accessed March 20, 2013.

MARKHAM, ANNETTE and ELIZABETH BUCHANAN. Ethical Decision-Making and Internet Research. Recommendations from the AoIR Ethics Working Committee (Version 2.0), 2012. http://aoir.org/reports/ethics2.pdf, accessed March 12, 2013.
OPPEL, RICHARD A. "Ohio Teenagers Guilty in Rape That Social Media Brought to Light." *The New York Times*, March 17, 2013. http://www.nytimes.com/2013/03/-18/us/teenagers-found-guilty-in-rape-in-steubenville-ohio.html?pagewanted= all&_r=0, accessed March 30, 2013.
O'TOOLE, EMER. "Delhi gang-rape: Look westward in disgust." *The Guardian* (Comment), January 1, 2013. http://www.guardian.co.uk/commentisfree/2013/-jan/01/delhi-rape-damini, accessed March 27, 2013.
PRENSKY, MARC. "Digital Natives, Digital Immigrants." *On the Horizon MCB University Press* 9, no.5 (October 2001). http://www.marcprensky.com/writing/Prensky%20-%20 Digital%20Natives,%20Digital%20Immigrants%20-%20Part1.pdf, accessed April 6, 2014.
PURVES, LIBBY. "Gang-rape shame could drag India into 21st century." *The Times*, January 1, 2013. http://www.theaustralian.com.au/news/world/gang-rape-shame-could-drag-india-into-21st-century/story-fnb64oi6-1226545829569, accessed March 17, 2013.
SHOHAT, ELLA and ROBERT STAM. *Unthinking Eurocentrism: multiculturalism and the media*. London/New York: Routledge, 1994.
WILSON, SAMUEL M. and LEIGHTON C. PETERSON. "The Anthropology of Online Communities." *Annual Rev. Anthropol* 31 (2002): 449–467.

Online Sources

Alexa.com. Site Info: reddit.com. 2014. http://www.alexa.com/siteinfo/reddit.com, accessed January 1, 2014.
Criminal Law (Amendment) Bill, 2013. http://www.prsindia.org/uploads/media/-Criminal%20Law,%202013/Criminal%20Law%20%28A%29,%202013.pdf, accessed February 1, 2014.
Reddit.com – the front page of the Internet. 2013. http://www.reddit.com, accessed March 27, 2013.
Reddit-Wiki. 2013. http://www.reddit.com/wiki/faq, accessed March 27, 2013.
/r/india – Truth alone Triumphs. 2013. http://www.reddit.com/r/india, accessed March 27, 2013.
/r/india-Wiki. 2013. http://reddit.com/r/india/wiki, accessed March 27, 2013.
/r/india discussion. 2012. "Delhi gang rape victim has died." http://www.reddit.com/r/india/comments/15ld2t/delhi_gang_rape_victim_has _died/, accessed March 30, 2013.
/r/india self-post. 2013. "Reaction to Delhi gang-rape incident on reddit." http://www.reddit.com/r/india/comments/161nns/reaction_to_delhi_-gangrape_incident_on_reddit/, accessed March 30, 2013.
/r/worldnews. 2013. http://reddit.com/r/worldnews, accessed March 27, 2013.
/r/worldnews discussion. 2012. "BBC News: Delhi gang-rape victim dies in Hospital." http://www.reddit.com/r/worldnews/comments/15ld8w/bbc_news_delhi_-gangrape_victim_dies_in_hospital/, accessed March 30, 2013.

Surveymonkey. 2012. http://www.surveymonkey.com, accessed March 27, 2013.

WILGER, MAREN. "Media Bias regarding the reporting of the Delhi gang rape? (Questionaire)". *Reddit.com*, Self-Post, February 1, 2013 (2013a). http://www.reddit.com/r/india/comments/199ka9/media_bias_regarding_the_reporting_of_the_delhi/.

WILGER, MAREN. "What do you think about the way, reddit discussed the Delhi Gang Rape Case?" *Reddit.com*, Self-Post, March 13, 2013 (2013b). http://www.reddit.com/r/india/comments/1a7pon/what_do_you_think_about_the_way_reddit_discussed/.

---

1   This pseudonym is connected to a film by Rajkumar Santoshi (1993) with the same title.
2   There were discussions as to whether the name of the victim should be published and used to name a planned "anti-rape-law", see Dhawan (2013). This is interesting in relation to the memorization of the incident after the case but is beyond the scope of this article.
3   "reddit" is a modification of: „I read it" (Reddit-Wiki 2013).
4   The traffic rating website Alexa.com states that 46.1% of the visitors are from the United States, 11.5% from India, 5.5% from Canada, 5.0% from the UK, 2.0 from Australia followed by Germany with 1.7% (Alexa.com 2014).
5   "The term [bias] seems to take on three major meanings. Sometimes, it is applied to news that purportedly distorts or falsifies reality (distortion bias), sometimes to news that favors one side rather than providing equivalent treatment to both sides in a political conflict (content bias), and sometimes to the motivations and mindsets of journalists who allegedly produce the biased content (decision-making bias)." (Entman 2007)
Within this framework I see media bias in terms of a basic attitude to report only certain events from one mainstream perspective, which already appeared on various channels, while others are completely marginalized. That means it would be situated between content and decision-making bias. A distortion or prejudices within reports can be for or against ethnic groups, minorities and religions. In relation to this article, 'bias' should highlight that Eurocentric opinions of media producers influence the way of reporting as well as discussing.
6   The content of reddit.com is structured around areas of interest called "subreddit". Each subforum is identified by its URL: the subreddit India is named "/r/india", a shortcut from http://reddit.com/r/india. In the following I will use this notation for identifying each subreddit.
7   'Rage Faces' are based on a popular internet phenomenon, in which everyday situations are transformed into simple comics. The faces of the protagonist represented emotions like rage, happiness, sorrow, etc. in online forums like reddit.com. A list of the faces used on reddit.com can be found here: http://www.reddit.com/r/fffffffuuuuuuuuuuuu/comments/ecnd4/every_fffffffuuuuuuuuuuu_face_a_reference_guide/, accessed March 28, 2013.
8   Web 2.0 is not a 'new version' of the internet, but rather the shift from static websites to increasingly user incorporating websites, which come alive through the dialogue between creators and users. Examples are social media- and networking sites, blogs and video sharing websites.
9   Video-and voice-oriented communication is also common and used regularly. Well-known examples include the software Skype, which allows online video chat, and chatroulette.com, a website that connects individuals randomly to each other for a video chat. These forms of communication are mainly used to communicate one-to-one and are not relevant to this article.
10 The term "digital natives" was coined by Marc Prensky and aims to describe the generation that grew up with digital technology and that is able to adapt to various digital technologies due to their socialization. See Prensky (2001).
11 Dayan and Katz define media events as follows: (1) they are *interruptions* of routine as they interrupt the normal broadcasting flow (2) they are broadcasted simultaneously through various channels, (3) the happening is *live*, (4) they take place and are generated outside of the media, (5) they are partly pre-planned productions (if they are no disruptive events), (6) they are presented with ceremony and reference, (7) they celebrate reconciliation, even though addressing conflict and (8) they reach a very large audience (Dayan/Katz 1992, 5–8).

12 Reddit.com describes their karma-system as follows: "*The number next to a username is called the user's "karma". It reflects how much good the user has done for the reddit community. The best way to gain karma is to submit links that other people like and vote for, though you won't get karma for self posts.*" (Reddit-Wiki 2013). Parallels to karma in its classical sense seem to be intended.
13 See: http://blog.reddit.com/2009/02/our-freedom-from-press-shirts-dont.html, accessed March 27, 2013.
14 A reddit banner ad reads: "*today´s headlines – chosen by readers, not editors*", http://sp.reddit.com/728x90A.gif, accessed March 27, 2013.
15 See reddit's blog entry: http://blog.reddit.com/2013/06/browse-future-of-reddit-re-introducing.html, accessed January 23, 2014.
16 On March 27, 2013 (/r/india 2013). One year later, in February 2014 /r/india has 20,317 readers. Since subreddits can be accessed openly these numbers are only benchmarks.
17 If users want to be able to restore their password, they can validate their account via email, but don't have to. While it offers access to anyone, this practice has also a couple of disadvantages, such as problems with the before mentioned trolls, youth protection or flourishing porn-related content.
18 Comment by user "Arto3": http://www.reddit.com/r/worldnews/comments/15ld8w/bbc_news-_delhi_gangrape_victim_dies_in_hospital/c7nmnhy, accessed March 30, 2013.
19 In retrospective it could have been fruitful to post O´Tooles comment on /r/worldnews and observe the following discussion, which actually did not happen until today.
20 SELFPOST: selfposts do not contain external links or information by other sources, but are questions and/or statements by users. Selfposts cannot generate karma and do not serve to gain a better reputation.
21 Former observations on reddit.com showed that time is an important factor: Users seem to want concise and fast deducible content. An example for that online attitude is the commonly used abbreviation "TL;DR" ("To long; did not read") as a response to too long entries or it is positioned in a self-reflexive manner under a long entry to add a short version for those who do not want to read the entire entry.
22 This mirrors the general male/female ratio on reddit.com – a survey conducted two years ago with a total of 26,887 participants resulted in a ratio of 84% male, 16% female redditors. http://www.reddit.com/r/reddit.com/comments/gzb2w/i_made_a_basic_reddit_demographic_survey_lets/, accessed January 20, 2014.
23 The respondents will be named in order of their participation, i.e. respondent 1 was the first participant, respondent 2 was the second, etc.
24 The Ohio rape case happened around the same time in the USA: Two college football players raped a 16-year-old, boasted about the event on social media websites and even shared pictures and short clips of the event. See for example: Oppel (2013).
25 See: "Girl, 14 raped by two men on bus… in Glasgow", 2013. http://www.reddit.com/r/worldnews/comments/1b8knv/girl_14_raped_by_two_men_on_bus_in_glasgow/, accessed March 30, 2013.
26 See: "(x-post from worldnews) See the difference, A girl is raped in Scotland, and the top most comment is 'Why is this on worldnews?'" http://www.reddit.com/r/india/comments/-1b9d2d/xpost_from_worldnews_see_the_difference_a_girl_is/, accessed March 30, 2013.
27 See the Bill No. 63 of 2013. Criminal Law (Amendment) Bill, 2013. http://www.prsindia.org/-uploads/media/Criminal%20Law,%202013/Criminal%20Law%20%28A%29,%2013.pdf, accessed February 1,2014.
28 See: http://web.archive.org/web/20130913125202/http://www.reddit.com/, accessed January 30, 2014.
29 One for the keywords "Indonesia" ("You know what men are like": Indonesia to ban mini-skirts over links to rape") as well as one for the keyword "USA". Ironically the headline and the linked article are about "five teenaged girls gang-raped in Pakistan" – this headline only pops up due to the users' username "chrisjohnson-usa" who posted the article. Results for the "India" Search: http://www.reddit.com/r/worldnews/search?q=india&sort=relevance&restrict_sr=on&t=all, accessed January 30, 2014.

URMILA GOEL

The Delhi rape case and international attention

An interview with Urvashi Butalia

On the occasion of the international women's day 2013 Urvashi Butalia, the Indian feminist activist and publisher, was invited to speak at an event about sexism and sexual violence in Berlin. Urmila Goel interviewed her a day later about the international attention on the Delhi rape case and her perception of current feminist discourses around it.

Goel: What do you think about the reaction of the West to the Delhi rape case, the demonstrations and what happened afterwards?

Butalia: The whole question was quite mixed. This became a big case for the media both in India and outside. The attention of international media, in particular Western media, but not only Western, was something which happens all the time. The international media tend to focus on all the terrible things that happen in India, because they are so used to seeing it as a place of terrible violence or a place of terrible poverty. They never really focus on the gains or the positive things that are happening. I do not say that the media attention was bad. That the case got so much international media attention pushed our government to take some action. Because they were embarrassed by this attention, because they did not want to be seen as a country that is violent towards its women. It destroys the image of India as the rising super power, as the country that is doing well economically, the shining India story is marred by something like this. So that media attention in some ways was certainly helpful, but in other ways it comes with a lot of baggage. The kind of questions all of us got asked were: 'Why is this happening in India? Why is Delhi the rape capital of the world? Why are people in India so violent towards each other? Why are women treated so badly? Why is there no response in India?' Now this is all rubbish. They talked about this being the first time there had been demonstrations. India has a strong and healthy tradition of protests. There have been protests on a range of issues: On the nuclear issue, on the issue of building damns, on the question of corruption and women's groups have been demonstrating and protesting throughout the last thirty, thirty-five years. In fact, the law on rape had changed as a result of the pressure put on by women's groups in 1983. That pressure was sustained from then until now to ask for further changes in the law. There was a bill in parliament when this incident happened, which women's groups had put there, which was looking at changes suggested in the rape law. So it is not as if the women's movement has been totally silent or inactive.

What disturbed me was not only the media's reaction, but also the reaction of a lot of Western feminists, who assumed that there is no women's movement in India and who started to jump up and down saying: we will go in there and help. There was a group of Harvard feminists, who created a project, which says: 'We must assist the Indian government and the justice Verma committee.' – This is the committee that the government set up to look into gender violence and so on. – 'We must assist them to better implement the recommendations, we have made.' Who are they to decide to implement them? Do we turn around and say, we must help American feminists to get the Equal Rights Amendment taken seriously or we must help American feminists to get abortion as a legal right? We do not say that. This is the old colonial attitude: 'This is the third world, there are terrible problems out there, we must go in there and help them out'. They just started to replay these things and nobody turned the mirror on themselves. If you look at the statistics on rape in the world, they are far higher in America than they are in India, but no American feminist said: 'We must look at the question of rape in America', because it is much easier to locate the problem somewhere out there and replay the hierarchy of first world and third world.

If you look at hate crimes or racial crimes in the West, what are they? A gang of white guys goes out, sees an Asian or a black guy walking around, they just kill him brutally because of the colour of his skin. How is it different from gang rape? It is a violation of somebody's autonomy, their bodies and these guys mostly get away with it. But nobody talks about those.

I also found it very interesting that many of us were asked to be on Chinese television. From the questions that were asked, it was very clear to me, that the Chinese media were revelling in this thought that India and China are constantly put together in a race that is neck at neck, in which India is doing better in terms of human rights and democracy and China is doing better in term of the products it makes. So the Chinese were very interested in proving that India is not so great in the question of protecting the rights of its citizens and in particular its women. The attention of the Chinese media was not interested in the particular case and this poor girl who died. It had much more to do with proving themselves superior to India. It showed in the way in which these programmes were constructed: They had an American expert on it, they had an Indian woman on it and they had somebody else. The Indian woman was put in a corner so that you could say: 'Yes, things are terrible in India'. Of course it is very difficult, because you do not want to fall into a chauvinistic position of being nationalist and protecting India. Things are terrible and you have to admit that some things are bad, but it is not all bad and you have to have a balance. So it was a very strange kind of media attention that raised all of these questions.

Goel: How did you deal with these hidden other agendas?

Butalia: A number of us were asked to be on the media and we discussed it with each other. We agreed that we would go onto some channels or talk in some newspapers and that we would not do others. It was really just a gut instinct from the kind of questions that we were asked. We felt that if we got up there and put our perspective forward it was important and so we did not hide the terrible nature of the crime that had taken place, the terrible gaps in the Indian law and the state's reluctance to take any steps towards the protection of women. You cannot pretend to cover up all of these things. But at the same time, we also talked about the importance of the protests. When the committee was set up and its recommendations were so good, we talked about that as well. We also talked about what we felt the international media were doing and how they needed to turn the mirror on themselves.

Similarly when the Harvard women put on the project description, we had a good laugh. All of us were so amused at the arrogance in that description. We wrote a letter back to them, which we thought was a very humorous letter. It made the point that we were not just people sitting there without a history of feminism and women's activism in India and we said to them: 'It is very good of you to bring American feminism and American feminist concerns to India, but next time you want some help in telling president Obama how to deal with women, ask us, we will tell you.'

Goel: Did you get any reaction from them?

Butalia: Apparently today. My office forwarded me an email, which I have not yet seen. There is a statement from them, saying: 'We never intended to implicate that there was no feminist movement in India.' But if you read what they said, it is such a – possibly unconscious – colonial attitude, even in the language. It was not only one feminist in India, who read it in this way, but many of us and we discussed it. We were all laughing and saying: 'It is the 21st century, how can feminism replicate all those old colonial patterns?' But you heard that yesterday also in the event for the international women's day. The German politician in her opening remarks completely replicated that. It was as if India is so terrible, does not have a women's movement, Indian women do not know what is going on and it is their job to help out as much as they can and now that they have found out how terrible things are in India, they must do something about it.

Goel: What kind of international solidarity would you like instead of this colonial one?

Butalia: Feminism is the one movement in the world, which has actually been very international, which has benefited from international links and connections. No matter what our political, social and developmental differences may be, there are certain issues which cut across, which are common to all of us: All of us deal with patriarchy in different ways, all of us deal with violence against women and the cultural forms it takes in different ways. It may be that a country that is wealthy does not have to address the issue of poverty, but in a country like India feminists cannot ignore the issue of poverty. Those things might be different given the political histories of our countries, but on certain issues like violence against women, on the whole question of war and the use of women's bodies in war, there has been a lot of international solidarity. This solidarity can continue and must continue, but it has to be based on recognition of difference. It has to be based on an understanding that all our feminisms are born out of the specific conditions of the nations in which we have grown up, even though our feminisms are not nationalist and should not be. The fact is that being a feminist in India my thought processes are influenced by the political realities of India, which would be very different from say yours and while we can sit across the table and talk and we may be able to ally on some things, the activism that we are involved is quite different in our different countries. What often happens is that feminism replicates the patterns of power that exist in the world and sees the West as the fountain of feminisms and everything else is miles behind it. This is wrong. It is wrong to see feminism as some kind of race, in which some countries are ahead and others are left behind and those that are ahead have a superior form and those that are left behind have an inferior form and once we reach where you are, where the Western countries are, we will be fine. That is a load of nonsense. Feminism has to recognise that there are differences and difference is what you must respect and once you start to respect that difference, then you do not see it as a race, in which some people have lost out and you do not necessarily see the same solutions for everybody.

For example feminists have always said that it is important to have economic power, because once you have economic power everything else flows from it. But in a country like India you often see that this is not true. You might be earning a lot of money, might have control of your income, etc., but at the same time the cultural barriers and familial ties hold you in a grip that is difficult to get rid of. Economic empowerment does not lead necessarily to a certain kind of liberation. On the other hand you may not be very wealthy, but you may be politically empowered and you might actually find that a route to liberation. You have to ask questions about what works for one, what does not work for the other. And if we start doing that, you suddenly start to realise the whole question of difference.

Goel: Yesterday at the event you were asked to say something about religion and you refused to do so.

Butalia: We were having a discussion on the issue of violence, I was specifically asked to speak about the December 16th case, the demonstrations that had taken place and its aftermath and I was trying to explain that. Then somebody from the audience got up and asked: 'I am really surprised that you have talked about India and you have not addressed the question of religion.' That is completely the kind of ridiculous assumption that I am talking about. It is not necessary that every time you speak of India you must speak of religion. This expectation is born out of people's stereotypical perception of India as that mystic exotic country steeped in religion. This is complete rubbish; India is a very modern country. Yes it is a deeply religious country, but religion is a private matter for people. There are ways in which in India (as in every other country in the world) religion has in recent years been used as a political tool for political mobilisation, for creating identity battles. It is happening here as well, it is happening all over Europe with the rise of fundamentalist parties, which are coming into power and are very attractive to the young. Religion and India are not a natural equation and I was very annoyed at that assumption. I am talking about a case of violence against women. It has nothing to do with religion. Why should I talk about religion? Just because I am from India, I should talk about religion?

Goel: Was this case instrumentalised by religious movements in any way?

Butalia: Everything that gets a public issue gets instrumentalised in some way or the other. The Hindu right wing political party came into it in a big way and used it to run down the ruling government of Delhi, saying the Congress party – the state of Delhi is ruled by the Congress party – has not done enough for women. But it is not as if the Hindu party has done anything for women either and its leaders made some stupid statements and the Congress leaders made some stupid statements as well. Religion did not come into it, except that occasionally the religious groups tried to jump on the bandwagon to make political capital. But they were very quickly shouted down and people were very unwilling to allow the case to be hijacked.

Goel: To come back to the event yesterday. It was an event to celebrate the international women's day. What did you think about this idea of getting you as a main speaker and letting you talk with a young British and a young German blogger?

Butalia: I was very pleased with both the German and the British blogger, because both of them are young and doing some really interesting work in the form of media that now so much appeals to young people and it is great to be able to talk across cultures. Both of them were very aware of the fact that this was not a problem that belongs elsewhere and only to somebody else. They were turning the mirror on their own societies as well and I think that was really important. That the event was framed by reference to the German twitter campaign against sexism and sexual violence, to all the German women coming out and talking about sexual harassment and the sexism they had faced, set the tone very well. Otherwise I would have been really uncomfortable, if it had been just like come and tell us about India, because we want to help. But it was not that, it was really saying this is a problem that touches all of us, it is wider than just one country.

Goel: There is a lot of talk now about this new net feminism. As an old feminist, who has been fighting for a long time, what do you think about the newer feminists?

Butalia: My thinking on it is very mixed. In some ways it is a very important development. Many of the people of my generation, we used to despair that our daughters did not have the same kind of awareness. You always think that about the new generation. I think the internet has given women of this age a way to connect and a way to discuss issues. It is not that they did not feel or did not want to be involved in issues in the same way, it is just that for their generation the issues were somewhat different. The internet has enabled them to discuss about those across cultures, which is very good. Out of that have been born some interesting, unique kinds of protest. However, I still feel that in a country like India, even though you can see the power of the internet – and after the post-December 16th protests I would never be sceptical about it – still it is a very class conscious medium. Internet access is nothing yet compared to the population. It leaves a whole lot of people out of its ambit. You might say that still the cell phone is there and every second Indian now has a cell phone. So it is true that the gap that the internet might have because of connectivity and access is something that is made up by the cell phone. You have to look at the new media seriously. You cannot dismiss them as a mobilisational tool. You may question how far it reaches; you can question the efficacy of internet activism as opposed to the efficacy of street level activism. If you are out in the streets demonstrating in large numbers how important is that as opposed to if you are putting petitions on the internet? What seems to be happening now is both things seem to be combining and that is important.

Goel: Thank you for the interview.

PART II
LINKING YOUTH, GENDER AND MEDIA STUDIES: MEDIA PRACTICES, NEW IM/MOBILITIES AND EVOLVING SEXUAL IDENTITIES

Thomas K. Gugler

New Media, Neosexual Activism and Diversifying Sex Worlds in Post-Liberalization India

Looking at the history of gay empowerment and social activism in Indian cities since 1991, I argue that the very project of sexual liberation is heavily influenced by capitalist change and its interests articulated in semantics melding the rhetorics of freedom, pluralism (i.e. the production of difference), (in)security and egoism. This discourse became meanwhile medialised in India, where the new urban middle-class sets the agenda for the production of norms for media society, and heavily impacted on the legal process. As I will show in this chapter both debates were crucial for processes of communication and recognition of distinct LGBTQ sexual identities.

Sex Trouble and Gender Trouble – Three Revolutions

Men have always engaged in penetration and yet fucking has never been the same. The symbolic attributions, emotions and the desire-specific framings of norms and expectations of society constantly change (Sigusch 2013, 24). As capitalist logic pressures people to label themselves, produce authenticity to mark difference and market more specific identities, sexual practices increasingly become identity resources. For instance, the oral intercourse among men described in Vātsyāyana's *Kāmasūtra*, the most widely known work of *ars erotica* of human history, is a quite different phenomenon from what happens inside gay brothels in contemporary India. Increased impact of media and the advertisement industry transforms the feminity hierarchy and role models become more commercial: today α-women are far more sexualised. Demographic masculinisation and the sex ratio imbalance has reached a peak in India since the Western export of pervasive sex determination techniques (ultrasound) in the 1980s – India is missing more than 65 million women today due to sex selective abortion, i.e. female feticide (Hvistendahl 2012). Political analysts even warn that the Asian surplus men pose a serious security threat to the West (Hudson and den Boer 2004). The commercialisation of role models and the concept of the pharmaceutical management of the human body as a step toward sexual liberation (cf. Preciado 2013, 230) are just two examples of how capitalist exploitation logic is squeezing out intimacy.

Gender, sex and sexualities are concepts constructed by society, rather philosophical in nature, they are far less physiological facts (Butler 1993, Voß 2011, Mildenberger et. al. 2014). Although the concept of homosexuality (and later heterosexuality) as a modern identity was born in Europe (Gugler 2014, Beachy 2010), MSM (men who have sex with men) have a long history in South Asia and elsewhere (Vanita 2002, Vanita and Kidwai 2000, Aldrich 2007).

Sigusch (2013, 226–230) distinguishes three sexual revolutions during the 20th century to explain the ongoing dispersion of sexual fragments. With Dr. Alyappin Padmanabbha Pillay (1889–1956), editor of the journals *Marriage Hygiene* (1934–1948) and *International Journal of Sexology* (1947–1955), India was blessed with one of the leading sexologists in the English-speaking world and a main figure in the first sexual revolution in the 20th century. The revolutions in detail:

i) the first sexual revolution started at the beginning of the century and revolved around perversion (Sigmund Freud's *Three Contributions to the Theory of Sex*) and reproductive hygiene/eugenics,
ii) a second, more commercial-antiauthoritarian sexual revolution (Foucault, Osho[1]) in the 1960s and 70s following the market launch of the contraceptive pill – the most used pharmaceutical molecules in the whole of human history, and
iii) the neosexual revolution starting in the 1980s – characterized by debates on HIV, gender, and ultimately the digital revolution (with the pornographic industries as the great mainspring of cybereconomy) fueling disturbing levels of isolation – new intimacies in solitude and new solitudes in intimacy – where "we look to technology for ways to be in relationships and to protect us from them at the same time" (Turkle 2011, xii), where we expect more from technology and less from each other.

HIV made not only MSM and sex workers (as well as later surplus men as their consumers) as high-risk groups more visible and turned them into a social issue, the HIV-discourse did quickly impact on heterosexual intimate relations as well: Already in 1984 – at a time in which AIDS has still been considered a *Gay Related* disease (GRIDS) – Osho was enforcing safe sex rules for his heterosexual followers too: kissing was prohibited and the use of condoms and disposable gloves made mandatory. Even today the *OSHO International Meditation Resort* in Pune can be entered only after a negative result from the mandatory HIV test in the *Welcome Centre*.

While older and more traditional forms of male same-sex activities in India could be classified mostly as either transgenderal, transgenerational or class-structured homosexuality (Joseph 2005, 203), it was the politics of economic liberalization and the social change accelerated by urbanization and medialisation as well as the increasing impact of globalization after 1991 that resulted in giving space for more egalitarian-modeled same-sex neosexualities and neosexual identities in broader society.

LGBTQ Activism

In particular in rural areas several young MSM still think that they are "alone", the *pink sheep of the village*,[2] being different with their mode of desire and often discover by encounter in the city or on the internet that there are other people like them. Family bonds are rather tight in South Asia and "not everyone who accepts homosexual orientation as a part of their personality necessarily identifies with it positively, for some may accept it as an ailment to be cured or sin to be repented" (Kugle and Hunt 2012, 260). Many choose to hide their desires and to lead covert lives in order to compromise with patriarchal expectations of family and community.

> "In coming out, a person acts to create a sense of wholeness by establishing congruence between interior experience and external presentation, moving the inner into the outer, bringing the hidden to light, and transforming a private into a social reality" (Weston 1997, 50).

However, coming out is harder in India as compared to European countries: Asian families are said to be more close-knit, family culture is more hierarchical, everyone knows what everyone else is doing and with the extended family there are simply a lot of people to tell (Weston 1997, 58, cf. Khan 2013).

"Activism happens when the distance between 'what is' and 'what ought to be' – the very breeding ground of alienation – is filled with creative and energetic action so that a person does not slip into despair, disillusion, and depression" (Kugle 2014, 220).

Seeking to secure rights or achieve some modicum of justice, LGBTQ activists adopted different modes of activism (cf. Kugle 2014). These modes range from engaging religious tradition ("God made me gay", "each soul is divine"), like the Hare Krishna offspring GALVA (*Gay And Lesbian Vaishnava Association*),[3] over family engagement to the secular politics activism of *Naz Foundation*. Many activists are connected to some organization that runs its own support group focusing either on information, counseling or partying to build a community in particular for those, who are more independent of their families. Weston (1997) coined the lucid concept of "chosen families" as opposed to the family given by birth for describing LGBTQ-kinship.

Since the 1990s the network of support groups has increased in viability with new technology.

Today there are hundreds of LGBTQ support groups and new media enables them to organize, share experiences and compile or link information – building communities and representing and communicating their specific concerns for reform toward more social pluralism, individual rights and diversity in gender identities. Activism means creative action in society and media supplies splendid tools for such.

Emerging Queer Mediascapes

In the 1980's the first Western-styled gay newsletters emerged in India. The newsletter *Gay Scene* started in Calcutta in 1980, but didn't run for long. In 1986 two Indian men founded *Trikone* in California as the first LGBT group for South Asians. The quarterly magazine *Trikone: Giving Voice to Gay, Lesbian, Bisexual and Transgender South Asians* includes personal ads from India and the website's online video diaries advice, amongst others on how to speak with parents and deal with incoming marriage proposals.[4] After a newspaper article on the work of Trikone was published in an Indian newspaper along with an Indian post office box in 1986, the group that organized the newspaper article was flooded with letters from gay men from all over India. Trikone then published an advertisement for the group later labeled "Red Rose", initiated among others by Dalip Daswani, and this resulted in over 50 men meeting in a café in New Delhi, where gay men could meet at the table marked with a red rose (Rangayan 2013, 176). In 1988 the bimonthly newsletter *Shakti Khabar* was started in London. Other groups were founded in the West for South Asian immigrants like New York City's SALGA (*South Asian Lesbian and Gay Association*) in 1991[5] and MASALA (*Massachusetts Area South Asian Lamda Association*) in 1994 (cf. Das Gupta 2006, 6 and 92–97), etc. These organizations still exist today and heavily engage in transnational politics and identity formation. They were role models for most of the local organizations and their impact on their counterparts in India can hardly be overestimated. Apart from US-based *Trikone*[6] and lesbian *Jiah* (just 3 issues) the most important Indian gay magazines or e-zines today include Mumbai's *Pink Pages,*[7] Pune's *TQC* (*The Queer Chronicle*),[8] and Bangalore's *Gaylaxy,*[9] founded by *Facebook*-activist Sukhdeep Singh in 2010. In comparison to gay magazines in Germany the Indian pendants are not dominated by advertorials (advertisement-editorials) as they are not (yet?) dependent on the funding from the pharmaceutical companies.

HIV prevention efforts and sexual health oriented activism became increasingly important in India during the early 1990s and the newly founded organizations include Mumbai-based MSM organization *Humsafar Trust* (1991)[10] and New Delhi-based *Naz Foundation* (1994), which also led the juridical war against Section 377 IPC.[11] Apart from counseling, informing, educating and simply providing space where MSM can hang around, talk freely and make new friends, they also provide medical help and testing for STDs (*Sexually Transmitted Diseases*). *Naz India* is a NGO founded in 1994 by Anjali Gopalan, an India-born medical doctor, who returned from the USA to New Delhi. Naz India provides (MSM) counseling, home based care, organizes several education programs and runs a residential care home for HIV-positive children. In 2003 several NGOs formed INFOSEM (*India Network FOr SExual Minorities*) as a network organization.[12] Another example would be MINGLE (*Mission for INdian Gay & Lesbian Empowerment*), financially supported by *Planetromeo Foundation*. The support groups hence have become more translocal and interconnected, forging alliances.

India's first gay magazine was *Bombay Dost*. Shopkeepers did not display it openly and pulled it from under the table only when requested. It was started in Mumbai in May 1990 by the retired journalist Ashok Row Kavi (b. 1947) and ran until 2002 when it stopped due to lack of funds. After joining Ramakrishna Mission as a monk, Ashok studied journalism at Berlin's International School of Journalism and became the first gay activist in India after coming out in an interview with *Savvy magazine* in 1986. He was founder-chairperson (along with Sridhar Rangayan) of *Humsafar Trust* and co-organizer of the first ever ILGA-Asia (*International Lesbian and Gay Association*) conference taking place in Mumbai in 2002. When *Bombay Dost* was re-launched after the 2009 Delhi court verdict, it did change totally, now displaying the cover model in color on the front-page and not monochrome inside on the first page as before.[13] Today, the magazine is sold openly for example at Mumbai's Oxford Bookstore.

In Calcutta activist Pawan Dhall started *Pravartak* newsletter in 1991 and later the Counsel Club which also organized Calcutta's pride parade *Walk on the Rainbow* in 2003. Other newsletters started in the 1990s include *Friends India* from Lucknow and *Good As You* (G.A.Y.) (1994) from Bangalore which existed also as a group. Newsletters and *yahoogroups* enabled the LGBTQ community to organize private parties to meet and mingle. *Voodoo's* in Mumbai started to operate practically as the first gay club when gays decided to flood it on Saturday evenings. In New Delhi *Peppers* followed to introduce a gay night on Tuesdays and in Bangalore the alcohol store *Ching Lung* started gay parties after official closing hours, serving unforgettable drinks like Indian red wine mixed with coke. In 1999 a huge posh private gay party in Mumbai was raided by police forces and the party's organizer was arrested in what became known as the White Party fiasco. Although the upper-class family of the organizer pulled strings that the media would not report that it was a gay party, newspaper coverage cited the police inspector saying he could not give details on the event as *"things were beyond limits of decency"* (Express News Service 1999). Accounts of these non-Western queer experiences can be found in several readers.[14] Today, there are gay parties taking place openly in most of the cities of India. In Mumbai *Azaad Bazaar* opened as India's first and only LGBT pride shop, but it has closed already.[15] *Queer Ink* is India's first LGBTIQ online bookstore. *Indjapink* is India's first gay travel company and located in New Delhi.[16]

With the launch of internet in India in 1995, virtual spaces quickly provided a "gay haven" (Campbell 2004) for Indian men: an online parallel queer universe to affirm their identities and explore sexual desires. As computers neither grow on trees nor fall from the sky, these new opportunity structures introduced by digital technology were obviously available first for the middle class once again. By allegedly guaranteeing anonymity the world wide web offers a magnitude of options to articulate and experience new identities, stimulating identity games that could be rather unlikely in direct communication (Turkle 1998). People put their most intimate fantasies on dating profiles, pedophiles share pictures of naked children, a cannibal can find a consenting human object to eat up and a serial killer in Lahore can make out online to postcoitally kill MSM "to teach homosexuals a lesson" (AFP 2014). Virtual communities are characterized by a specific awareness of commonalities that are thematic.

The first Indian egroup was *GayBombay* and it started in 1998.[17] It follows in several aspects the example set by the worldwide *Khush*-list founded for LGBT South Asians in 1992 in the West (Roy 2003). Shahani (2008) provides a highly readable virtual ethnography on the online presence of *GayBombay* and its list activities. The group successfully managed to take things offline as well and started biweekly meetings at a McDonald's in Mumbai (Roy 2003, 196). Was the Internet seemingly used first for finding porn and sex partners, support and information, it increasingly became a tool to organize collective action. Virtual communities became real and started to take over a club[18] or a street for specific events. Following what Niklas Luhmann would probably call functional differentiation, many LGBTQ groups later developed more specific agendas. In 1999 Sunil Menon founded *Sahodaran* in Chennai to empower Kothis[19] who worked mostly as sex workers. Other examples are queer book clubs as *Queer Reads Bangalore*[20] and QUILT (*Orinam's Queer Literature Group in Orissa*)[21] or the gay sports group GRAB (*Gay Running and Breakfast*) in Bangalore in 2005, which meets for jogging at Cubbon Park every Sunday morning and afterwards take breakfast together at Airlines Hotel – with many more people just joining the breakfast. Other examples are Bangalore's *Queer Bowling League, Pink Divas* dance group or other LGBTQ groups for trekking, picnic, kite flying etc.

Cell phones were another technological improvement that impacted dramatically on dating activities as most people engaging in MSM would not share a landline number with sex partners out of the fear that family members could take the call.

The success of transnational gay chat fora with instant messages triggered another dating revolution, making the guys on the bazaar of pleasure searchable by pictures and personal details like age, HIV status, sexual preferences or fetishes and cock size. German-founded *Gayromeo* for example has 111,797 registered users in India and *manjam* 27,323 (27.02.2014). *Whatsapp* and gay geosocial networking applications such as "gaydar" *Grindr* (launched in 2009 by Nearby Buddy Finder), awarded the "Best Mobile Dating App" at the iDate Awards 2011, are highly popular among MSM in India and dramatically impact on dating activities as computer access is not necessary anymore to scan potential sex partners in the immediate environment, enabling the exchange of the exact GPS coordinates by one click only. Again, *iPhones* don't fall from the sky and are not affordable to a majority of Indians. Nevertheless phone calls are increasingly outdated already – *"no need to call"* (Turkle 2011, 187ff) – emoticons are easier and more trendy! }:) ☺ New media, however, does not unfold its opportunity structures equally among the South Asian nation states. It is important to note that in India sexual and in particular gay-content homepages like porn-blogs,[22] chat rooms and dating apps are not blocked by the government unlike in neighboring Pakistan.

On Medialisation

Different cultural spheres continuously overlap and interact with each other. As media culture – there are more than 800 TV channels and over 80,000 newspapers with a total daily circulation of about 110 million copies in India – is omnipresent in the contemporary digital age, it increasingly permeates society as well as other cultural spheres: Media culture can pressure people into conformity to established organizations and moral standards of society and yet media technology provides resources to empower individuals against it (Kellner 1995, 3). Today we hear voices that have been silenced in the past, and the field of media plays a crucial role in supplying the technical tools to communicate these voices (cf. Narrain and Bhan 2005). Media culture is *constitutive for reality*, among others in deciding which themes are relevant for the cultural program of society (Schmidt 2008, 67). Media provides powerful sites for symbolic and cultural production. Sexual minorities have until recently been rather marginalized on mainstream media in South Asia. By mass media consensus they were for long not considered a kosher topic to report on in an unbiased or even supporting way. In Bollywood films queer characters (such as *Bobby Darling*[23]) were displayed to laugh about. India's first gay film was the filmlet *Bomgay* by Riyad Vinci Wadia in 1996; in 1999 Nishit Saran followed with the filmlet *Summer in my Veins*. When commercial broadcasting networks like NDTV (New Delhi Television Limited) started to report on gay life in India, gay voices were expected to express contriteness[24] hereby intentionally or unintentionally confirming the American neoimperialist and homonationalist narrative of suppressed sexual minorities in developing countries (Puar 2007) after the sudden conversion of large parts of the Bush regime to feminism in order to mobilize for an enduring military invasion in Afghanistan (Kandiyoti 2010).[25] This pattern did change significantly meanwhile. Soon gays were represented in increasingly positive ways starting with mainstream TV formats like *Big Boss* (Indian version of *Big Brother*) or the soap *Jassi Jaisi Koi Nahin* (Indian-themed version of *Yo soy Betty, la fea* / *Ugly Betty* / *Verliebt in Berlin*) over gay movies like *Dunno Y...Na Jaane Kyon* up to big Bollywood blockbusters (*Dostana, Fashion, My brother... Nikhil, Honeymoon Travels Pvt. Ltd., Do Paise ki Dhoop, Page 3, Life in a...Metro* etc.). And this change of patterns accelerated after the 2009 landmark decision of the Delhi High Court to decriminalize same-sex activities among consenting adults. The cultural-normative border between usual and unusual sexuality is shifting in India and this is reflected in the scale of anxiety experienced on the level of the individual. The legal debate is hence crucial in transforming a history of repression of sexual minorities into a story of emancipation.

Criminalization, Decriminalization and Recriminalization of Homosexualities in India

In 1533, Henry VIII renegotiated the boundaries between the Catholic Church and the British state by secularizing sodomy, transforming it from a sin against God into a crime against the state. The statute was first and foremost deployed against Catholic monks.

> "Once the law was passed, Henry's commissioners began to inspect the monasteries; within a year Henry declared them dissolved and their goods forfeit to the state" (Fone 2000, 216).

Europe's homophobia is hence less rooted in Christianity than in concepts of the secular state.

i) Criminalization

In British India, in particular after the so called "Mutiny" or "Great Rebellion" in 1857, it became even more imperative for the rulers of the imperial state to maintain their sexual purity (first and foremost within the army). The colonial anti-sodomy statute, Section 377, was introduced into Chapter XVI "Of Offences Affecting the Human Body" of the Indian Penal Code on 06 October 1860 by the Indian Law Commission (Bhaskaran 2002, 15). It reads:

> "Whoever voluntarily has carnal intercourse against the order of nature with any man, woman or animal, shall be punished with imprisonment for life, or with imprisonment of either description for a term which may extend to ten years, and shall also be liable to fine.
> Explanation. Penetration is sufficient to constitute the carnal intercourse necessary to the offence described in this section.
> Comment. This section is intended to punish the offense of sodomy, buggery and bestiality. The offense consists in a carnal knowledge committed against the order of nature by a person with a man, or in the same unnatural manner with a woman, or by a man in any manner with an animal."

Although the law de iure also applies to heterosexuals and married couples who indulge in oral or anal intercourse, it has been mostly deployed against gays and transgenders. In the United Kingdom sex between consenting male adults has become legalized in 1967 (Jeffery-Poulter 1991).

ii) Decriminalization

The first manifesto to demand gay rights in India was *Less than Gay* by ABVA (*AIDS Bhedbhav Virodhi Andolan* – an activist organization founded by Siddharth Gautam[26]) in 1991. In August 1994 ABVA organized a protest against police harassment outside the Delhi police headquarters (Misra 2009, 22). ABVA filed the first public interest litigation calling for the repeal of Section 377 in 1994 (!), however, the case was not heard until 2001. As ABVA did not have the funds to employ a full-time lawyer to keep track of the case, it was dismissed in 2001 as ABVA did not get to know about the hearing and hence failed to appear in court.

In September 2001 *Naz Foundation* preferred a writ petition against the criminalization of homosexuality by Section 377 of the Indian Penal Code (IPC). Naz Foundation challenged the constitutional validity of Section 377 IPC, claiming that it infringes on the fundamental rights guaranteed under Articles 14, 15, 19 and 21 of the Constitution of India. The petition argues that Section 377 is based on Judeo-Christian moral and ethical standards, which are outdated and have no place in postcolonial India. Section 377 is a weapon for police abuse and blackmail; it perpetuates negative and discriminatory beliefs toward sexual minorities that jeopardize HIV prevention efforts by driving homosexual activities underground, creating a class of vulnerable people. The fundamental rights infringed are the protection of life and personal liberty (Article 21), the right against discrimination as the expression "sex" would include "sexual orientation" (Article 15), the right to equality (Article 14) as Section 377 distinguishes between procreative and non-procreative sexual acts and the right to freedom (Article 19) as MSM are not allowed to make personal statements about their sexual preferences. The writ petition was dismissed by Delhi High Court on 02 September 2004 as *"purely academic"* and hence Naz was denied the right to sue. Its review petition was dismissed on 03 November 2004. On 03 February 2006, however, the Supreme Court (Civil Appeal No. 952/2006) set aside this order from the Delhi High Court, observing that the matter does in fact require consideration.

In September 2006 Indian novelist (and gay activist) Vikram Seth authored an open call to the Indian public to collectively fight Section 377 IPC, which was signed and supported by many of India's intelligentsia among others by Nobelist Amartya Sen, Arjun Appadurai, Ashis Nandy, Arundhati Roy, Veena Das, and Sudhir Kakar. The Union Minister of Health and Family Welfare, Dr. Anbumani Ramadoss, also stated, that Section 377 IPC *"must go"* in August 2008 (Express New Service 2008). On 02 July 2009 Delhi High Court declared Section 377 IPC unconstitutional as it is violative of Articles 21, 14 and 15 of the Constitution (High Court of Delhi 2009). It left the issue of violation of Article 19 open.

All of a sudden the criminal stigma of being gay was gone in India. Homosexuality was decriminalized among consenting adults. This judgment is of historical relevance and quickly many "came out", gay parties started to be organized openly, gay magazines were launched, homopages and hundreds of queer Indian Facebook groups mushroomed up as did gay spas or saunas[27] and LGBT student groups on university campuses such as Delhi's *Queer Campus*.[28]

Large companies started displaying gayfriendly images in advertisement campaigns to catch the pink rupee and present their products as specifically modern. Several celebrities have come out as gay in public, among them are fashion designers like Krishna Mehta, Rohit Bal or Wendell Rodricks (who registered a PACS (*pacte civil de solidarité*) in 2002 with his French partner) – and most reported: His Royal Highness Prince Manvendra Singh Gohil from Rajpipla. The "gay prince" – out, proud and princely – introduced the Indian gay lifestyle magazine *Fun* in July 2010 and relaunched India's first gay magazine *Bombay Dost*.

Only days after the Delhi court decision the Pakistan Supreme Court ruled to grant equal rights for transgenders. Members of the third sex, so called *hijras* or *khusras*[29], are meanwhile officially regarded as neither male nor female in national identity cards in Pakistan. They have become a judicially recognized neosex in India as well.

iii) Recriminalization

However, several (22) individuals and organizations requested the Supreme Court to intervene against the Delhi High Court verdict – among them were several Hindu astrologers, who make their living with matching marriage horoscopes. The interventions were allowed on 07 February 2011 and the petitioners were heard in 2012.

On 11 December 2013, the Supreme Court overturned the 2009 Delhi High Court verdict which had decriminalized consensual sex among adult men. By declaring Section 377 IPC constitutionally valid, it thus recriminalized homosexual acts in India (Supreme Court of India 2013).

Thousands from the LGBTQ community in India who had become open about their sexual identities after the 2009 Delhi High Court order are now facing the threat of legal prosecution and police harassment. Sonia Gandhi, president of the then ruling coalition, commented (Zee Media Bureau 2013):

"I am disappointed that the Supreme Court has reversed the previous Delhi High Court ruling on the issue of gay rights. The High Court had wisely removed an archaic, repressive and unjust law that infringed on the basic human rights enshrined in our Constitution. This Constitution has given us a great legacy, a legacy of liberalism of openness, that enjoin us to combat prejudice and discrimination of any kind. We are proud that our culture has always been an inclusive and tolerant one."

Media commentators used harsh terms for these "cruel and inhuman" (TNN 2014) developments, speaking of a "perversion of Indian culture" and the "world's largest homophobic democracy" (Ghoshal 2014). Hindu organizations such as the *Hindu American Foundation* issued strong statements criticizing the court.[30] The *Times of India*, India's most widely read English language newspaper, bluntly even added its own view (Mahapatra 2013):

> "This paper has consistently supported the decriminalization of consensual gay sex between adults. (…) The Supreme Court brings back a discriminatory law that was created over 150 years ago by our colonial masters. It deals a body blow to the very idea of individual choice. It recriminalizes homosexuality, which carries a maximum jail sentence of life, and gives the police one more excuse to harass, extort and jail law-abiding people whose only 'crime' is that they do not conform to the traditional view of sexuality. The government and our political parties need to correct this injustice. Over the past couple of years, the UPA has time and again criticized the courts for 'judicial over-reach' and for invading executive and legislative turf; but such activism is due, at least in part, to our MPs and MLAs not doing their main job, which is to legislate. An amendment of 377 is something Parliament should have done on its own a long time ago."

The decision of the Supreme Court has triggered protests in all major cities in India as well as in front of Indian embassies in 17 countries with Indian activists holding up banners saying for example: "Quit homophobia India", "377 sucks", "same sex / same rights", "love is the law" or "No balls in our court". As Foucault and Freud have already noted, nothing propagates the sexual as its repression.

Shades of Gay on Display: Making Space for Pride and Solidarity

Marching for visibility, praise and pride has a long and broad history in South Asia, gods are taken out on the streets for *rathayātrās*, Muslims stage Muharram processions, families and friends march on weddings and funerals (Jacobsen 2008). Pride, Stonewall or Christopher Street Day parades, however, are a global LGBT phenomenon.

The first Indian *friendship walk* was held in Calcutta in 1999 and only 15 activists are reported to have participated. In 2001 the *Kolkata Rainbow Pride Week* was made an annual event. The *Walk on the Rainbow* marches held after 2003 attracted around 300 activists already (Shahani 2008, 182) and were the first to be held at the same time in which pride weeks happen all over the world. Only in 2008 New Delhi and Mumbai followed the example set by Kolkata. Outside of Kolkata, the first formal LGBTQ pride parades took place on 29 June 2008 (however, there have been informal protest marches in Mumbai before as well). The main political theme of the pride parades was to fight Section 377.

On 29 June 2008 India's first coordinated pride parades took place on the same day in New Delhi, Bangalore, Pondicherry and Kolkata (Chennai followed the day after), with about 2,200 overall participants. This was the first pride event in India's capital, New Delhi, and it rallied before the police headquarter (cf. Dave 2012, 164).

"The marchers were anxious at first, outnumbered probably ten to one by police and journalists. But the group of revelers soon swelled to a euphoric, drumbeating, slogan-shouting thousand, outnumbered no more." (Dave 2012, 2).

The parade displayed mostly young men with torso-hugging clothes and apart from rainbow hand flags, carnival-type masks were handed out to those participants, who would not feel comfortable to show their faces (Gohil 2013). Activists shouted slogans against Section 377 and distributed flyers by hand. Prime Minister Manmohan Singh took the opportunity to appeal for great social tolerance towards sexual minorities the next day. Mumbai's first formal pride parade took place on 16 August 2008, one day after India's Independence Day.

Attendance at pride parades did increase significantly (cf. Rangayan 2013, 175) after decriminalization in 2009, for example 3,500 people were reported to have participated in New Delhi's 2010 pride march and 1,500 in Bangalore the same year. In June 2012 the first international pride parade was held in the temple town of Madurai (Gopishankar 2012). In particular for Delhi, a striking increase of participants has been reported by now.[31] And participation is larger in South Indian cities like Bangalore or Chennai (in 2008 around 300 activists in Kolkata, 600 in Bangalore). Slogans include "samānatā" (equal), "We're here, we're queer. Marching without fear", "love is stronger than fear", "I'm proud of my gay child", "Love is a Human Right", "Love – Equal – Accept" etc.

The relatively new identities of sexual minorities need to be united and reinforced and one way to publicly confirm such an "umbrella" minority identity is the LGBTQ pride parade. Several neologisms were created in Hindi around this event and its concepts, for example *samlaingik* (Sanskrit term for same-sex)[32] or *kvīyar garvotsav* (skt. garva = pride, proud speech; skt. ut-sav(a) = festival, blossoming). Pride marches are both love parade parties and political protests aiming to turn sexual minority identities into "a reason for pride, not a reason to hide". Media plays a crucial role in communicating such positive role models.

Several homepages were launched to advertise pride parades' parties and awareness programs, organize fund raising etc. Examples are *Delhi Queer Pride*,[33] *Queer Azaadi Mumbai*,[34] *Chennai LGBT Pride*,[35] *Bengaluru Pride* etc.[36]

Mainstream media reports of Indian pride parades are by and large positive[37] – even by the more conservative media like *Al Jazeera* (however, the comments of readers are more doubtful) (Gaedtke 2014). And of course there is today a large number of queer amateur blogs (Mitra 2010) reporting additionally like *The Reluctant Observer*,[38] *Queer Media Watch*,[39] *Crazy Sam's Bloginess*,[40] *Queeristan*,[41] *Out in My Head*,[42] *Bengaluru Pride*,[43] *The Unsung Psalm*[44] etc. But with around 13 per cent, India's internet accessibility is quite patchy.

Indian pride parades are smaller and less organized than in the West. There is drum-beating instead of dance music from trucks. In a direct comparison of Indian pride parades with its Western equivalent, apart from the masks used to cover faces the most striking difference is the importance of pride film festivals that are being organized during these pride days.

India's largest *gay event* is the *Kashish Mumbai Queer Film Festival* that takes place in May annually since 2010, attracting lots of media attention.[45]

However, there are also critics: gay activist Ashley Tellis for example considers LGBTQ activism in India an elitist and quite neoliberal affair, "taken over by marauding (…) upper caste twits who have been seeing too much US TV and think queer" (Tellis 2013).

Media logic or the rationalities of mass communication highly impact on other institutions of society, social fields and systems (Hepp 2011, 42). According to Norbert Elias (1997) the civilizing process is shaped by transformation of affect control, i.e. a shift in sensing prudency or embarrassment. Media's power to interpret can support or even accelerate such dynamics. Media cultures are crucial in processes of production, representation, adoption and governmental regulation of mediated codes constitutive for affect control in society. In India and Nepal as well as European locations (where same-sex marriage is legal), Hindu priests and temples are increasingly comfortable to organize religious marriage ceremonies for same-sex couples. Vanita (2005) compiles a most interesting collection of material on same-sex marriages among Indians.

Capitalist Logic of Producing Plurality and Difference

If there is a market price for it, how much are people willing to pay for recognition? In 2013 an entrance fee of INR 5000,– (85,– USD/60,– EUR) is common and hence considered "normal" for the queer middle class crowd in India to be allowed to enter a gay bar in the city. Capitalist change results on the one side in forcing more and more men to leave their families and move into megacities of an informal urban proletariat (what Davis 2006 called "planet of slums") to seek wage labor and on the other side the neoliberal discourse produces a pluralisation of lifestyles, advocating immediate fun and consumption while promising the freedom to choose any way of life by increasingly individualizing responsibilities formerly associated with society. The social relevance of the family of origin decreases, divorce rates increase, couples marry later and the length of "single life" lasts longer in particular when love-marriages become idealized or economic expectations – not only for dowry – grow disproportionately – not to forget the surplus men, who are statistically doomed to stay single. As capitalism reduces economic security and social justice, individual sexual freedoms increase (Sigusch 2005, 7 and 19). Hence sexual minorities could be considered among the winners of the ruptures resulting from capitalist change. These developments sparked the dissociation of the sexual, the dispersion of sexual fragments and diversification of intimate relations (Sigusch 2011, 158, cf. Turkle 2011 and Dean 2009). Capitalism celebrates the freedom of individual choice, it constantly creates new needs and commodities while forcing the consumer to choose. Later TV and social media created citizens of a digital *confessional society* (Bauman 2013, 30), where making public exposures of the private is a public virtue and obligation, in which people compete for being watched/followed/liked, accumulating social capital by commodifying themselves to attract followers on *Twitter* and allocate *likes* on *Facebook* etc. Cultural influences from the diasporas and human rights movements of oppressed groups impacted on the social and economic change in Indian society additionally. Globalization added sex tourism and the Gay International.

In particular among India's growing middle class the priorities of life shift from survival to self-fulfillment. The increasing pluralisation and diversification of life-worlds and (sexual) identities – that takes place because it is more and more irrelevant for the consumer society or regime of capitalism *what* individuals do or think (Sigusch 2011, 110) as long as they choose (freely) and consume or their difference can be capitalized as a resource of creativity (Voß and Wolter 2013, 41 and 106, McKinsey&Company 2011) – leads to a new market basket of late-capitalist neosexual identities: from the by now canonized LGBTTIQQ catalogue (i.e. lesbian, gay, bi, transsexual, transgender, intersex, queer, questioning) over cis (born in the right body),[46] BDSM, e-sexuals and agenders all through to the emerging trend of asexuality[47] – "Happy and proud to be asexual!" (Nair 2010).

At the same time neosexual practices become more and more accepted in the societies of pharmacopornographic-technosexual (Preciado 2013) modernity: childless couples shopping Brahmin/Sunni/Shia sperm from infertility solutions firms (TNN 2012), buying testosterone on *ebay*, selfsex, solosex and civilizing sexuality through hardcore-pornography or erotic home entertainment (Pastötter 2003), medical virility of Sildenafil citrate (as in Viagra) – one of the most commonly used drugs in India (Vasudev 2009) –, Tadalafil & Vardenafil, poppers, mobile porn (Bhalla 2012), phone sex, cybersex, serosorting & similar risk reduction strategies for HIV transmission among barebackers (Dean 2009, 12–16), etc.

Sex worlds diversify; sex lives today become increasingly self-confident, variegated, exiling fear. Masturbation and sex work seems legitimate. Premarital, extramarital, anal, oral, fetishist, homosexual or SM intercourse hardly shock anybody today. Traditional sexual morals lose ground and give space for individual choices, preferences and rules. The advertisement and pornographic industries worked hard for this hand in hand with sexual reformers and LGBTIQ activists (cf. Heider 2014, 310). In particular sexual minorities strive for visibility in society in order to reify their specific identities. Sexualities come out of the private and go public – closet is out and "out is IN".⁴⁸ "Out & proud" LGBT parades and their surrounding activities, like awareness programs, are designed to attract a maximum of attention and consumers, while transforming the swarm of its consumers into commodities, catching the eye for more consumers. The sexual becomes more and more commercial as well as trivial. The downside of the sexual becoming more banal is that men increasingly turn toward violence to experience some sort of kick. Even if, as some fear, the Hindu nationalist bloc would strive to launch a sexual counter-revolution in India, the further pluralisation and diversifaction of sex worlds seems unstoppable.

Bibliography

AFP. "Serial killer from Lahore wanted to teach homosexuals a lesson." *Dawn*, April 28, 2014. Accessed May 5, 2014. http://www.dawn.com/news/1102826/serial-killer-from-lahore-wanted-to-teach-homosexuals-a-lesson.

AIDS Bhedbhav Virodhi Andolan. *Less Than Gay: A Citizens' Report on the Status of Homosexuality in India*. New Delhi: ABVA, 1991.

ALDRICH, ROBERT, ed. *Gleich und anders: Eine globale Geschichte der Homosexualität*. Hamburg: Murmann, 2007.

BAUER, THOMAS, and BERTOLD HÖCKER, WALTER HOMOLKA, KLAUS MERTES. *Religion und Homosexualität: Aktuelle Positionen*. Göttingen: Wallstein, 2013.

BAUMAN, ZYGMUNT, and DAVID LYON. *Liquid Surveillance*. Cambridge: Polity, 2013.

BEACHY, ROBERT. "The German Invention of Homosexuality." *The Journal of Modern History* 82, no.4 (2010): 801–38.

BHALLA, NITA. "India ministers quit after caught watching porn in parliament." *Reuters*, February 8, 2012. Accessed March 2, 2014. http://in.reuters.com/article/2012/02/08/us-india-porn-idINTRE8170VD20120208.

BHASKARAN, SUPARNA. "The Politics of Penetration: Section 377 of the Indian Penal Code," in *Queering India*, edited by Ruth Vanita, 15–29. London: Routledge, 2002.

BOONE, JOSEPH ALLEN. *The Homoerotics of Orientalism*. New York: Columbia University Press, 2014.

BUTLER, JUDITH. *Bodies That Matter: On the Discursive Limits of Sex*. New York: Routledge, 1993.

CAMPBELL, JOHN EDWARD. *Getting It On Online: Cyberspace, Gay Male Sexuality, and Embodied Identity*. New York: Harrington Park, 2004.

DAS GUPTA, MONISHA. *Unruly Immigrants: Rights, Activism, and Transnational South Asian Politics in the United States*. Durham: Duke University Press, 2006.

DAVE, NAISARGI N. *Queer Activism in India: A Story in the Anthropology of Ethics.* Durham: Duke University Press, 2012.

DAVIS, MIKE. *Planet of Slums.* London: Verso, 2006.

DEAN, TIM. *Unlimited Intimacy: Reflections on the Subculture of Barebacking.* Chicago: University of Chicago Press, 2009.

DWYER, RACHEL. "Zara hatke (Somewhat different): The New Middle Classes and the Changing Forms of Hindi Cinema." In *Being Middle-Class in India: A Way of Life,* edited by Henrike Donner, 184–208. London: Routledge, 2011.

ELIAS, NORBERT. *Über den Prozeß der Zivilisation.* (2 Vols.), Frankfurt a.M.: Suhrkamp, 1997.

Express News Service. "Ramdoss backs gay rights, says 377 must go." *The Indian Express,* August 8, 2008. Accessed February 25, 2014. http://archive.indianexpress.com/news/ramadoss-backs-gay-rights-says-sec-377-must-go/346649/.

Express News Service. "Red faces at The White Party." *The Indian Express,* June 8, 1999. Accessed January 30, 2014. http://www.expressindia.com/ie/daily/19990608/ige08025.html

FONE, BYRNE. *Homophobia: A History.* New York: Metropolitan Books, 2000.

GAEDTKE, FELIX. "In pictures: Mumbai's gay pride parade." *AlJazeera,* February 3, 2014. Accessed March 3, 2014. http://www.aljazeera.com/indepth/inpictures/2014/02/pictures-mumbai-gay-pride-parade-20142215145797937.html.

GAYATRI, REDDY. *With Respect to Sex: Negotiating Hijra Identity in South India.* Chicago: University of Chicago Press, 2005.

GHOSHAL, SOMAK. "This Valentine's Day our roses are for queer love, deemed criminal by the Supreme Court." *Live Mint,* February 8, 2014. Accessed February 26, 2014. http://www.livemint.com/Leisure/HaqZOKVu3VpVBeAfj7yN1H/The-Love-Issue--Tough-love.html.

GOHIL, MANVENDRA SINGH. "Gay pride? Then why hide behind the mask." *DNA,* October 8, 2013. Accessed March 3, 2014. http://www.dnaindia.com/analysis/column-gay-pride-then-why-hide-behind-the-mask-1900495.

GOPINATH, GAYATRI. *Impossible Desires: Queer Diasporas and South Asian Public Cultures.* Durham: Duke University Press, 2005.

GOPISHANKAR, M. "Voices unheard." *The Hindu,* June 20, 2012. Accessed March 9, 2014. http://www.thehindu.com/features/metroplus/society/article3550406.ece.

GUGLER, THOMAS K. "Okzidentale Homonormativität und nichtwestliche Kulturen." In *Was ist Homosexualität?,* edited by Florian Mildenberger et. al., 141–79. Hamburg: Männerschwarm, 2014.

HAJRATWALA, MINAL, ed. *Out! Stories from the New Queer India,* Mumbai: QueerInk, 2012.

HEIDER, ULRIKE. *Vögeln ist schön: Die Sexrevolte von 1968 und was von ihr bleibt.* Berlin: Rotbuch, 2014.

HEPP, ANDREAS. *Medienkultur: Die Kultur mediatisierter Welten.* Wiesbaden: VS, 2011.

HERZOG, DAGMAR. *Paradoxien der sexuellen Liberalisierung.* Göttingen: Wallstein, 2013.

High Court of Delhi. *WP(C) No. 7455/2001.* New Delhi, 2009. Accessed February 2014. http://www.nazindia.org/judgement_377.pdf.

HIRSCHFELD, MAGNUS. *Weltreise eines Sexualforschers im Jahre 1931/32.* Frankfurt a.M.: Eichborn, 2006.

HIRSCHFELD, MAGNUS. *Geschlechtskunde auf Grund dreißigjähriger Forschung und Erfahrung bearbeitet. II. Vol.: Folgen und Folgerungen.* Stuttgart: Püttmann, 1928.

HUDSON, VALERIE M. and ANDREA M. DEN BOER. *Bare Branches: The Security Implications of Asia's Surplus Male Population.* Cambridge: MIT Press, 2004.

HUSSEIN, AMEENA. ed. *Blue: The Tranquebar Book of Erotic Stories from Sri Lanka.*, Chennai: Tranquebar Press, 2011.

HVISTENDAHL, MARA. *Unnatural Selection: Choosing Boys over Girls, and the Consequences of a World Full of Men.* New York: Public Affairs, 2012.

JACOBSEN, KNUT A. ed. *South Asian Religions on Display: Religious Processions in South Asia and in the Diaspora.* London: Routledge, 2008.

JAFFREY, ZIA. *The Invisibles: A Tale of the Eunuchs of India.* New York: Pantheon, 1996.

JEFFERY-POULTER, STEPHEN. *Peers, Queers, and Commons: The Struggle for Gay Law Reform from 1950 to the Present.* London: Routledge, 1991.

JEFFREY, ROBIN. "The Mahatma didn't like the movies and why it matters: Indian broadcasting policy, 1920s–1990s." *Global Media and Communication* 2, no.2 (2006): 204–24.

JOSEPH, SHERRY. *Social Work Practice and Men who have Sex with Men.* New Delhi: Sage, 2005.

KANDIYOTI, DENIZ. *Islam and the Politics of Gender: Reflections of Afghanistan.* Berlin: Wissenschaftskolleg zu Berlin, 2010.

KELLNER, DOUGLAS. *Media Culture: Cultural Studies, Identity and Politics between the Modern and the Postmodern.* London: Routledge, 1995.

KHAN, SARAH. "Staat und Familie in Pakistan: Von Onkels und Regenten." *Frankfurter Allgemeine Zeitung*, June 5, 2013.

KUGLE, SCOTT SIRAJ AL-HAQQ. *Living Out Islam: Voices of Gay, Lesbian, and Transgender Muslims.* New York: New York University Press, 2014.

KUGLE, SCOTT and STEPHEN HUNT. "Masculinity, Homosexuality and the Defense of Islam: A Case Study of Yusuf al-Qaradawi's Media Fatwa." *Religion and Gender* 2, no.2 (2012): 154–279.

LAWRENCE, PAREENA G. and MARIA C. BRUN. "NGOs and HIV/AIDS Advocacy in India: Identifying the Challenges." *South Asia: Journal of South Asian Studies* 34, no.1 (2011): 65-88.

MAGOO, ISH KUMAR. *Law Relating to Sexual Offences and Homosexuality in India.* Delhi: Capital Law House, 2006.

MAHAPATRA, DHANANJAY. "Supreme Court makes homosexuality a crime again." *Times of India*, December 12, 2013. Accessed February 27, 2014. http://timesofindia.indiatimes.com/india/Supreme-Court-makes-homosexuality-a-crime-again/articleshow/27230690.cms?referral=PM.

McKinsey&Company. *Vielfalt siegt! Warum diverse Unternehmen mehr leisten.* November 2011. Accessed April 15, 2014. http://www.mckinsey.de/sites/mck_files/files/Vielfalt_siegt_deutsch.pdf.

MERCHANT, HOSHANG. ed. *Yaraana: Gay Writings from India.* New Delhi: Penguin, 1999.

MILDENBERGER, FLORIAN and JENNIFER EVANS, RÜDIGER LAUTMANN and JAKOB PASTÖTTER. eds. *Was ist Homosexualität? Forschungsgeschichte, gesellschaftliche Entwicklungen und Perspektiven*. Hamburg: Männerschwarm, 2014.

MISRA, GEETANJALI. "Decriminalising homosexuality in India." *Reproductive Health Matters* 17, no.34 (2009): 20–28.

MITRA, RAHUL. "Resisting the Spectacle of Pride: Queer Indian Bloggers as Interpretive Communities." *Journal of Broadcasting & Electronic Media* 54, no.1 (2010): 163–78.

NAIR, PREETHA. "They are happy and proud to be asexual." *India Today*, March 24, 2010. Accessed March 11, 2014. http://indiatoday.intoday.in/story/They+are+happy+and+proud+to+be+asexual/1/89619.html.

NANDA, SERENA. *Neither Man, Nor Woman: The Hijras of India*. Belmont: Wadsworth, 1990.

NARRAIN, ARVIND and GAUTAM BHAN. eds. *Because I Have A Voice: Queer Politics in India*. New Delhi: Yoda, 2005.

NATARAJAN, MAHESH. *Pink Sheep*. New Delhi: Gyaana Books, 2010.

NATH, JAYAJI KRISHNA and VISHWARATH R. NAYAR. "India." In: *The Continuum Complete International Encyclopedia of Sexuality*, edited by Robert T. Francoeur and Raymond J. Noonan, 516–32. New York: Continuum.

OSELLA, CAROLINE and FILIPPO. *Men and Masculinities in South India*. London: Anthem, 2006.

PASTÖTTER, JAKOB. *Erotic Home Entertainment und Zivilisationsprozess: Analyse des postindustriellen Phänomens Hardcore-Pornographie*. Wiesbaden: Deutscher Universitätsverlag, 2003.

PATTANAIK, DEVDUTT. *The Man Who Was a Woman and Other Queer Tales from Hindu Lore*. New York: Harrington Park, 2002.

PILLAY, ALYAPPIN PADMANABBHA and ALBERT ELLIS. eds. *Sex, Society and the Individual*. Bombay: International Journal of Sexology, 1953.

PRECIADO, BEATRIZ. *Testo Junkie: Sex, Drugs, and Biopolitics in the Pharmacopornographic Era*. New York: Feminist Press, 2013.

PUAR, JASBIR K. *Terrorist Assemblages: Homonationalism in Queer Times*. Durham: Duke University Press, 2007.

PULLEN, CHRISTOPHER. ed. *LGBT Transnational Identity and the Media*. Basingstoke: Palgrave, 2011.

RANGAYAN, SRIDHAR (2013): "Breaking free: Eine persönliche Geschichte über das sich wandelnde Gesicht der indischen Lesbian-, Gay-, Bisexual und Transgender-Community." In *Speak Up! Sozialer Aufbruch und Widerstand in Indien*, edited by Elina Feig, Madhuresh Kumar and Jürgen Weber, 175–85. Berlin: Assoziation A.

RAO, R. RAJ and DIBYAJYOTI SARMA. eds. *Whistling in the Dark: Twenty-One Queer Interviews*. New Delhi: Sage, 2009.

RATTI, RAKESH. ed. *A Lotus of Another Color: An Unfolding of the South Asian Gay and Lesbian Experience*. Boston: Alyson, 1993.

REVATHI, A. *The Truth About Me: A Hijra Life Story*. New Delhi: Penguin, 2010.

ROY, SANDIP. "From Khush List to Gay Bombay: Virtual Webs of Real People." In *Mobile Cultures: New Media in Queer Asia*, edited by Chris Berry, Fran Martin and Audrey Yue, 180–97. Durham: Duke University Press, 2003.

SCHMIDT, SIEGFRIED J. *Systemflirts: Ausflüge in die Medienkulturgesellschaft*. Weilerswist: Velbrück, 2008.
SCHNEIDER, NADJA-CHRISTINA. "Medialised Delhi: Youth, Protest, and an Emerging Genre of Urban Films." *Südasien-Chronik* 3 (2013): 86–110.
SEABROOK, JEREMY. *Love in A Different Climate: Men Who Have Sex with Men in India*. New York: Verso, 1999.
SETH, VIKRAM et. al. *Open Letters Against Sec 377*. August 2006. Accessed February 27, 2014. http://www.nytimes.com/packages/pdf/international/open_letter.pdf.
SHAHANI, PARMESH. *Gay Bombay: Globalization, Love and (Be)Longing in Contemporary India*. New Delhi: Sage, 2008.
SIGUSCH, VOLKMAR. *Neosexualitäten: Über den kulturellen Wandel von Liebe und Perversion*. Frankfurt a.M.: Campus, 2005.
SIGUSCH, VOLKMAR. *Auf der Suche nach der sexuellen Freiheit: Über Sexualforschung und Politik*. Frankfurt a.M.: Campus, 2011.
SIGUSCH, VOLKMAR. *Sexualitäten: Eine kritische Theorie in 99 Fragmenten*. Frankfurt a.M.: Campus, 2013.
SINGH, DAYANITA. *Myself Mona Ahmed*. Zürich: Scalo, 2001.
SPIVAK, GAYATRI CHAKRAVORTY. *Righting Wrongs – Unrecht richten: Über die Zuteilung von Menschenrechten*. Zürich: Diaphanes, 2008.
Supreme Court of India. *Civil Appeal No. 10972 of 2013*. Accessed February 26, 2014. http://de.scribd.com/doc/190889099/Sc-Verdict-on-Article-377.
SYED, RENATE. "Hijras: Nicht Mann, nicht Frau – Indiens und Pakistans drittes Geschlecht und seine Inszenierung von Körper, Geschlecht und Sexualität." In *Frauenbilder – Frauenkörper: Inszenierungen des Weiblichen in den Gesellschaften Süd- und Ostasiens*, edited by Stephan Köhn and Heike Moser, 439–58. Wiesbaden: Harrassowitz, 2013.
TELLIS, ASHLEY. "On Being a Gay Activist in India." *Café Dissensus*, June 25, 2013. Accessed April 17, 2014. http://cafedissensus.com/2013/06/25/on-being-a-gay-activist-in-india-ashley-tellis/.
TNN. "A mother and a judge speaks out on section 377." *Times of India*, 26.01.2014. Accessed May 14, 2014. http://timesofindia.indiatimes.com/home/stoi/deep-focus/A-mother-and-a-judge-speaks-out-on-section-377/articleshow/29383723.cms.
TNN. "Brahmin sperm in high demand among childless couples." *Times of India*, May 13, 2012. Accessed May 2, 2014. http://m.timesofindia.com/PDATOI/articleshow/13114610.cms
TURKLE, SHERRY. *Leben im Netz: Identität im Zeichen des Internet*. Reinbek: Rowohlt, 1998.
TURKLE, SHERRY. *Alone Together: Why We Expect More from Technology and Less from Each Other*. New York: Basic Books, 2011.
VANITA, RUTH. *Love's Rite: Same-Sex Marriage in India and the West*. New York: Palgrave Macmillan, 2005.
VANITA, RUTH and SALEEM KIDWAI. eds. *Same-Sex Love in India: Readings from Literature and History*. New York: Palgrave, 2000.
VANITA, RUTH. ed. *Queering India: Same-Sex Love and Eroticism in Indian Culture and Society*. London: Routledge, 2002.

VASUDEV, SHEFALEE. "Prakash Kothari: I've saved so many marriages prescribing Viagra." *Outlook*, December 14, 2009. Accessed March 2, 2014.
http://www.outlookindia.com/article.aspx?263154.
VERMA, RAVI K. et. al. eds. *Sexuality in the Time of AIDS: Contemporary Perspectives from Communities in India*. New Delhi: Thousand Oaks, 2004.
VOß, HEINZ-JÜRGEN and SALIH ALEXANDER WOLTER. *Queer und (Anti-)Kapitalismus*. Stuttgart: Schmetterling, 2013.
VOß, HEINZ-JÜRGEN. *Geschlecht: Wider die Natürlichkeit*. Stuttgart: Schmetterling, 2011.
WESTON, KATH. *Families We Choose: Lesbians, Gays, Kinship*. New York: Columbia University Press, 1997.
Zee Media Bureau. "Sonia Gandhi expresses disappointment over SC verdict on Homosexuality." *Zee News*, December 12, 2013. Accessed May 1, 2014.
http://zeenews.india.com/news/nation/sonia-gandhi-expresses-disappointment-over-sc-verdict-on-homosexuality%5C_896238.html.
ZWILLING, LEONARD and MICHAEL J. SWEET. "The Evolution of Third Sex Constructs in Ancient India: A Study in Ambiguity." In: *Invented Identities: The Interplay of Gender, Religion, and Politics in India*, edited by Julia Leslie and Mary McGee, 99–132. New Delhi: Oxford University Press, 2000.

---

1 Chandra Mohan Jain (1931–1990), also known as Acharya Rajneesh from the 1960s onwards, as Bhagwan Shree Rajneesh during the 1970s and 1980s, and as Osho from 1989, was an Indian mystic, guru and spiritual teacher. He advocated a more open attitude towards sexuality and started to attract many Western followers from the 1970s onwards. His international following has continued beyond his death. His Ashram in Pune is today known as the Osho International Meditation Resort. See: http://en.wikipedia.org/wiki/Rajneesh, accessed August 22, 2014.
2 Highly readable selection of short-stories by Natarajan 2010.
3 http://www.galva108.org/, accessed March 3, 2014.
4 For example: http://www.dailymotion.com/video/xbixvz_meet-the-parents_people, accessed February 27, 2014.
5 http://salganyc.org/, accessed February 2, 2014.
6 http://www.trikone.org/index.php/magazine/publication, accessed March 11, 2014.
7 http://pink-pages.co.in/, accessed March 10, 2014.
8 http://issuu.com/thequeerchronicle, accessed March 11, 2014.
9 http://www.gaylaxymag.com/, accessed March 10, 2014.
10 http://www.humsafar.org/, accessed February 27, 2014.
11 http://www.nazindia.org/, accessed February 27, 2014.
12 http://infosem.org/about.htm, accessed March 6, 2014.
13 http://www.bombaydost.co.in/Bombay_Dost_-_Archives.html, accessed March 6, 2014.
14 For example Hajratwala 2012, Rao and Sarma 2009, Narrain and Bhan 2005, Merchant 1999, Seabrook 1999, cf. Ratti 1993 and Hussein 2011.
15 http://www.azaadbazaar.com/, accessed March 6, 2014.
16 http://www.indjapink.co.in/home.html [06.03.2014]. Cf. http://www.outjourneys.com/, accessed March 13, 2014.
17 http://www.gaybombay.org/, accessed March 13, 2014.
18 A colorful example of this is Boston's Queer Guerrilla Bar, who regularly organizes hundreds of gays attacking straight bars and other locations under the #DestinationTakeover program:

http://thewelcomingcommittee.com/boston-takeovers/, accessed March 14, 2014.
19 Kothis are feminine men or boys who take a feminine role in same sex relationships with men. See: http://en.wikipedia.org/wiki/Kothi_(gender), accessed August 22, 2014.
20 http://whaq.blogspot.de/2012/10/queer-reads-bangalore-first-meeting.html, accessed March 10, 2014.
21 http://orinam.net/orinams-quilt-meeting-dec-30-2012/, accessed March 10, 2014.
22 Examples for Indian porn blogs are:
http://www.indiangaysex.com/, accessed April 22, 2014,
http://desigayindia.blogspot.de/, accessed April 22, 2014,
http://desi-gay-desires.blogspot.de/, accessed April 22, 2014,
http://desidicks.tumblr.com/, accessed April 22, 2014.
23 http://www.youtube.com/watch?v=jqaSTv_OMOs, accessed March 14, 2014.
24 https://www.youtube.com/watch?v=BteMne0lmFk, accessed March 4, 2014.
25 In Germany the war propaganda machine revolved around girls' schools and bridge-building.
26 Anti-AIDS Discrimination Campaign.
27 For example Spartacus in Delhi: http://www.spartacusdelhi.com/, accessed March 5, 2014.
28 http://queercampus.blogspot.de/search/label/QueerCampus, accessed March 13, 2014.
http://mingle.org.in/mingle-youth-and-campus-survey-2011/, accessed March 13, 2014.
29 Syed 2013, Revathi 2010, Jaffrey 1996, Singh 2001, Gayatri 2005, and Nanda 1990.
30 http://www.hafsite.org/HAF_Disappointed_by_Indian_Court_Verdict_Homosexuality, accessed April 22, 2014.
31 Cf. http://www.buzzfeed.com/stacylambe/few-but-proud-gather-for-delhi-pride-parade, accessed March 14, 2014 and: http://www.pri.org/stories/2013-11-25/delhis-lgbt-pride-parade-shows-what-difference-decade-can-make-india, accessed March 14, .2014.
32 http://www.sumlaingik.com/, accessed March 7, 2014.
33 http://delhiqueerpride.blogspot.de/, accessed March 2, 2014.
34 http://queerazaadi.wordpress.com/, March 2, 2014.
35 http://orinam.net/ChennaiLGBTPride2009.html, accessed March 2, 2014.
36 https://sites.google.com/site/bengalurupride2/, accessed March 2, 2014.
37 For example NDTV: http://www.youtube.com/watch?v=-AMlXoXp4Vs, accessed March 14, 2014.
Cf. https://sites.google.com/site/bengalurupride2/mediacoverage, accessed March 14, 2014.
38 http://mike-higher.livejournal.com/, accessed February 27, 2014.
39 http://www.queermediawatch.blogspot.in/, accessed February 27, 2014.
40 http://samsbloginess.blogspot.de/, accessed February 27, 2014.
41 http://queeristan.blogspot.de/, accessed February 27, 2014.
42 http://www.outinmyhead.com/, accessed February 27, 2014.
43 https://sites.google.com/site/bengalurupride2/, accessed February 27, 2014.
44 http://unsungpsalm.wordpress.com/, accessed February 27, 2014.
45 www.mumbaiqueerfest.com, accessed March 13, 2014.
46 Hirschfeld 1928, 81 discussed age-cisvestites (*Alterszisvestiten*) and class-cisvestites (*Standeszisvestiten*), i.e. people changing their dress to appear to be of a different age or class.
47 In China there is a highly successful matrimonial dating website exclusively for asexuals: http://www.wx920.net/, accessed March 11, 2014.
48 http://mingle.org.in/living-life-openly-mingles-coming-out-guide-for-lgbt-indians-released/, accessed March 12, 2014.

NADJA-CHRISTINA SCHNEIDER

Filming Urban Spaces and Entangled (Im)mobilities: Experimental Documentaries by & about Young 'Muslim Women' in Delhi

The following article introduces two experimental documentary filmmakers from Delhi and showcases two of their recent films: Fathima Nizaruddin ("Living 'My' Religion", 2004) and Ambarien Alqadar ("The Ghetto Girl", 2011).

Fathima Nizaruddin is a documentary filmmaker from Kerala, now based in Delhi, who has explored issues of religion, gender and identity in three of her self-reflexive documentaries – including her own identity as a young 'Muslim woman' from South India who moved to the capital in North India in the early 2000s. Alongside her work as an independent documentary filmmaker, Fathima has been a lecturer at the A.J.K. Mass Communication Research Centre at Jamia Millia Islamia in Delhi since 2007. In 2009, she went to London to complete her master's degree at Goldsmiths College. Since 2013, she is pursuing a practice-based PhD project at Westminster University in London, on the subject of the anti-nuclear movement in the South Indian state of Tamil Nadu.

Ambarien Alqadar spent a formative period of her youth in Delhi in the 1990s. Like Fathima Nizaruddin, she is also an alumnus of the renowned A.J.K. Mass Communication Research Center at Jamia Millia Islamia University in New Delhi where she currently teaches integrated courses in Digital Film Production, Post Production and Screenwriting. Gender performativity, religious identities and urban localities are some of the themes Ambarien explores in her experimental films. In 2012, Ambarien finished her documentary "The Ghetto Girl", a film about a girl who "obsessively walks the streets" in a predominantly Muslim neighbourhood in South Delhi, which is often referred to as one of India's new "mini-Pakistans".

The interpretation of the two documentaries presented in this article is not exclusively based on my reading of them, but also on various conversations and two longer, semi-structured interviews I conducted with the two directors in Delhi (2011) and Berlin (2012) about their understanding of documentary forms, their own filmmaking practices as well as their continued exploration of gender-related issues.[1] I propose to approach their work and documentary practices from the perspective of entangled (im)mobilities that so many young women and men who were born in the 1980s and 90s have experienced in particular urban spaces and localities which have undergone dramatic socio-economic changes and upheavals due to the interwoven processes of neoliberal restructuring and resurgence of religion-based identity politics in India (see Rajagopal 1994).

1 Who can speak of 'Muslim women' in India? Old and new (im)mobilities and the question of representation

For some time now, 'mobility' has been seen as a new paradigm within the social sciences and humanities, even though it may not refer to a clear-cut or self-explanatory concept, since we have to deal with multiple levels of meaning – such as spatial, physical or social mobility, but also communicative or digital mobility, which are becoming increasingly important. Not least, another important level of meaning has been added to the ongoing discussion by Kevin Robins who introduced the concept of an imaginative, emotional and intellectual mobility in his research on media usages and practices of Turkish migrants in Western Europe (Robins 2004, 114–132). Even though we have to deal with this diversity of forms and ideas about mobility, they are nevertheless connected in many complex ways. Historically speaking, this is certainly not a new phenomenon, but what is new indeed is the fundamentally new dimension and densification of mobility (Sheller and Urry 2006). In addition to this, there are a number of new places and technologies which serve to enhance the mobility of some people while reducing the mobility of others, if one thinks for example of national borders or the so-called 'digital divide'. Questions of mobility, either of too much or too little, or of the wrong time or place, are decisive for many individuals as well as for organizations or institutions. Accordingly, the different forms of mobility and also the control exercised over mobility reflect and reinforce current power relations (ibid.).

In that sense, mobility is a resource and not everyone has the same relation and access to mobility. The mobility paradigm can thus be helpful in highlighting the nexuses that provide some people and groups with new forms of connectivity or connectedness and 'empowerment', while engendering isolation and processes of exclusion for others. Research on human mobility on a global level thus pays more attention to 'local' questions and problems of mobility, such as transport, material culture and spatial relations of mobility and immobility, as well as to technological questions such as mobile communication technologies and, not least, surveillance and security infrastructures. At every turn, these multiple and entangled (im)mobilities, as I provisionally like to call them, also include image distribution and the circulation of perceptions and information in local, national and global media. The politics of mobility as well as the representation of immobility should thus be central to any analysis, as Sheller and Urry argue.

In the post-liberalization context of the 1990s and 2000s, the idea of mobility as it is invoked in innumerable advertising messages has become a central, if not the most powerful metaphor within Indian society (Chakravarty and Gooptu 2000). Mobility can in this context refer to the creation of possibilities to increase one's social standing or to one's personal freedom of movement; in the context of an increasingly media-supported communication both inside and outside of India, it can also refer to a technology- or media-related form of mobility. Right from the beginning, however, the concept of an increasing mobility on the individual level had been closely tied to the general 'progress or rise of the Indian nation'. In sharp contrast to this, Indian Muslims in particular have been increasingly blanked out of the media-led orchestration and construction of a 'mobile, national family' since the 1980s, most glaringly in Hindi cinema (Desai 2007). Moreover, through an excessive emphasis upon their "backwardness" and alleged "unwillingness to reform" (Ataulla 2007), they have been frequently portrayed as the very incarnation of the 'immobile other' – especially in contrast to the newly branded category of the highly mobile 'global Indian'. This in its turn affects in a particular way the strongly essentialized depiction of Muslim women in India who are still perceived predominantly as 'immobile' in every sense – socially, physically and also with regard to mediated communication.

The responsible editor of the magazine *Islamic Voice* from Bangalore, Nigar Ataulla, speaks of a "dangerous triangle". As soon as the conversation turns to a subject such as the status of Muslim women in the Indian context, the focal point of discussion is inevitably placed upon three topics, she argues, namely the infamous out-of-court repudiation of a wife through the so-called "Triple Talaq", the matter of polygamy and finally the "veiling" of the woman (Ataulla 2006). Furthermore, opinion polls and studies revealed that even though the portrayal of the "veiled/secluded" woman, which was dominant in the Indian media for many decades, is not a realistic portrayal of Indian Muslim women, the majority of non-Muslims surveyed still attributed their low status to discriminatory treatment under the Muslim Personal Law in India, and to the religion itself. According to their understanding, Islam suppresses women to a greater extent than other religions do; Muslim women, compared to women of other religions, are thus largely perceived as "submissive," "reserved" and "fragile" and, due to their social conditioning, unable to fight for their own rights (see Kidwai 2003, 104–128).

In contrast to this perception, Muslim women in India have of course never been as quiet and passive as they are frequently portrayed and there are many historical examples of women who have committed themselves in public and private spheres and staked their claims to their rights as full members of their communities.[2] Nida Kirmani describes how a more recent academic interest in research into the subject of 'Muslim women' first crystallized in the 1970s, in the context of a generally increasing interest taken by Western feminists in "third-world women", where the 'Muslim women' were often assumed to be the most oppressed members of this group (Kirmani 2009). At the same time, this construction and representation of the category of the 'Muslim woman' in the field of academic research is also founded in a wide range of publications that attempted to explain the social realities faced by Muslim women in India from the perspective of their legal status under Muslim Personal Law and the gender-specific roles ascribed to them within the religious framework of Islam. It was only in the very recent past that this de-contextualized category of the 'Indian Muslim woman' has also been strongly called into question by the world of academic research itself. The demand has been raised that the peculiarities of region, location, context and social caste be more strongly taken into account and that the idea of a clearly definable, coherent group be questioned more strongly than in the past (see Searle-Chatterjee 2000 and Mehta 2010).

Furthermore, it can be argued that things are not exactly the same after the so-called Arab spring in 2011 when all of a sudden, a large proportion of the visual and textual representations of Muslim women would differ quite markedly from the otherwise predominant depiction of 'veiled femininity' and the 'oppression of women in Islam'. Along with the headlines of those days, one would find a very different kind of visual and textual imagery which added to a new representation of Muslim women as social agents or actors, as very active and courageous citizens, whose activism was crucial in bringing forth the revolutionary movement in Tunisia and Egypt. There is also a growing number of young women who actively seek the opportunity to position themselves vis-à-vis the hitherto dominant discourse and to express their individuality, self-determination and agency. At least to a certain degree, similar discursive shifts can be presently observed with regard to the perception and self-perceptions of Muslim women in India, and Indian Muslim women themselves who have recently started the process of redefining, reinterpreting and of re-appropriating this category. They do so in various ways and through very diverse actions, articulations and performative practices. While poetry and literature are still two very important media of expression, they are by no means the only ones which are available, especially for a 'post-liberalization' generation of women that has grown up with the rapidly increasing densification of mediated communication and availability of media technology in India, just as elsewhere in the world. Two of them shall be introduced in the two following sections.

As mentioned in the introduction, Fathima Nizaruddin was born in the southern Indian state of Kerala, where she also grew up. At the turn of the century, she travelled more than 2500 km from her hometown Varkala to the Indian capital Delhi to study journalism at the renowned A.J.K. Mass Communication Research Centre at Jamia Millia Islamia. Following her studies, in 2004, she started to work for a large Indian news station in Mumbai called *Times Now*, a joint venture between Reuters and Bennett, Coleman and Co. Ltd. However, she very quickly became disillusioned with her working conditions and the subject matter in news reporting and eventually turned to the documentary film. In three of her films, Fathima sought to deal with the different points of view of Muslim women on the questions of gender, identity and religion, an idea she had already explored during her studies at Jamia Millia Islamia University when she filmed "Living 'My' Religion" (2004) with her classmate Nida Khan. The second film of the trilogy, "Talking Heads [muslim women]" was developed in 2009–2010 during her M.A. studies at Goldsmith College in London and was filmed almost exclusively on location in the British capital. The third film on women, religion and identity is entitled "My Mother's Daughter" (2011) and deals with the matriarchal structure of Fathima's familiy in Kerala; the subjective identity of her mother and not least, with the difficult relationship between mother and daughter which has been overshadowed for some years now by the question of when Fathima will finally be ready to marry and/or allow her family to find her a husband.

The second young filmmaker is Ambarien Alqadar, also from Delhi. In 2011, she finished her documentary "The Ghetto Girl", a film about a girl who "obsessively walks the streets" in a predominantly Muslim neighbourhood in South Delhi, which is often referred to as one of India's new "mini-Pakistans". Her first film "Who Can Speak of Men?" (2002) is a documentary about three women who cross-dress (i.e. dress up as men) and who used to live in the same neighbourhood in Jamia Nagar.[3]

By focusing on the two directors from Delhi, I suggest that the increasing imaginative and intellectual mobility as well as the ability to express and articulate their own positionality and reflections about the category 'Muslim women' needs to be contextualized in the larger field and discussion about urban spaces and entangled (im)mobilities in India.

2 Forced mobility and immobilization of Muslims in Delhi during the 1990s and 2000s

Increasing discrimination against Muslims in India coupled with anti-Muslim violence – culminating first in December 1992 in the razing of the Babri mosque in Ayodhya and then in the anti-Muslim massacres that shook the western state of Gujarat scarcely ten years later in the spring of 2002 – led to the relocation of large numbers of Muslims to overwhelmingly Muslim-inhabited areas of Delhi.

> "The regrouping of Delhi's Muslims into religiously 'homogenous' colonies was [...] the result of two cumulating trends: the overcrowding of the Old City and the state of fear induced by communal riots [...]. Those Muslims leaving the walled city for the less congested periphery (and in particular Jamia Nagar) generally belonged to wealthy bazaar families who retained their shops into the Old City while moving their place of residence. From a trickle, this movement of Muslims within the city turned into a stream after a state of fear engulfed the whole country in the 1990s (Gayer 2012, 219)."

In a large number of cases, they were and are even now unable to secure lodgings in those areas of Delhi that were not inhabited by a majority Muslim population, simply because of their Muslim names. When the English-language newspaper *The Hindu* carried out an investigative research in Delhi in the summer of 2012, the current situation was labelled as an ongoing "housing apartheid" in the newspaper (Ashok and Ali 2012). This is also confirmed by one interviewee in Ambarien Alqadar's film "The Ghetto Girl" who narrates how after his marriage, when he was looking for a new flat in other parts of Delhi, real estate agents repeatedly told him that they had apartments but not for him, because he was a Muslim. Eventually, he moved to Jamia Nagar too.

This relocation in turn led to widespread criticism of a perceived "self-segregation" and "ghetto-building" of the Delhi Muslims. Gayer criticizes that the notion of immobile "insular existences" which accompanies these terms and media representations is particularly problematic and misleading as it overlooks the social realities of many Muslims in the Old City or in Jamia Nagar who are in no way cut off from the media-communicative connectivity or from various interactions that arise in the course of their actual working lives in completely different parts of the city every day (Gayer 2012, 236).

An expression of this common perception is the scene in "Living 'My' Religion" in which co-director Nida Khan speaks about the forced (im)mobilezation and marginalization of the Delhi Muslims since the 1990s while we see her driving in a car through the city. She describes that she feels "embarrassed" about her residential address in Ghaffar Manzil (Jamia Nagar), to which there is the subtext that "it's a ghetto, a mini-Pakistan, if you please". Nida analyzes the argument of the supposed "security" regained or retained by Muslims who withdraw to areas that are inhabited by a majority Muslim population. Unlike her father, who presents this argument himself, for Nida when she was growing up, the new family home was connected with the experience of a pervasive control over her clothes and the weight of expectations for her to behave "correctly" as a "Muslim woman". Despite this perceived narrowness and restriction of her personal liberty, she is also aware that she shares the same constant feeling of uncertainty and living under threat as other Delhi Muslims:

"But then again, at some level, I do understand the anxiety, the fear, the trepidation of my community. I have them as well. But do we really have to be amongst our own to be safe in India? Though I hate to admit it to myself, I know that in a riot, perhaps I'll be safer here than anywhere else."

Nida's reflections resonate strongly with one scene in Ambarien Alqadar's film "The Ghetto Girl" in which the voiceover narrator asks her mother when exactly people started migrating to this area and the mother replies (in Hindi and English, with English subtitles as quoted here):

"This began once the Babri mosque was broken and the Hindu-Muslim thing began. Crowds started coming in after the riots that followed the demolition of the Babri mosque. In Seelampur, homes were set on fire. Some people came from there. My mother's shop was burnt down. Girls who had gone missing at the time have still not been found. The kind of security one needs when you think of what happened in Gujarat, the riots that happened in Bhagalpur. If you consider all that, we are definitely more safe [sic] here."

If Gayer argues that the social trajectories of Muslims in Delhi, just as in many other parts of India, are informed by a memory of violence which extends beyond time and space and which often lingers on long after the abatement of said violence, then this certainly seems to be evidenced by the two statements in the documentaries by Ambarien Alqadar and Fathima Nizaruddin. A very interesting representation of the spatial mobility between different parts of the city is Fahmida Khatoon's story in "The Ghetto Girl". Fahmida works in a beauty salon in Zakir Nagar, but lives in Old Delhi. In order to get home, she has to take a cycle rickshaw from her workplace to the Batla House bus stop, from where she takes a bus or shared taxi to the old city. Like two other interviewees in the film, she was filmed in the evening or during night-time, while travelling and talking about how difficult it is for women to move within this locality by night. As soon as she reaches there, Fahmida says in the film that she "flings" the hijab which she doesn't like wearing at all and then "roams in the city".

By doing so, she already practices in her everyday life what Shilpa Phadke, Shilpa Ranade and Sameera Khan invite women in Indian cities to do, that is to "loiter" without purpose in order to express their claim to public space:

"So when we ask to loiter then, we see loitering as a performance with the capacity to enable a subjectivity that can claim the position of a 'legitimate citizen'. [...] It is only when the city belongs to everyone that it can ever belong to all women. The unconditional claim to public space will only be possible when all women and all men can walk the streets without being compelled to demonstrate purpose or respectability, for women's access to public space is fundamentally linked to the access of all citizens (Phadke, Ranade and Khan 2009, 198)."

3 Being young and a 'Muslim woman' in post-liberalization Delhi

"There are times in life when you have answers and times when you are all confused. Right now, I'm in the second stage. If you ask me, I wouldn't exactly know who I am. Somehow, I find that, quite often, what others take me for is first as a Muslim. Maybe it's due to my scarf" ("Living 'My' Religion").

It is with these words that the first of three documentary films begins in which Fathima Nizaruddin grapples with her individual identity, the meaning of her religion for her own self-understanding and the way in which she is perceived by others. "Living 'My' Religion" was also her final assignment for her undergraduate degree at the A.J.K. Mass Communication Centre of Jamia Millia Islamia University in New Delhi. She produced the film together with one of her classmates, Nida Khan, her idea for the film having germinated in conversations they had together about "being Muslim". In the film, the two co-directors are also two of the three 'talking heads', whilst the third character is Atiya (her second name is not given in the film), a student of Islamic studies whom Fathima had met in the halls on the Jamia Millia campus. Atiya's appearance in the film differs strongly from the two other young main characters because she wears the *niqab*, meaning that only her eyes and hands are visible in the film, her feet also being revealed in one scene. "There was nobody in my family who used to cover themselves from head to foot," she says; her family opposed her veiling and did not like it in the beginning. "In fact, my father used to call me a walking tent." Her decision to read Islamic Studies at university was also initially met with resistance from her family, since she had been expected to pursue a professional career as an IT specialist; indeed, she had already completed the necessary training to study IT at university and acquired some professional experience in the field. While Atiya speaks about this in the film, she is shown repairing a computer, and other scenes are being crosscut with shots of the university campus and also the occasional photograph of their life on campus. On several occasions throughout "Living 'My' Religion", we see the three young women engaged in discussions about their religion, as well as about their gender roles, not only in Islam, but in Indian society at large. In these discussions, the question is raised time and again as to what 'being Muslim' actually means and whether it is possible to define this for others, or whether this remains at the discretion of the individual.

We hear the voice of the second protagonist, Nida, alternately as both the voice-over and directly in interview situations, and she introduces herself with the following words:

> "I come from a family of believing, practicing Muslims. I've been brought up as a Muslim girl, but even at 23, when people around me seem to be all sorted out about everything in their lives, I'm still groping around for my answers."

At the Jama Masjid mosque in Old Delhi, we see Nida dressed in a traditional *shalwar kameez*, while she is predominantly seen in jeans and a T-shirt in other scenes in the film. The issue of dress, and more precisely, the issue of dressing in a manner that is considered 'appropriate' and 'correct' for a Muslim woman, represents one of the central themes of the film and is discussed repeatedly by the three women. The differences between – and indeed the incompatibility of – their positions on the *hijab* lead Fathima to conclude that the film was "a discovery of our differences" and thus, on the one hand, perfectly illustrates how important this documentary was for the three who set up and engaged in a dialogue which probably would not have taken place without this film project. At the same time, the fact that Islam can be understood as a discursive tradition is illustrated very clearly to the audience, and the scenes depicting the engaged discussions during which the three characters articulate their very different positions about their religion, are particularly impressive.

Contrary to the generalizations of the Indian mainstream media, which are often based on the collective ascription and essentialization of identities, "Living 'My' Religion" paints the individual portraits of each of the protagonists and brings subjectivity to the fore, where identities are neither solely and inextricably linked with the women's religious affiliations, nor with their own statements and actions. Instead, it is made clear through their many discussions and reflections on their lives that the women's attempts to negotiate and reflect on their own positions and identities are constantly being rehashed and can thus be seen as being part of continuous, fluid process.

The question of dress and more specifically, the 'appropriate' dress for Muslim girls and women emerges also as another important theme in Ambarien Alqadar's documentary "The Ghetto Girl". As she describes in her director's statement, it was a gradual process which led her mother to "choosing to cover herself out of her free will and refusing to be photographed because of her acquired Islamic beliefs". In spite of this, after many years of working as a teacher, she decided to open a beauty salon called "La Femme" in Jamia Nager which is also shown as a very vivid social space for women:

> "One morning she declared that she wanted to open an aromatherapy salon-this with no formal beautician's training and her constant disciplining of me in my growing up years against 'doing' things to the body. The salon was named La Femme, a block away from home, directly opposite the main mosque; it was a place where I regularly saw women happily contradict themselves – they invented stories to justify fashions/trends and wore the hijab as a part of broader strategies to negotiate freedoms. Out on the streets there was the myth of the madman – a man who hit women if they ever walked with uncovered heads."

The director argues that this transformation was an inevitable part of her mother's negotiating the place where the family built their home in Zakir Nagar and where she felt "suffocated" in the beginning. This constant and often tedious negotiation about their physical-spatial mobility is also illustrated in other interviews with two young women and one middle-aged woman who either moved to the area some time ago, grew up there or who commute between the old city and this part of New Delhi. The growing pressure and social control of women's "proper" dress and behavior is clearly interwoven with the dramatic socio-demographic changes in these areas which are now predominantly inhabited by Muslims, but also with the perception that places like Jamia Nagar and other "Muslim colonies" are under constant surveillance by the police and state. At the same time, it is strongly felt that "the State gives no facilities to people who live here".

Rising discrimination against Muslims in India, coupled with massive anti-Muslim violence were crucial experiences made both personally or through the media by directors born in the early 1980s throughout childhood and adolescence, and these events thus very much shaped their world-view and self-perception. Interestingly, in "Living 'My' Religion" we hear Nida Khan's statements concerning her fear of riots as a voice-over to clips from Mani Ratnam's film *Bombay* (1995), in which the South Indian director staged the violent riots between Hindus and Muslims in 1992–93 in such a visually striking and nightmarish way that these are actually very likely to have become a part of the visual memories of the real violence for many who saw the film.[4] This aspect of a medialized memory and of media-related autobiographical memories is also touched upon in a sequence where Fathima Nizaruddin tells of one of her early childhood experiences of a "riot" in her hometown in Kerala. From the start of her story, her voice sounds like the backing track to a film as she describes how, at around ten years old, she saw a television series that depicted an abandoned little boy that frightened her so much because she was suddenly and directly confronted with her own experience of otherness as a Muslim woman, and with an unfamiliar sense of isolation:

> "The riots in my city didn't last long. Quite a few people died. I noticed something had changed when I went back to school. Now my class teacher had a kind of pity in her eyes when she looked at me. I didn't know how to react, to resent or to be thankful for it."

Not willing or able to provide insight into her personal memories of the violence or her individual fears and concerns about possible violent anti-Muslim riots, Atiya responds to questions about the Babri mosque by saying that, in her opinion, Muslims should not focus too heavily on the past. They should instead concentrate on matters of education and "economic empowerment", "giving the women the Islamic rights" and leading a good Islamic life. On the one hand, Atiya's statements seem to be indicative of her intense engagement with the discourse of Islamic feminism, in the same way that they show that she advocates a publicly visible religion that is not confined to the privacy of the home. Nida is the one most strongly opposed to this view, arguing that, in the secular sense, religion is the private affair of each individual because it concerns the personal relationship of each individual with God.

The continuing debate on the public visibility of (other) religions vs. a consistent 'privatization' of religion is particularly apparent in the growing polarization and hardening of attitudes in Europe in recent years. Two clear tendencies can be identified in the mainstream media's portrayal of the debate. On the one hand, the contrast between the two positions is often globally represented as a conflict between the supposedly "enlightened West" and "backward Islam". The widespread assumption that Muslim immigrants had brought a "pre-Enlightenment" or traditional understanding of religion to Europe that would now shake the confidence of or even directly challenge the supposedly secular majority living there, as it is also evoked in Jürgen Habermas' notion of "post-secular societies" in Europe (see Habermas, 2008), overlooks the various trajectories of secularism in many of the former colonies and newly-founded nation states outside of Europe. Furthermore, the positions of religious Muslims who advocate secular principles are largely ignored in this highly polarized debate and are thus absent from the public's understanding of the issue. As José Casanova argues, the rifts within contemporary societies run neither along European and non-European, nor along religious and non-religious fault lines, but right between those groups, institutions and actors representing both the secular and laical positions, and those that assign a different role to religion within the public sphere than had thus far been deemed legitimate (Casanova 2006, 23–44). The very same rifts seem to have divided a group of young Muslim students – all of the same age – at Jamia Millia Islamia University in New Delhi, and just as no acceptable compromise or agreement has been reached so far in the debate raging in the public arena, no point of consensus has been found on the micro level, thus impeding continued communication and interaction between the three protagonists. As Fathima Nizaruddin summarizes in the film, "in the end, we reached no conclusion or answers. There were times when we couldn't agree about a single thing". Thus "Living 'My' Religion" goes beyond merely revealing the diversity of modern-day spirituality and the notions of religious identity held by young Muslim women in urban India today, even if the desire to show an alternative, "opposite" representation to the dominating media discourse and stereotypical ideas about 'the' Muslim woman was originally one of the reasons why Fathima Nizaruddin wanted to make this film.

In a personal interview, Ambarien Alqadar referred to a similar motivation to pluralize the mediated image of Muslim women:

"[…] I think that was the starting point that I used to feel that where are these women that I used to see every day when I go back home from my university? I see these women every day. And it's not that these women are talking about themselves, they, the language they're using is a language that is challenging a lot of the constructions that are happening in the mainstream, let's say the news media, and films, Bollywood films a lot of times would have Muslim women just play very limited roles. So I thought of my documentary practice as a dialogue […], like if there is one voice, there should be many more voices and I thought of my work and still think of my work as one of the many different voices that pluralize an image (personal interview, April 2012)."

In the interview, Ambarien Alqadar stressed her interest in women's "strategies around the everyday" and the various ways in which they challenge the construction of the Muslim woman. It is tempting indeed to understand the girl's loitering without a purpose or "obsessive walking the streets" as an act of resistance or at least a "conscious or contentious act of defiance" against the lack of "spatial solidarity" (Bayat 2000, 540) and inclusion by the men who often deny women access to and equal participation in public spaces. This lack of solidarity and denial is most vividly illustrated in the "The Ghetto Girl" by several interviews with two younger and a middle-aged woman, and even more so by the filmmaker's attempts to capture the gestures and explanations men use to legitimize this denial, for example at a local mosque or tea stall. But as Asef Bayat aptly criticizes, the attempt to challenge the essentialism of such categories as "submissive Muslim women" and stress their agency instead has led many writers to "overestimate and read too much into the acts of the agents" (Bayat 2000: 544). In his view, however, because of the fact that these acts "occur mostly within the prevailing systems of power", the actors "may hardly win any space" from the state or other sources of power, like capital and patriarchy (Bayat 2000, 545). Instead of using the term "resistance", Bayat thus suggests to look at these strategies as "coping strategies" (ibid.).

And yet, exactly because of the fact that regular walks or walking is considered a *routine*, a strategic practice of walking in public spaces and by women who are not encouraged or even prevented from doing so, appears as a potentially powerful practice of change and transformation indeed. In the fourth minute of the film, we hear the director's voiceover saying:

"The girl was in love with loitering on the streets. She felt, this was a safe way to be. That like this, she could stay invisible and yet look at the street. There is a magical quality to walking the streets, she would say, the kind of magic you feel when you do forbidden things."

4 Experimental documentary filmmaking and the problem of form

The exploration of the questions of what it means to be a 'Muslim woman' today in a world dominated by a media-visual regime, and what consequences these stereotypical images have for the sense of self and one's own identity, is also a key theme in Fathima Nizaruddin's 2010 documentary "Talking Heads [muslim women]". Fathima made this film during her M.A. studies at Goldsmiths College in London, but she had the idea behind the film much earlier; she was just unable to realize her ideas until 2010, when she was finally able to secure funding – a very frustrating experience, but one that nevertheless had a silver lining for the director in retrospect, because "by the time I got funding, I had reached a certain maturity, also with regard to the film I had arrived at the kind of film I want to make, my kind of approach" (personal interview, September 2011). Central to her approach is a self-reflexivity that is clearly recognizable in the form, structure and content of her work. It would have felt too easy to make a film that was, in Fathima's own words, purely "positive about Muslim women", because "it has to be both, making an argument, but you need to respect the form also, form has a politics." This statement perfectly encapsulates both theoretical analysis and the professional experience that Fathima gained during her first graduate job at a television news station about which she reflects very critically (personal interview, September 2011):

"Do you really legitimize that form by following that form in the work that you do to counter their content? I think there should be a break in form also. You have to de-legitimize that form itself. You know, and not just say that what they're saying is not correct and this is the correct way" (ibid.).

In an article published towards the end of the 1970s entitled "The Image Mirrored: Reflexivity and the Documentary Film", film scholar Jay Ruby described the (then) new tendency to reflexivity in the documentary in the context of a general cultural turn towards greater (self-)reflexivity. Ruby's observations referred specifically to the North American context in the 1970s and thus one has to question their applicability to non-Western contexts and countries such as India. On the one hand, Arvind Rajagopal argued in a very illuminating discussion with documentary filmmaker Paromita Vohra that the documentary film is a "global form" which – unlike the feature film – cannot be described in the exclusive context of national historical writings (Rajagopal and Vohra 2012, 15). This statement is particularly apt in view of the global growth and densification of media-communicative connectivity over the last thirty years, as well as of the fact that Indian documentary filmmakers not only actively follow international developments, but are also becoming more visible and present with their own films, meaning that their audience is also becoming increasingly global (ibid.; see also Sen and Thakker 2011, 32; Sarkar and Wolf 2012, 1-6). As Sen and Thakker state, this development can generally be supported in the case of South Asia, but it also applies to a degree to the current global interest in 'women documentary filmmakers' from this region, who seek to deal with urban social realities in their films:

> "Documentaries are new Indian art. The consumers are insatiable. [...] A decade ago, film curators, and galleries supporting resident artists from developing economies would have turned to the Middle East in search of city-based films, especially since they challenged the gap between the 'Orient and the Occident' while retaining their unique, urban legacies. In contemporary times, however, it is the summer of South Asian filmmakers, and several documentaries about cities are finding their place in the sun" (Sen and Thakker 2011, 32).

Notwithstanding this observation, it is still important to remember that it was a long and heavily disputed process through which the recent generation of documentary filmmakers in India slowly gained new freedoms during the last decades to explore and experiment with the form of and various processes specific to the documentary film (see Wolf 2002, 107f). The developmentalist understanding of the media in general, regarded first and foremost in newly-founded, postcolonial nation states as a tool for bringing about development, social change and democratization, appears to have been particularly characterized in India by the perception of the media and, indeed, the form of the documentary film, which is largely attributed to the shaping influence of John Grierson and his "displeasure with discussions about aesthetics".[5] For many decades, Rajagopal and Vohra asserted that the only "significant forms" were the "reality-based or agit-prop influenced [forms], that were easily categorized as the political film" (Rajagopal and Vohra 2012, 8).

Although many filmmakers in India have long since departed from the normative concept that "formalist discussions are a luxury which India cannot afford" (Sarkar and Wolf 2012, 4) and that the documentary film must always be "strongly grounded in realism, avoiding the habits of fiction" (Rajagopal and Vohra 2012, 8), this does not mean that the argument is finally over and, more importantly, that the acceptance and support of increasingly experimental, young documentary filmmakers by (national) funding authorities and film critics in India can be taken as a given.

> "Even critics, at least in India, seem to be more reserved when responding to documentaries that foreground an aesthetic or artistic interest. Perhaps they feel that these are less easy to categorize because they do not meet familiar and established codes of the heretofore legitimate documentary aesthetic and require more active, maybe even individual decisions about their political value" (Rajagopal and Vohra 2012, 10).

Fathima Nizaruddin nevertheless speaks about a perceived tendency over the past few decades towards a departure from normative concepts within the youngest generation of documentary filmmakers, who no longer wish to adhere to formal categories and conventions:

> "With the younger generation, I see a shift, doing more things with the form, they want to experiment more – they want to have a break, want to do something new" (personal interview, September 2011).

So far the matter of securing funding and finding institutional support for these new approaches, as well as for the wish to experiment with formal aesthetics, remains one of the greatest hurdles to independent documentary film in India, as vividly described by filmmaker Ambarien Alqadar in the interview:

> "I wonder if there is really funding for that kind of experimental documentary work. There is funding for documentary work which is working in the activist mode because that's how festivals and funders evaluate work, or how funders evaluate proposals. It's in the usefulness of the documentary, how useful it is going to be and in going to change, changing certain things, you know, if it's a powerful documentary, if it's a moving documentary. I mean, what if you do not want to make a moving documentary and you want to do experimental work?" (personal interview, April 2012).[6]

At the same time, the lines between activist and experimental documentary films have become increasingly blurred in recent years, thus leading to sometimes unexpectedly positive decisions concerning the promotion or screening of films in the context of large festivals. Ambarien Alqadar, herself, experienced this with her film "Four Women and a Room" (2008), her first documentary film to be funded and promoted by the Public Service Broadcasting Trust (PSBT), which deals with the "complex ways in which women understand and experience motherhood" and the issue of sex-selective abortions through experimental filmmaking techniques.

Given the lack of sufficient distribution structures for the documentary film in India at present, the fact that the number of documentary film festivals in the country is growing exponentially is vitally important in getting the films out there for the public to see and in being invited to further screenings (see also Waugh 2012, 90ff.). The dialogues and conversations with the audience that are so crucial to directors occur less often at the larger festivals than in less anonymous settings such as private screenings followed by discussions with the audience. Shuddhabrata Sengupta passionately describes an exchange with one audience in India that was very much interested in the documentary film as a medium and in the discussion thereof:

> "We know for certain that documentary films, contrary to the expectations of media pundits, strike chords and touch raw nerves in the consciousness of a generation that is condemned to a low and shifting visual attention span by the same media pundits. We have watched hundreds of people, at a time, immerse themselves in our films and come out with insights and responses. We know now that after each screening, the problem has not been about whether people would say anything but whether people would stop speaking once they got started. [...] Every film is a catalyst for never-ending conversations" (Sengupta 2006, 144).

Conclusion

Twelve years ago (2002), Nicole Wolf found that in the view of the documentary filmmakers she had interviewed, the great promise of the pluralization of audiovisual media through the liberalization of the Indian market had not been fulfilled. Indeed, attempts to establish dedicated documentary film channels have collapsed and although air time was reserved on the public channel *Doordarshan* for independent documentaries and non-commercial films, this is very limited. Securing funding and finding reliable distribution structures are perennial problems for independent filmmakers, above all for those looking to innovate and experiment with form. They are still viewed, as before, with skepticism. In what followed the transitional period of the 1980s and built on a nationalist Hindu ideology, the increasingly market-oriented policy on audiovisual content on public television channels in India favored the "portrayal of a nation comprising a predominantly Hindu, urban middle and upper class" (Wolf 2002, 102). Minorities in religion, caste and class were thus barely visible or plaid underprivileged, stereotypical roles (i.e. the employees in the background) (ibid.).

Today, however, a little more than a decade later, the Indian documentary film landscape continues to develop with exceptional dynamism, despite the fact that fundamental problems like funding and insufficient distribution structures are still very much present. The number of film festivals organized in this vein in the country has also risen, allowing documentary films from India to gain a new global visibility, which in turn makes the industry increasingly interesting and relevant for academic discussion. Contrary to feature films, this discussion is led not just by academic circles, but also by documentary filmmakers themselves, who are often motivated and interested in contributing to and promoting the academic study of the past and present of the documentary film in India. Jay Ruby accurately stated that "both social scientists and documentary filmmakers are interpreters of the world" (Ruby 1977, 10). It is no surprise then that the development of a new research area, Indian Documentary Studies, has also been and continues to be informed to a large degree by highly relevant conversations between filmmakers and academics (see Sen and Thakker 2011; Sarkar and Wolf 2012).

A central question, to which this article contributes discussion at best, but is in no way able to conclusively answer, concerns the terms and interpretations that can be used to represent and analyze these new constitutions of more fluid identities within the academic discussion. At the same time, it is important to understand why, despite misgivings to the contrary, filmmaker Ambarien Alqadar finally decided to work with this term and category. Indeed, there would otherwise be no way of entering into a dialogue defined by the parameters which have thus far framed the discussion, as she argues:

"And again, I used to think and I still think that how valid it is to call my characters 'Muslim women', myself 'Muslim woman', and I think that I do so in the context that I feel that the framing has already been done. I think the framing, and the framing is done in the mainstream media that these are the Muslim women, so the parameters are already set. So how do you then dialogue with these parameters if you're not using that very language? [...] So a lot of us have used the word 'Muslim' in the context of that naming that already happened and it's sometimes as if we were not framed as a minority, perhaps we would not be using the word. But I wonder if it's important then to claim your identity and then say that well it's not just that, it's a much more diverse identity and howsoever you might want to fix us in this term, it is nevertheless a fluid term (personal interview, April 2012)."

Especially following the anti-Muslim pogroms in Gujarat in the spring of 2002, it became an almost moral issue for the director to adopt a position that she had consciously labeled as 'Muslim woman'.

However, as I have proposed in the beginning of this article, instead of trying to understand Ambarien Alqadar and Fathima Nizaruddin's films primarily as 'alternative representations' of 'young Muslim women in the city', I suggest to look at their work and documentary practices – as well as their own biographies – from the perspective of entangled (im)mobilities that so many young women and men who were born the 1980s and 90s have experienced in particular urban localities in Indian cities which have all undergone dramatic changes during the last three decades and this transformative process also informs and shapes their own understanding of documentary forms, their explorations and filmmaking practices.

As regards the new conversations and dialogues with audiences that may or may not be made possible through the numerous new media practices and forms that are currently emerging very strongly, of which experimental and reflexive documentary forms are a particularly incisive and increasingly visible example in India and beyond, I hope that this will be the subject of further analysis and discussion over the coming years.

Bibliography

Films

1. Fathima Nizaruddin
   - Living 'My' Religion (2004)
   - Talking Heads [muslim women] (2010)
   - My Mother's Daughter (2011)
2. Ambarien Alqadar
   - Who Can Speak of Men? (2002)
   - Four Women and a Room (2008)
   - The Ghetto Girl (2012)
3. Mani Ratnam
   - Bombay (1995)
4. Aparna Sen
   - Mr & Mrs Iyer (2002)

Literature

AFTAB, TAHERA. *Inscribing South Asian Muslim Women: an annotated bibliography & research guide,* Leiden: Brill, 2008.

ALI, MD. "13 unauthorized colonies of Jamia Nagar get NOC from ASI". Published online at *TwoCircles.net*: http://twocircles.net/2010nov11/13_unauthorized_colonies_jamia_nagar_get_noc_asi.html#.U9Zru7FaJ30 (last checked 28.07.2014).

ASGHAR ALI, AZRA. *The emergence of feminism among Indian Muslim women,* Pakistan: OUP, 2000.

ASHOK, SOWMIYA and MOHAMMAD ALI. "Housing apartheid flourishes in Delhi". In: *The Hindu.* [online edition] July 8. Available at: http://www.thehindu.com/news/national/article3613994.ece (last checked 14.09.2012), 2012.

ATAULLA, NIGAR. "Indian Muslims and the Media", in: *Countercurrents,* [online] retrieved from: http://www.countercurrents.org/ataulla050607.htm (last checked 24.09.2012), 2007.

ATAULLA, NIGAR. "Muslim Women: The Dangerous Triangle", in: *Countercurrents,* [online] retrieved from: http://www.countercurrents.org/ataulla050808.htm (last checked 24.09.2012), 2007.

BAYAT, ASEF. "From 'Dangerous Classes' to 'Quiet Rebels': Politics of the Urban Subaltern in the Global South". In: *International Sociology,* Vol. 15, No. 3, 533–557, 2000.

CASANOVA, JOSÉ. "Religion, European Secular Identities and European Integration", in: MICHALSKI, KRZYSZTOF (ed.): *Religion in the New Europe,* New York: CEU Press, 23–44, 2006.

GAYER, LAURENT. "Safe and Sound: Searching for a 'Good Environment' in Abul Fazl Enclave, Delhi", in: GAYER, LAURENT; CHRISTOPHE JAFFRELOT (eds.): *Muslims in Indian Cities. Trajectories of Marginalisation*, London: Hurst, 213–236, 2012.

HABERMAS, JÜRGEN. "Die Dialektik der Säkularisierung", in: *Eurozine*, [online] retrieved from: http://www.eurozine.com/articles/2008-04-15-habermas-de.html (last checked 24.09.2012), 2008.

KIDWAI, SABINA. *Images of Muslim women: A study on the representation of Muslim women in the media, 1985–2001*, New Delhi: WISCOMP, 2003.

KIRMANI, NIDA. "Competing constructions of Muslim-ness in the south Delhi neighbourhood of Zakia Nagar". In: *Journal of Muslim Minority Affairs*, Vol 28. No. 3, 355–370, 2008.

KIRMANI, NIDA. "Deconstructing and reconstructing 'Muslim women' through women's narratives". In: *Journal of Gender Studies*, Vol. 18, No. 1, 47–62, 2009.

LAMBERT-HURLEY, SIOBHAN. *Muslim women, reform and princely patronage: Nawab Sultan Jahan Begam of Bhopal*, New York: Routledge, 2007.

MEHTA, SHALINI. "Commodity Culture and Porous Socio-Religious Boundaries: Muslim Women in Delhi". In: *South Asia Research*, Vol. 30, No. 1, 1–24, 2010.

METCALF, BARBARA. *Perfecting Women: Maulana Ashraf Ali Thanawi's Bihishti Zewar: A Partial Translation With Commentary*, Berkely: UCP, 1990.

MINAULT, GAIL. *Secluded scholars: women's education and Muslim social reform in colonial India*, Delhi & New York: OUP, 1998.

PERNAU, MARGRIT. *Bürger mit Turban. Muslime in Delhi im 19. Jh.*, Göttingen: Vandenhoeck & Ruprecht, 2008.

PHADKE, SHILPA, SHILPA RANADE and SAMEERA KHAN. "Why loiter? Radical possibilities for gendered dissent". In: Butcher, Melissa and Selvraj Velayutham (eds.). *Dissent and Cultural Resistance in Asia's Cities*. Routledge: London/New York, 185–203, 2009.

RAJAGOPAL, ARVIND. "Consumer Identity and Image-Based Politics". In: *Economic and Political Weekly*, Vol. 29, No. 27, Juli 2nd, 1994, 1659–1668, 1994.

RAJAGOPAL, ARVIND and PAROMITA VOHRA. "On the Aesthetics and Ideology of the Indian Documentary Film: A Conversation". In: *BioScope: South Asian Screen Studies*, Vol. 3, No. 1, SPECIAL ISSUE: INDIAN DOCUMENTARY STUDIES: CONTOURS OF A FIELD, ed. by Bhaskar Sarkar and Nicole Wolf, 7–20, 2012.

ROBINS, KEVIN. "Beyond Imagined Community? Transnationale Medien und türkische MigrantInnen in Europa". In: HIPFL, BRIGITTE, ELISABETH KLAUS and UTA SCHEER (eds.). *Identitätsräume: Nation, Körper und Geschlecht in den Medien. Eine Topografie*. Bielefeld: transcript, 114–132, 2004.

RUBY, JAMES. "The Image Mirrored: Reflexivity and the Documentary Film". In: *Journal of the University Film Association*, Vol. 29, No. 4, THE DOCUMENTARY IMPULSE: CURRENT ISSUES (Fall 1977), 3–11, 1977.

SARKAR, BHASKAR and NICOLE WOLF. "Editorial". In: *BioScope: South Asian Screen Studies*, Vol. 3, No. 1, SPECIAL ISSUE: INDIAN DOCUMENTARY STUDIES: CONTOURS OF A FIELD, 1–6, 2012.

SCHNEIDER, NADJA-CHRISTINA. "Being young and a 'Muslim Woman' in post-liberalization India: Reflexive Documentary Films as Media Spaces for New Conversations". In: *ASIEN*. SPECIAL ISSUE: Islam, Youth and Gender in India and Pakistan: Current Research Perspectives, ed. by Nadja-Christina Schneider, No. 126 (January 2013), 85–103, 2013.

SEARLE-CHATTERJEE, MARY. "Women, Islam and Nationhood in Hyderabad". In: DAMODARAN, VINITA and MAYA UNNITHAN-KUMAR (Eds.): *Postcolonial India. History, Politics and Culture*, Delhi: Manohar, 145–162, 2000.

SEN, ATREYEE and NEHA RAHEJA THAKKER. "Prostitution, pee-ing, percussion, and possibilities: Contemporary women documentary film-makers and the city in South Asia". In: *South Asian Popular Culture*, Vol, 9. Issue 1, SPECIAL ISSUE: BEYOND BORDERS, 29–42, 2011.

SENGUPTA, SHUDDHABRATA. "The Hum of Conversations". In: MEHROTRA, RAJIV (ed.): *The Open Frame Reader. Unreeling the Documentary Film*, Delhi: Public Service Broadcasting Trust, 142–145, 2006.

SHELLER, MIMI and JOHN URRY. "The new mobilities paradigm". In: *Environment and Planning A 2006*, Vol. 38, 207–226, 2006.

WAUGH, THOMAS. "Miffed! Or 'Gasping for [Polluted?] Air". In: *BioScope: South Asian Screen Studies*, Vol. 3, No. 1, SPECIAL ISSUE: INDIAN DOCUMENTARY STUDIES: CONTOURS OF A FIELD, ed. by Bhaskar Sarkar and Nicole Wolf, 87–93, 2012.

WOLF, NICOLE. "Portraits of Belonging". In: *Frauen und Film*, ed. by Annette Brauerhoch et al., No. 63, March 2002, 99–114, 2000.

---

1   An earlier and differently structured version of this article was published in ASIEN: The German Journal on Contemporary Asia under the title: "Being young and a 'Muslim Woman' in post-liberalization India: Reflexive Documentary Films as Media Spaces for New Conversations". ASIEN 126 (January 2013), 85–103, 2013.

2   Historians like Gail Minault (1998), Barbara Metcalf (1990), Azra Asghar Ali (2000), Siobhan Lambert-Hurley (2007) and Margrit Pernau (2008) – to name but a few – have shown that Muslim women and men alike have constantly strived for new or re-definitions of existing women's rights since the second half of the 19th century. With regard to the contemporary situation, however, Tahera Aftab argues in her groundbreaking bibliography 'Inscribing South Asian Muslim Women' that studies on the situation of Muslim women in South Asia are still scarce. According to Aftab, South Asian Muslim women are generally represented as "oppressed", "backward" and "victims of the double tyranny" of their religion and the specifically South Asian form of patriarchy which is grounded in the "traditional Hindu view of femininity" (Aftab 2008, xxxi).

3   Jamia Nagar, literally 'university town', designates a larger conglomerate of so-called Muslim localities which had originally been built up around the Jamia Millia Islamia University. "Spread over fourteen acres, with approximately 375,000 residents, 90% of whom are thought to be Muslims (the small non-Muslim population is mostly composed of OBCs [author's note: members of the Other Backward Castes] and Dalits], Jamia Nagar constitutes one of the largest concentrations of Muslim populations in Delhi along with Seelampur and Old Delhi. This Muslim population is almost entirely Sunni, although a small Shia population harmoniously coexists with fellow Muslims of Barelvi, Deobandi, Tablighi or Ahl-e-Hadith persuasion" (Gayer 2012, 223; see also Nida Kirmani 2008, 355–370). Of the 20 unauthorized colonies or localities in Jamia Nagar, 13 got authorized in 2010, among them Abul Fazl Enclave, Okhla Vihar and Ghaffar Manzil Extension, while the 7 other colonies are likely to get legalized in the near future, among them Batla House and Zakir Nagar where Ambarien Alqadar's family lives (see Ali 2010).

4   Other film clips in "Living 'My' Religion" are taken from Aparna Sen's film "Mr & Mrs Iyer" (2002).
5   John Grierson's contemporary and joint founder of the National Film Commission in Canada (later: National Film Board, NFB), James Beveridge, spent several years in India and supported the development of a documentary film production unit in Mumbai for the Burmah Shell Corporation. According to his daughter, Nina Beveridge, James produced some forty documentaries in India, between 1954–58, these being filmed up and down the country. She wrote the following about his approach to filmmaking: "After WWII and the formation of UNESCO in 1945, there were concerted efforts to use film as a tool for nation-building around the world. India was defined as one of the key emergent countries, rising out of the ashes of colonialism. Dad applied his Griersonian principles in earnest, helping to shape India's national film board 'The Indian Films Division' following the NFB model. His filmmaking followed similar NFB principles ([online] Available at: <http://www.beevision.com/JAB/father3.shtml> [Accessed September 22, 2012]). At the start of the 1980s, Beveridge was also involved in the development of the A.J.K. Mass Communication Research Centre at the Jamia Millia Islamia University (cf. Rajagopal and Vohra 2012, 9).
6   Aside from a dearth of funding opportunities, Ambarien believes above all that a wider set of spaces and platforms (e.g. art residencies and workshops) is needed where a genuine dialogue on experimental practices can take place.

Kabita Chakraborty

Young people's mobile phone cultures in the urban slums of Kolkata

Introduction

This chapter explores the local mobile phone culture amongst young people in the *bustees* (urban slums) of Kolkata. The context of this study are the rapidly modernizing slum communities of India where both social and economic changes have seen an expansion of mobile phone use by local youth. The chapter presents research data from 2003 to 2013 to show how in this period of time the mobile phone has impacted upon young people's identity and relationships. Drawing on fieldnotes, interview transcripts and other qualitative data, the chapter demonstrates the role mobile phones play in local youth culture. This investigation into mobile phone practices reveals how mobile phones intersect with gendered social, employment and educational changes in the *bustees*, and how mobiles are changing the landscape of romantic relationships. By exploring mobile phone use over this ten year period of time we can see that similar to youth culture around the world, for a select group of young people the mobile has become an ordinary feature of their lives, and plays an important role in everyday communication and leisure. We can also predict a future *bustee* where, with decreasing ownership and maintenance costs, the mobile phone becomes an ordinary part of local youth culture.

The chapter reviews in a linear way how between 2003 and 2013 the mobile has made its way into youth culture. I show how young people's initial relationship with this technology was one of novelty and deeply tied to class. The potential for the phone to impact class mobility was a felt possibility for many early on in my fieldwork. I trace how, with easier access and greater affordability, the mobile has become an ordinary fixture in youth culture.

Bustees are slum communities in India and they often have a history that responds to poverty, but not all *bustees* in India are poor. Around the country *bustees* take different shapes and have different cultures; for example *bustees* can crop up overnight around construction sites or after natural disasters.

These slums may remain for a short period of time, with the state moving on residents by different means. They may become quite permanent, housing generations of dwellers in a tenanted community. The slums in which this research has been conducted are two very dense and largely Muslim populated spaces in the urban city of Kolkata, West Bengal, India. The two slums are side-by-side, and approximately 2.5 sq/km in area with a population of over 300,000. I have written about the fieldsite in depth elsewhere (Chakraborty 2009, Chakraborty 2012). The *bustees* are made up of both established (*pukka*) tenanted and legal residences, and non-established (*jhupri*) squatter communities and the data presented in this chapter draws from participants from both communities. The population is a mostly migrant and displaced Muslim population. Migrants are predominantly from within India, especially Bihar state, thus these are Hindi/Urdu-speaking *bustees*. Intermixed with the majority Muslim population are pockets of Christian and Scheduled Caste/Other Hindus, mostly from migrant backgrounds. The established slums are permanent in nature, with tenanted settlements and populations having access to different permanent infrastructure and political representations, they have a long history in the area, with families able to trace their history over 50 years in the same space. The *jhupri* community is a community which is a mixture of tenanted and untenanted residential communities surrounded by industries. While they have a shorter history in the area, many families have come to the area because of similar reasons as established dwellers, namely as a response to rural poverty from states like Bihar and Odisha. The young people I worked with over 2003–2013 are all Muslim, and both young men and women participated in the study, although my research generally focused on young women's lives. The young people represented in this chapter are between the ages of 14–24 (with some young men up to the age of 25) and mostly unmarried. This age range and marital context represents both cultural and legal understandings of 'youth' (National Youth Policy 2012) and 'child' (UNCRC 1989) in India, thus there is overlapping terminology between child/youth, and young people/girls and boys, throughout the chapter. Between 2003 and 2013 most young women were school going and some participated in home based employment, with the exception of a few young women who had public paid jobs at an NGO, while young men were schooling or at different stages of employment (unemployed, part time, full time and casual). The NGO[1] the young people worked at is the same one I also am affiliated with in the field. In 2013 I obtained reports from this NGO and another one which suggested that young people under the age of 25 make up between 30 to 50 percent of all residents in the slums.

Because of the density of under-25s, these urban slums are an important research site where we can study and understand the mobile phone revolution and how it has been received in local youth culture in India. Many young people in the *bustees* are challenging normative lifecourses typical in the slums and are striving to participate in national social and economic changes. An example of this is young women taking computer lessons to move away from home-based textile work in order to gain a footing in the exploding IT or private banks sectors in Kolkata. In this context "the mobile phone finds pride of place in the media ecosystem of contemporary Indian teenager's [lives]" and Rangaswamy's research reminds us that "youth living in urban slums are no exception" (Rangaswamy and Yamsani 2011, 1). Rangaswamy's ongoing research (Rangaswamy and Cutrell 2012a; Rangaswamy and Nair 2010; Rangaswamy 2009) on mobile phone culture in the urban slums of India has been at the theoretical and methodological forefront of study in the field, but this work is certainly the exception.

Research on young people's relationship with the mobile phone has been lacking across India, probably due to the tremendous expansion of the technology. Mobile phones have gone from being an expensive and elite technology to being a quotidian part of life across many classes and groups in a very short period of time (see Doron and Jeffrey 2013 for a comprehensive overview of the mobile phone in India). This chapter shows how the mobile went from being a unique tool to an ordinary fixture of lower class youth culture in less than 10 years, and in presenting this data the chapter resonates with a global youth culture which has described a similar trend. Research around the world has shown how the mobile phone in many youth communities is now a normative way to communicate, and provides important entertainment, social, educational and economic services (for example Wang 2005, Balakrishnan and Raj 2012, Hameed 2008, Komulainen et al 2010, Ling 2007, Schwittay 2011, Arora 2010, Donner 2008).

Contemporary mobile phone ownership and use amongst young people in the *bustees* is very widespread, particularly in the established *bustees*. The ordinariness of the phone had many young people question why I should study mobile phone use, "why are you so interested in me using the mobile *didi*[2], it is so normal, why don't you study the education change for girls instead, it will be more interesting for the readers" (personal communication 2013, Ruksar, female 20)[3]. Indeed, as the mobile becomes an ordinary part of life, research on mobile phone culture amongst contemporary youth in India results in unoriginal information. For example, Rangaswamy and Cutrell note that youth mobile culture in India "are dominated by mundane, non-instrumental, and entertainment-driven needs" (Rangaswamy and Cutrell 2012a, 51), and data on the subject becomes repetitive quite quickly. However, they remind us that ethnographic study allows us to understand "what drives a specific user population to adopt technologies in particular ways. Clearly there is a link between context and use, and understanding this may be invaluable for development research. Adopting a narrow development lens of technology use may miss the actual engagements and ingenious strategies marginal populations use to integrate technologies into their daily lives" (Rangaswamy and Cutrell 2012a, 51). My own research is situated in youth and childhood studies. I am interested in the nature and significance of children's culture and how young people create their own culture (which is different from the culture created by adults for children). In this chapter I show the use and meanings of the mobile phone in young people's lives, thus mapping how technology is embedded in young people's own unique culture in the slums.

Overall the chapter shows that mobile phones are impacting upon local youth culture. By investigating mobile phone culture amongst youth we see how the mobile has a bearing on romantic relationships and plays a role in class identity for many youth. We also understand how the mobile both strengthens and challenges normative gendered relations in the slums. This nuanced look at mobile phone practice reveals the need for further research in the subject.

Mobile phones in India

The mobile phone revolution resulting in an increase in mobile phone ownership and multifaceted mobile phone praxis is a global one. India is at the cutting edge of this revolution, and is positioned as a rapidly growing market for mobile phone use and consumption. The mobile phone in India is now the most important communication device in the country. Long gone are the days of being placed on the wait list for years in order to get a landline. Kumar and Thomas comment that in India today "many states companies are competing to gain customers and there is no waiting list. Mobile telephone services have become so cheap now that subscriptions have outpaced fixed line connections" (Kumar and Thomas 2006, 297).

According to the Telecom Regulatory Authority of India (TRAI 2014) there are 933 million telephone subscriptions in the country, of which 904 million are mobile phone subscriptions. While this does not mean there are over 900 million unique mobile phone users, the large number does suggest the popularity of the mobile phone for telecommunication. By comparison the latest figures suggest that there are only 28 million unique landlines in India, a majority of which are in urban locales, and one can assume represent mostly business lines (TRAI 2014). Indeed, in the urban slums of Kolkata landlines are not popular; outside of poor infrastructure in the *bustees*, landlines are notoriously expensive and unreliable as they are affected by weather and jumbled wires. The vast majority of mobile phone subscriptions in India are for personal communication (TRAI 2014), but it is not unusual for businesses to use mobile phones as their primary phone connection, and this is particularly true in the *bustees* where small business owners usually only have mobile phones.

In the *bustees* young people who do have mobiles use their phone primarily for personal communication and entertainment. Globally much contemporary research on young people's mobile phone culture is related to the role of the phone in communication and leisure and social media (for example, Lenhart, Purcell, Smith, Zickuhr 2010). More recently the advent of smart phones has widened the scope of use expanding traditional phone and text to include application-rooted communication formats (including popular Skype and Whatsapp applications), service (mobile banking and consumption assistance) and entertainment (including games, video and music). In the slums 3G connectivity is expensive, and smart phones are not the norm. Most young people use 2G phones for communication and entertainment, and this did not change between 2003 and 2013. Although the average cost of ICT in India has fallen steadily (see Doron and Jeffrey 2013, chapter on the Mechanics of the Mobile to understand the importance of the cheap China Mobile, which in the slums is called "*Chinese-model*", on mobile use amongst the poor) smart phones, tablets and personal computers are out of reach for many *bustee* youth. Outside of the budget which is needed to buy these technologies, the upkeep including regular (i.e., 'always on') data and service packages is a big ask, particularly for young women in the urban slums who often do not engage in public paid employment.

When I first started working in these two particular communities in 2003 none of the young people I knew had a mobile phone. At the time I was working with an international NGO and I was conducting a study on violence against children in the two slums (Chakraborty 2003, see also Ennew and Pierre-Plateau 2004). During our focus groups on solutions for reducing violence in the community, the children's helpline 'Childline' was brought up in earnest by participants. This phone hotline was being promoted by civil society as a way for children to get advice and find support for issues such as violence, sexual abuse and mistreatment. I distinctly remember asking a focus group of 20 children who was the best person to contact when facing violence, and them shouting 'we'd call Childline *didi*!' almost in unison. When asked if they have ever called Childline, or knew of friends who used the service, they all responded they had not (Chakraborty 2003).

In 2003 the way most young people used the telephone was through the ISD/STD shop – a landline booth run by local entrepreneurs (see also Doron and Jeffrey 2013). These shops were numerous, and almost every neighbourhood in urban Kolkata had several. The shops were often in very public places, like on the main road. While some had individual phones in small booths inside the shop, it was not uncommon for the phone to be on an open countertop, for the entrepreneur to dial the number for you, and for bystanders to be privy to your conversation. The lack of privacy was just one of the reasons why in 2003 none of the children had any experience with Childline. While phone calls were never prohibitively expensive at the time (unlike in the 1990s), it was a cost that could add up, thus money was another obstacle in use. The phone as a communication device was also limited in 2003 because of who you could call – certainly not friends and family, as they did not have their own phone. Calling businesses, government services and during emergencies calling another ISD/STD booth to contact your family were some occasional uses of the telephone early in my research. Mobile phones did exist, of course, especially amongst some adults in the slums who were more economically secure. They were also part of youth culture – in middle and upper class circles in India (see also Donner et al 2008, Steenson and Donner 2009 for further detail). Thus the mobile was tied deeply to class and age status when I first began working in the slums.

A developing youth mobile culture in the *bustees*: Teaching and sharing

It was only during my doctoral research in 2005 that I became aware of a developing mobile phone culture amongst young people. My fieldnotes reveal a curious youth community, where the phone was 'cool' (or *bindass*). At the early stages of my research mobile phones were a novelty amongst youth. Owning a phone signaled steady employment, a modern sensibility and advanced technological know-how. Afsgar (male, 21) was a tannery worker from the *jhupris* (the less established slum community) and the boyfriend of Rima (female, 17), a young woman who worked closely with me during the research. On the first day he brought the mobile out to show his friends, his phone ownership was met with enthusiasm and excitement. I noted quite a few times in my fieldnotes his role of expert, and the importance of sharing in local mobile phone culture amongst youth.

> Afsgar got a new phone today, a new fancy LG. He came to the centre to see Rima, and he proudly showed me. It was secondhand, it was black and had some kind of radio or something where you can play music and everyone was trying to sort out how that worked. He was so proud, he kept changing the ring tone, it was really shrill, and probably on its loudest setting, and they were really getting a kick out of it. They would watch him and make suggestions about the best ringtone; he would also let them fiddle with it, changing the tones (Fieldnotes, November 2005).

At the time of writing I was conducting participant observation on the roof of a local home. This space was a unique one, which was private and secure. It allowed young people to gather in relative safety to perform multiple desires and identities that are considered to be risky in the slums – for example they were able to try on revealing Western clothes, dance in mixed-sex groups, and develop relationships (see Beazley and Chakraborty 2008, Chakraborty forthcoming). On the roof a Bollywood dance rehearsal was being organized to prepare for a grand show. In this space over 20+ youth gathered throughout the day to participate in a dance subculture that was unique to the community. When Afsgar came up to the roof with his new phone I noted the dance practice was abruptly cut off, so everyone could play with his new mobile.

The rehearsals were stopped as soon as Afsgar took out his phone. First a few boys left their dance partners to see the phone, and the girls followed and soon enough they were all engaged with the phone. Afsgar also showed everyone some game that was on the phone, it was some kind of bouncing ball game, and SQ started playing it and Afsgar was tutoring him on how to win. Everyone was huddled around SQ, and he played for a while, then passed it to Mickey, who also played for a while and passed it to Farhana. Everyone was really enjoying themselves, and they all took reasonably short times to play so everyone had a chance, just like operating the CD player. (Fieldnotes, November 2005).

There were young women on the roof who had mobile phones which they owned previous to the dance rehearsals. On the roof they "disrupted the concept of original and homogeneous culture" (Khan 1998, 464) which expected men to be the masters of technology. Like Afsgar, young women like Layla (female, 20 from the established *bustees*) who owned a mobile passed them around friendship circles and explained to others the phone's features. Girls were also observed teaching their girlfriends how to change the ring tone and screen saver image. Like boys, they preferred popular Bollywood tunes for their phones. Female mobile phone owners visibly enjoyed the attention that they received from other girls.

Both Layla and Afsgar's example points to how sharing is an integral part of local mobile phone youth culture in the slums. Whether you shared your mobile, food, clothing or knowledge, sharing indicates that you are a team player in a communal society which privileges joint family and other communal systems. Sharing is also an important equalizer for youth who are less economically secure. Not sharing indicates a 'selfish' or 'cheap' friend, someone who develops a *badnam* (poor reputation) for being a bad friend. Both Layla and Afsgar were good friends and let friends share in the excitement of their cool mobile phone. Rules around sharing – waiting your turn, taking a short time to play with the phone before giving it to someone waiting, and being extra careful with someone else's things – were already established before Layla and Afsgar brought their mobile to the roof.

Sharing one's mobile phone is a practice which scholars have described in youth culture around the world (Walton et al 2012 for example in South Africa). In other parts of India mobile phone sharing amongst youth is also a critical part of group membership. Steenson and Donner (2009) describe how during the early days of mobile ownership amongst middle class youth, the mobile phone was shared between younger and older members of a family, as well as amongst friendship groups (see also Schwittay 2011 and Donner et al 2008). They show an example of distributed sharing, where parents trying to reach their daughter by calling the mobile of her friends. Steenson and Donner describe the rules of this sharing in this example; namely friends must agree to pass the phone onto the child and the daughter must be physically present with her friends during the phone call (Steenson and Donner 2009, 235). In their qualitative research on (mostly) young men's participation on the Indian mobile text communication site Gupshup, Rangaswamy and Cutrell (2012b) found that young people shared hacks and tips with other members of the site for fun as "a useful, feel-good, service-oriented activity" (604). In the *bustees* young people with phones saw their role within the peer group to be that of a technological expert and thus they had a duty to educate their peers. On the roof other forms of technology, such as a CD player, also existed and in my fieldnotes I recount how young people all took turns to operate the player, and patiently taught newcomers how to work the system by giving them time to practice on different days. While no formal schedule was in place, young people made room for all of their peers to have a chance to operate the system.

With ownership of a mobile phone both Layla and Afsgar's role on the roof was that of an expert. Indeed Layla (female, 20, 2006) once confessed to me that she felt like a "mobile phone expert on the roof". Layla's new sense of expertise emerged as a result of the third space of the roof, a claim supported by Bhabha who argues, "once it [the third space] opens up, we are in a different space, we are making different presumptions and mobilising emergent, unanticipated forms of historical agency" (Bhabha 1995 in an interview with Mitchell, 114). While theoretically we can see a unique mobile phone culture develop amongst youth on the roof, as we will see later in the chapter, with the expansion of the technology Bhabha's third space no longer provides a sufficient framework for young people's mobile phone practices. In 2005 mobile phones were not affordable for most young people. Only after the popularity of the *Chinese-model*, a cheap, made-in-China no frills/no warranty phone which would become the staple of youth culture just one year after my initial fieldwork – did the mobile make the transition from a unique technology to an ordinary feature in youth communication and leisure. But in 2005, when I first began doctoral work, the phone was expensive. In 2005 I asked Afsgar about his phone and he shared with me his pride in being the expert and the conditions of consumption: "I worked really hard to save for the mobile. I worked for the last 5 months just to save up for it and when I look at it, yeah, I feel pride that I did this (buy the phone). Of course I am proud, but not in an arrogant way…you know because I am learning new things, new technology, I want to also learn the computer and share with my friends this knowledge". This conversation with Afsgar reveals how, at the time, ICT was very expensive, and young people had to save for months before buying a phone. Afsgar also saw that his phone opened doors to other ICTs and the possibility of greater participation in a connected India. His hope that the mobile phone was the beginning of a journey towards a more technology savvy lifecourse was also shared by others.

The mobile phone as a gateway technology

Afsgar's desire to use the mobile as a gateway to other technologies is an important observation as it points to young people's hope to use technology to improve their lives. For Afsgar technologies "help you to learn so you can work in an office", which he believed might be a possibility "not now, but maybe for later?" (personal interview, February 2006). I understand this aspect of modern history to be very important in capturing the spirit of the mobile phone in India. For young people in the *bustees* in 2005 the mobile phone was seen as a gateway to greater things. It represented a coveted technology which was new and modern and something that young people felt would have the potential to change their employment possibilities in the future. Like the personal computer, the mobile at the time was viewed as a ticket to upward mobility, as Rima stated in 2005, "I want to learn the computer so we can work in an office" (Rima, female, 17). By 2013 no young man I knew of had made the transition from "learning the mobile" to "learning the computer" to "working in an office". However, many young men did use technology in their small business ventures (small to medium enterprises or SMEs).

Young men's relationship with the mobile phone as a gateway technology in the slums is the small and medium enterprises (SME) connection. Almost all of the young men I knew at the beginning of my doctoral fieldwork were working in labour oriented fields such as the tanning, textile and transportation industry. In 2013 several young men did work in the IT arena through their SMEs. One known male participant opened up his own small shop where old personal computers were equipped with computer games, for example. For a few rupees local children would come to the game shop a couple of times a week to play. Doron's 2012 exploration of the exploding small business of mobile phone repair and care in North India shows how poor Indians are learning skills to supply a demanding secondhand phone market catering to poor and excluded populations. In their 2013 publication *The Great Indian Phone Book*, Doron and Jeffrey note that since the *Chinese-model* had no warranties, mobile repair was often sought (see Chapter Mechanics of the Mobile). A few young men in the *bustees* were actively involved in these economies of care and repair. Some boys had side-businesses where mobile phone accessories including mobile cases, batteries and plugs were sold to locals, while others were learning to repair mobile phones. These latter examples represent extracurricular work where young men were employed in the day and earned extra money with mobile-centred SMEs after work. With affordable secondhand phones poor Indians are able to engage in a globalizing India which often excludes them. While the secondhand phone industry allows the poor to communicate across borders, they often cannot participate in a contemporary consumer culture where newer and faster mobiles are privileged. Thus while they are participating in a modernizing India, their phone ownership keeps them "at a certain distance from the forms and symbolic capital of the new economy" (Doron 2012, 563).

Like young men, young women in 2005 hoped the mobile phone would act as a gateway to other employment possibilities. The desire to learn technology was made clear during focus groups and mapping exercises I conducted with young women. All of the girls I worked with dreamed of entering the paid workforce, and technology played an important role in this vision, like Putul (female, 14) who told me she wanted to "work with the computers for an airline and be an air stewardess and travel". In 2005 the opportunities to "learn the computer" were limited in the slums. Computer classes were not a guarantee at local poorly resourced public and private schools. The digital literacy gap at the time was slowly being filled by NGOs and other civil society organizations. By 2011 there were several popular, and free, computer centres in or close to the *bustees*. I have written about young women's participation in these computer centers and in internet cafes elsewhere (Chakraborty 2012). During my 2011 fieldwork it was obvious that these centres were used by primarily young women who were eager to learn computer skills and it was common to have entire classes made up of female students. While young men I spoke with at the time were also keen to learn computer skills, many were working during the day, when most of the young women were at school. Computer centres were a natural extension of young women's schooling and tuition routine, and this was one reason why more young women participated in these classes. But young women also felt that young men were not as interested in further learning, and some commented that young men in the community were, educationally, falling behind the girls (see Chakraborty 2012).

The relationship between the mobile phone and computers in 2005 was strong; like young men many young women saw the phone as a technology that was useful to learn to prepare for the future. Layla (female, 21), for example, was one of the few young women at the time working in a paid public position at one of the local NGOs. She had a mobile phone and she once explained to me that she was "very good at sending SMS, faster than anyone at the office". She told me that when she first got her mobile she was not that fast, but using the phone a lot to text her boyfriend and "typing on the computer everyday also helps". At her job she was responsible for typing reports about school outcomes. While these two typing methods were very different, they complimented each other and for Layla practicing both on the keyboard and the mobile phone allowed her to become very fast at sending SMSs. While not many young women made the transition from 'learning the mobile' into white-collar public employment, it was obvious that by 2013 there were more young women working in the NGO offices and the library centre than local boys. In fact, all of the newly hired youth outreach workers who were responsible for coordinating schooling and entering data at the NGO were young women. While it would be inaccurate to claim that young women are successfully making roads into more technologically-centred work compared to boys, evidence from the two slums suggests that young women's technological literacy was at a greater level than boys' as a result of computer classes, and that there is potential for young women to make the leap into public paid technical work in the future. However it remains to be seen if they are able to gain this work outside of the *bustees* itself.

Money matters

Because of the purchasing power one needed to buy and operate the phone, fewer young women had mobiles in my early research compared to young men. In 2005 paid public work was not the norm for young women; indeed very few women I knew worked in public, and those who did, like Layla, worked for the local NGO where I also worked. The culture of *purdah* which operates in more conservative Muslim spaces in Kolkata including the slums sees the separation of men and women, particularly in public places. One of the comments I get from people visiting the *bustees* is that "there are hardly any women to be seen". Maintaining *purdah* means that public roads and larger public spaces such as tea stalls and shops are used by men while women occupy more private spaces (homes, back alleyways) or use the *burqa* to maintain a separation between men. In the *bustees* public work often pays considerably more than private work, but such employment was fraught with accusations of being too modern or of loose character (see Chakraborty forthcoming, also Rajan, Dhanraj, Lalita 2011) and public work by women very much challenges the *purdah* culture of the slums. This did not mean young women did not work, rather they often helped their own mothers and aunts with their home-based employment, which was fitted between schooling, tuition and home care responsibilities. Cutting shoe soles, applying embroidery to fabric, setting leather decals for shoes are some examples of in-home paid work. The pay in 2005 was minimal, with some young women receiving 30 rupees a day for their work, about $1 USD at the time. By 2013 the pay had increased to almost 100 rupees (about EUR 1,23), which was still minimal compared to more lucrative public fields such as rag picking where families make tens of thousands of rupees a month. Thus in 2005 how young women got money to buy phones was a predicament, but there were a few young women who did have mobile phones at the time. Layla had bought her own secondhand mobile through her paid work at the NGO. Dalia's (female, 18) strategy involved gathering money from multiple avenues including her boyfriend and money she had saved in other ways, such as not spending pocket money, part time home-based work and saving money she received during festivals to buy her secondhand Nokia phone.

By 2013 most of the young women I worked with had secondhand mobiles which they bought themselves, were gifted, or were hand-me-downs from other family members. The prices of mobile phones dropped considerably since I began my fieldwork. Currently in the *bustees* you can get a secondhand 2G mobile for under Rs 500 (about $8 or EUR 6,00), a far cry from the hundred (indeed thousands) of rupees for a secondhand phone needed a decade ago. In contrast to the phone ownership price, phone operation between the time I started my fieldwork and my most recent fieldwork did not change at all. Pay-as-you-go recharging was the norm for all young people, even those with full time permanent employment. Prepaid recharge vouchers are as little as Rs. 10 ($0,16 or EUR 0,12) and different vouchers exist – including vouchers specializing in texting only, data only and talk time only. With affordable plans and a litany of secondhand phone options mobiles are becoming an important part of the everyday lives of young people in the slums.

To be clear what has not materialized since arriving in the community in 2003 is the link between the mobile phone, learning the computer and more white-collar working opportunities that people envisioned some years ago, particularly for young men. Instead of preparing youth for future careers in offices and banks the mobile has become an ordinary feature of communication and entertainment. But we do see some gendered change: young men have been able to carve out new SMEs businesses by dealing with mobile and technology games, accessories and economies of care and repair (see Doron's 2012 discussion of repair culture in Banaras). For young women I see that the mobile phone is helping parents stay in touch with their female children as they extend their schooling career. This constant contact has tried to reduce the insecurity of parents who are worried for their daughters' safety when they are outdoors. But it has also brought on another set of issues, with parents worried that girls are not "misusing their schooling freedoms…and the mobile" (mother of a participant) to develop romances. We can thus see that Muslim gendered practices of mobility for young women are being influenced by the mobile phone. Since the mobile allows parents to reduce their own anxiety of having daughters in public participating in schooling and other tasks, the phone may be playing a role in giving parents the confidence to send young women into the public world of work, but more research on this is required. There has been a very slow shift within the slums of accepting female public employment, especially within the social service sector like NGOs and teaching, and further research is needed into how the mobile phone is feeding this acceptance of female public employment, particular amongst more middle class residents in the *bustees*.

In 2013 the daily mobile phone practices of young women were predictably ordinary: lots of text messaging and missed calling (see Donner 2007 for a detailed analysis of missed-phone culture around the world), music playing and game playing (see Rangaswamy and Cutrell 2012a for greater detail). The ordinariness of the mobile meant that for most youth the mobile was expected in day-to-day practice – whether providing the number at schooling registration, or sending a text to a boyfriend, or miss-calling your parents if you were going to be home late – the mobile phone is now imbedded in everyday life. However it is important to note that these phones are not smart phones. Since phones were mostly 2G and operating on a prepaid basis, Internet on mobile phones was not very popular, and I have discussed elsewhere how young people access the Internet in different ways (Chakraborty 2012). The cost of internet access on the phone was the major barrier for most young people. Like Rangaswamy and Cutrell (2012a) have described in their research in the slums of Hyderabad, when young people in the *bustees* use mobile Internet, they do so opportunistically.

For mobile Internet a large enough data recharge voucher was required. Large carriers offer different plans including data only packages that last for a certain amount of time. At the time of writing, Airtel, for example, offered a 75MB data plan which lasted three days for Rs. 18 ($0,30 or EUR 0,22). Both young men and young women determined how much recharge they could afford based on their current economic conditions and their needs. The more extra spending cash often meant larger recharge vouchers which saw young people downloading games or Bollywood music videos and songs. But most young people did not take to mobile Internet, "to me it's not worth it, it is cheaper to just spend Rs. 20 at the cyber café and chat and watch videos for an entire hour with all my friends on a big screen than using the mobile' (Ruksar, female, 20, 2011). To circumvent costs, young people used services like yahoo chat on mobile or Gupshup – rather than chatting online for example – to participate in activities that were more suited to 3G and 'always on' data systems.

Class and status

Young people's savviness to circumvent expensive data and phone plans, and their reliance on pay-as-you-go operation points to the still obvious consideration of cost in mobile phone operation. While costs are a contemporary consideration, monetary negotiations should not be confused as relational to poor class status. In India the prepaid recharge is the most popular way to use the mobile amongst every class group (see for example Rangaswamy and Yamsani 2011, 6). This is not to say that the mobile in the *bustees* does not have class links; when I began my fieldwork the mobile phone was tied deeply to class identity, aligning closely to a middle class lifestyle. In 2005 the link between class identity and the mobile phone was very prominent. An example that stands out to me was from my own fieldwork when I had first lent my mobile to a *tana* (rickshaw) puller, who was a poor older man from the slums. I noted in my journal that local boys began to tease him when he spoke on the phone, with some shouting *"dhek dhek tanawala mobile* use!!"[4] and *"mobile theek se rakna"*[5]. This incident in particular reminds us that in 2005 the mobile phone was considered to be very much related to class membership. For a poor old *tana* uncle to have the privilege to participate in a culture which in fact excluded local boys was met with feelings of both jealousy and exclusion by youth. Recalling this incident I also am reminded that *tana* uncle was very pleased with himself when talking on the mobile, smiling to me and thanking me for the mobile upon returning it.

This example depicts some important class demarcations that exist in the slums. While dominant public discourses suggest that the slums are an urban poor neighbourhood, it is not a uniform space (see for example Davis' Introduction chapter in *Planet of Slums* 2007). A majority of the population do struggle to accumulate savings, there were many families in the established community that were comfortably middle class, which according to the NGO in 2013 meant a family income of Rs.10,000 or more. In terms of his status, age and occupation the old rickshaw puller who was taking me to the centre was very poor and of the lowest class. Seeing him use the mobile phone resulted in taunting by young men who felt his status was not high enough to be able to use the mobile phone. While the young men were probably themselves unemployed, the way I read this incident is that the teasers felt they had more ownership and expertise over the technology than the driver had. The young men might have even felt a little jealous that the driver was being trusted with the mobile, while they were not. When I gave the puller the mobile I saw his facial expression change from concern over not being able to find the destination, to pride. I read this expression as being trusted to use the phone and sheer excitement in using a technology which at the time in the *bustees* was not common.

The mobile phone in contemporary youth culture in the slums has different class roots than that presented when I first started my fieldwork. My most recent fieldwork in 2013 revealed that owning a phone in itself is no longer 'cool' but that the 'cool' factor is now increasingly aligned with global consumer culture (Doron 2012). In 2005 there was definitely the sense amongst youth that mobiles are aligned with a particular class and because of costs any old phone would do, because the cost of even a secondhand phone was prohibitive for most youth. With the decreasing prices, and greater technological knowledge, young people currently participate in sustaining a hierarchy of cultural consumption based on brands. Namely in the *bustees* Samsung is better than Nokia and Sony, which are better than *Chinese-model*. I do not wish to imply that brand awareness was nonexistent earlier on; in conversations with young women in 2005 I knew branding was important: "the mobile of Akshay Kumar in *Aitraaz* is the latest. The flip? That is one I think all the boys are dreaming about (laughs)" (Mumtaz, female, 15). However, the costs of the phones kept youth from participating in a larger consumption culture which favoured some brands over others. In 2013 young people could purchase the best brand, a secondhand 2G Samsung, at a reasonable cost. For youth, the class consciousness has moved away from being middle class just by owning a phone, to being more middle class based on the kind of phone you had, such as a smart phone (which is referred to in 2013 as *touch* in local lingo).

Currently in the slums there is a wealth of knowledge about mobile phones and branding that just did not exist in 2005. Young women were able to explain phone features and specifications to me, and they advised me on my own phone purchase as well. During my 2013 research I asked several young women about purchasing a new fieldwork phone. Reena, a 16 year old girl from a conservative household, advised me during an interview,

> "*Didi* you should get the new Samsung mobile; it looks just like a TAB (tablet), it is *touch* it can take two SIMs, very *hifi*… and the sound quality is very good for music, much better than the LG, but the LG is good for rough use, so you need to think where you will use it first before buying. For here in the *bustee* get the LG because *phonemaar* is common and you would feel so upset if someone took it."

Reena taught me the differences between the Samsung and LG phone and described the features of both phones; she also explained to me that there was a culture of phone theft – particularly of branded phones (*phonemaar*) and that as a result I should get a phone which was not too fancy (*hifi*) and would be the target of theft. When I got the new LG phone she also showed me how to find popular ring tones and make them work, including the dual SIM which she explained was good to have two mobile numbers and different phone plans. She herself had a secondhand LG phone and was not looking for a new phone, and more importantly, she had never seen the new Samsung phone to which she is referring to, making her knowledge on the subject even more impressive. I asked her how she knew all these details without even seeing the new Samsung phone in real life, she explained,

"Everyone just shares their opinion, I hear my brother advising of phones, my friends and boyfriend too, in films like *Chennai Express* they share the details of some phones, and all the ads share the details, about speakers and quality and so on, so I just put it all together (laughs). But based on my own experience with the LG it is why I recommend that one to you".

Youth in the slums, like young people in Rangaswamy and Cutrell's (2012a) research, obtain their knowledge of new mobile phone technologies by piecemealing information gathered from different sources. Bollywood popular culture and television and print advertising play an important role in educating young people about phone specifications, particularly about items young people have had little interaction with. Peer groups and other elders in the community were another source of knowledge, and young men also spent time asking phone shop owner's questions and gathered information in that way as well. Another important source of mobile phone knowledge for young women in particular, as Reena mentions, was boyfriends.

The mobile phone and romantic relationships

While socially unacceptable in *bustee* culture, many young women in the community did have boyfriends. Young women pursued their clandestine romances with a great deal of tension because of the *haram* (forbidden) nature of premarital mixed-sex interactions in local culture. The risks of getting caught weighed heavily on young women, as they were under greater threat of violence, slander and mistreatment by their family and community if caught. Young men in the *bustees* were able to benefit from a double standard of sexual morality which saw young women bear the brunt of social repercussions of being caught in mixed-sex relationships (see Chakraborty 2010a, 2010b). However, in 2005 it was apparent that young women who did not pursue part time work often were able to obtain a secondhand phone from within their relationships. To be clear, a 'good boyfriend' was always thought of as a respectable young man who treated young women nicely and gave gifts such as *showpiece* (a knick-knack), but in 2005 discourses of a 'good boyfriend' began to include the mobile phone, either as a giver of a mobile, or as a boyfriend who answered their phone and made time to talk, or one who gave recharge vouchers to ensure communication. By 2013, with most youth able to access a mobile phone of some kind, recharge vouchers were a very well received gift within relationships. Mobiles are also strongly featuring in dowry discussions. *Hifi* and *touch* mobiles and TAB (tablets) are currently being requested along with other indicators of status including motorbikes in dowry negotiations.

The mobile phone has impacted clandestine romantic relationships in very complicated ways. Since most romantic relationships are secret, young women in particular were very protective of their mobiles because they could provide evidence of a relationship. Reyhana (female, 17) explained to me in my 2013 fieldwork how she deleted text messages to ensure that if her phone was found by her dad, her relationship would not be revealed. "I keep his name as 'Noori' on the phone so it looks like all the missed calls are from a girl, but the SMS is deleted if they are romantic in nature, that will be too suspicious if kept". Other young women also employed similar strategies as Reyhana, using female names in their address book to not cause suspicion, deleting romantic text messages that were obviously from a suitor, and placing a passcode to ensure the phone could not be opened by just anyone. The passcode, however, was not always possible for some young women, "I just delete everything because my parents said that if I have a mobile, then they must know the passcode as my mother also shares use of the phone, so I cannot keep a passcode secret" (Mina, female, 18).

The mobile allowed young people to communicate at different times throughout the day with their boyfriends. This was not always possible in pre-mobile phone days, and for some this increased the intimacy in relationships (see also Donner et al 2008 for a similar discussion in middle class Bangalore). In 2013, Aysa, a married female participant who I have known since 2003, explained to me how the mobile impacted her romantic life:

"Oh I remember when we used to meet before the mobile (laughs) he sent his cousin to call for me or to pass me letters…I would long for our meet ups, but then once I had my mobile we would talk everyday and it was even easier to fight, Allah what fights! I used to ignore his calls and this would make the fights even bigger, nothing has changed in married life in that way!! (laughs)" (Aysa, female, 24).

Young people's ability to contact their romantic partner throughout the day has changed the way courtship and dating progress in the slums. I have detailed romantic and dating processes in the *bustees* elsewhere (Chakraborty 2010a), but briefly, before the mobile phone young men used to approach young women who were on their way to school or through other means. During the courting phase love letters were often passed through mutual friends or young family members by both parties, and arrangement for meeting in person was a preoccupation for most. Obtaining mobile phones has replaced the need for letter exchanges, but some still do exchange letters from time-to-time. For example, Nargis is a local young woman whose partner was someone she met when she was with the NGO on a long-distance fieldtrip. As he was not from the local community, frequent meeting up was not possible, but phone calls and text messages were ongoing. When they did meet up they often exchanged letters and cards and gifts, while the mobile was used to keep tabs on each other on a pretty regular basis. For Nargis the mobile was very useful to catch up but she did not spend hours on the phone with him. She explained to me in 2013: "you can't just say everything from your heart on the mobile all the time…it is not like you can talk for 3 hours so for your deep heart feelings to come out you need time and really long thinking and contemplation, so for that he writes me letters and I write him letters and when we meet we exchange…not always but sometimes" (Nargis, female, 20). Nargis reminds us that mobile phones are not used by youth in the slums for long communication. Here we see how costs impact on young people's mobile culture; Nargis sent missed calls and text messages to communicate, while long drawn conversations were done face-to-face. However, to Nargis the mobile does add to the intimacy of the relationship, "at least in this way I know how he is, if he has eaten, he can also check how I am…it makes you grow your caring feelings when you don't see them". In this way data in the slums is similar to other research in middle class communities in India where the mobile phone is used to increase intimacy in a relationship (see for example Donner et al. 2008, 330), even if in middle class communities partners are able to speak for more extended periods of time.

The ready access to one's partner in the slums as a result of the mobile phone has been convenient for some, as Nargis described in the above example. However, with this ready access came another set of problems, as described by Reyhana in 2013:

"With the mobile now it is constantly checking, calling and checking where you are, checking who you are with, checking what you are doing. One night I received over 20 missed calls from him, and about the same number of SMS... it is too much" (Reyhana, female, 17).

Reyhana's description of the flipside of convenient communication reveals how the mobile phone is rooted in a patriarchal *bustee* culture for many young women. The ability of the mobile to keep track of one's romantic interest has facilitated a culture of monitoring young women's mobilities by men in particular. In this way the mobile has not necessarily challenged normative gender roles in the community but can support existing patriarchal cultural practices. The mobile has, however, been able to disrupt the normative discourses that men are experts in technology. We see in the slums that the mobile phone has been able to uplift the status of young people – both male and female – as technological experts, while community elders are seen as populations that are falling behind in their knowledge of modern technology. This latter trend is similar to findings in global youth culture worldwide (Schwittay 2011, Ling 2007, Livingstone 2002).

Conclusion

This chapter very modestly reviewed the mobile phone cultures of some youth living in the urban slums of Kolkata. Overall this review of the role of the mobile phone in the *bustees* reveals a changing youth culture where the mobile is an important tool. While only 10 years separate my contemporary research findings from my first set of research data, this review shows the ease at which mobiles are now a part of normal life for youth. The role that the mobile is playing in destabilizing the normative construction of a good Muslim girl as being homely and *purdah*-observing to being a well-educated public-working citizen has been briefly discussed, as has how the mobile retains patriarchal power within romantic relationships. The social roles and responsibility of mobile ownership amongst youth has been explored, and I have also shown how the desire for upward mobility amongst *bustee* youth is deeply tied to the idea that 'technology' will be the ticket towards greater socio-economic status. While it is easy to take for granted the role of mobiles in communication and leisure in contemporary youth culture, it is important to explore and understand the specific local history of technology. How the mobile phone went from being a middle class and male dominated technology in the slums to an ordinary part of youth culture for both young women and men mirrors gendered, economic and social changes occurring nationwide. These changes have seen more young women in the slums taking up graduate level schooling and white-collar employment compared to men, for example. It is crucial that we understand the history of the mobile phone evolution to make sense of the future of youth culture in the slums, and to develop a contemporary theoretical framework which helps to explain youth cultural changes in urban poor communities in India.

Bibliography

ARORA, P. "Online Social Sites as Virtual Parks: An Investigation into Leisure Online and Offline." *The Information Society* 27, no.2 (2010):113–120.

BALAKRISHNAN, V and R.G RAJ. "Exploring the relationship between urbanized Malaysian youth and their mobile phones: A quantitative approach." *Telematics and Informatics* 29, no.3 (2012): 263–272.

BEAZLEY, H. and K.CHAKRABORTY. "Cool Consumption: Rasta, Punk and Bollywood on the Streets of Yogyakarta, Indonesia and Kolkata, India." In *Youth, Media and Culture in the Asia Pacific Region,* edited by U. M. Rodrigues and B. Smaill, 195–214. Newcastle UK: Cambridge Scholars Publishing, 2008.

BHABHA, H. "An interview with Homi Bhabha by J. Mitchell." *Artforum* 33, no.7 (1995): 80–84.

CHAKRABORTY, K. *Young Muslim Women in India: Bollywood, Identity and Changing Lives*. London: Routledge (Women in Asia Series), forthcoming.

CHAKRABORTY, K. "Virtual Mate-Seeking in the Urban Slums of Kolkata, India." *South Asian Popular Culture* 10, no.2 (2012): 197–216.

CHAKRABORTY, K. "Unmarried Muslim Youth and Sex Education in the *bustees* of Kolkata." *South Asian History and Culture* 1, no.2 (2010a): 268–281.

CHAKRABORTY, K. "The Sexual Lives of Muslim Girls in the *bustees* of Kolkata, India." *Sex Education* 10, no.1 (2010b): 1–21.

CHAKRABORTY, K. "'The Good Muslim Girl': Conducting Qualitative Participatory Research to Understand the Lives of Young Muslim Women in the *bustees* of Kolkata." *Children's Geographies* 7, no.4 (2009): 421–434.

CHAKRABORTY, K. *Violence against Children in Three Slum Communities in Kolkata: A Comparative Study*. Kolkata: Save the Children UK (Print), 2003.

DAVIS, M. *Planet of Slums*. London: Verso, 2007.

DONNER, J. "Research Approaches to Mobile Use in the Developing World: A Review of the Literature." *The Information Society* 24, no.3 (2008): 140–159.

DONNER, J. "The Rules of Beeping: Exchanging Messages via Intentional 'Missed Calls' on Mobile Phones." *Journal of Computer-Mediated Communication* 13, no.1 (2007): 1–22.

DONNER, J, N. RANGASWAMY, M. STEENSON and C. WEI. "'Express Yourself' and 'Stay Together': The Middle-Class Indian Family." In *Handbook of Mobile Communication Studies*, edited by J. Katz, 325–338. Massachusetts: MIT, 2008.

DORON, A. "Consumption, Technology and Adaptation: Care and Repair Economies of Mobile Phones in North India." *Pacific Affairs* 85, no.3 (2012): 563–585.

DORON, A. and R. JEFFREY. *The Great Indian Phone Book. How the Cheap Cell Phone Changes Business, Politics, and Daily Life*. Cambridge, Mass.: Harvard University Press, 2013.

ENNEW, J and D. PIERRE-PLATEAU. *How to research the physical and emotional punishment of children*. International Save the Children Alliance: Bangkok (Print), 2004.

HAMEED, S.S. "The Effects of Mobile Telephony on Singaporean Society". In *Handbook of Mobile Communication Studies*, edited by J. Katz, 285–298. Massachusetts: MIT, 2008.

KHAN, S. "Muslim Women: Negotiations in the Third Space." *Signs* 23, no.2 (1998): 463–94.

KOMULAINEN, S., M. KARUKKA and J. HAKKILA. "Social music services in teenage life: a case study." *Proceedings of the 22nd Conference of the Computer-Human Interaction Special Interest Group of Australia on Computer-Human Interaction*, 2010. Accessed at http://dl.acm.org/citation.cfm?id=1952303.

KUMAR, K and A.THOMAS. "Telecommunications and Development: The Cellular Mobile 'Revolution' in India and China." *Journal of Creative Communications* 1, no.3 (2006): 297–309.

LENHART A., K. PURCELL, A. SMITH, and K. ZICKUHR. Social Media and Mobile Internet Use Among Teens and Adults. Pew Research Center Publications 2010. Accessed at: http://pewinternet.org/;/media//Files/Reports/2010/PIP_Social_Media_and_Young_ Adults_Report_Final_ with_toplines.pdf

LING, R. "Children, Youth and Mobile Communication." *Journal of Children and Media* 1, no.1 (2007): 60–67.

LIVINGSTONE, S. *Young People and New Media* London: Sage, 2002.

National Youth Policy. Press Information Bureau, Government of India, 2012. Accessed at http://pib.nic.in/newsite/erelease.aspx?relid=84622.

RANGASWAMY, N and E. CUTRELL. "Anthropology, Development and ICTs: Slums, Youth and the Mobile Internet in Urban India." *Information Technology and International Development* 9, no.2 (2012a): 51–63.

RANGASWAMY, N and E. CUTRELL. "Re-Sourceful Networks: Notes from a Mobile Social Networking Platform in India." *Pacific Affairs* 85, no.3 (2012b): 587–606.

RANGASWAMY, N and S. NAIR. "The PC in an Indian Urban Slum: Enterprise and Entrepreneurship in ICT4D 2.0." *Journal of Information Technology for Development* 18, no.2 (2012): 163–180.

RANGASWAMY, N and S. YAMSANI. "'Mental Kartha Hai' or Its Blowing my Mind: Evolution of the Mobile Internet in an Indian Slum." *Microsoft research*, 2011. Accessed at http://research.microsoft.com/en-us/people/nimmir/mobileinternet_teens_ urbanslum_india__final.doc.

Rangaswamy, N. and S. Nair. "The Mobile Phone Store Ecology in a Mumbai Slum Community: Hybrid Networks for Enterprise." *Information technology and International Development* 6, no.3 (2010): 51–65.

Rangaswamy, N. "The non-formal business of cyber cafes: a case-study from India." *Journal of Information, Communication and Ethics in Society* 7, no.2/3 (2009): 136–145.

Rajan, D., D. Dhanraj and K. Lalita. "'Bahar Nikalna': Muslim women negotiate post-conflict life." *Inter-Asia Cultural Studies* 12, no.2 (2011): 213–224.

Schwittay, A. "New Media Practices in India: Bridging Past and Future Markets and Development." *International Journal of Communication* 5 (2011): 349–79.

Steenson, M. and J. Donner. "Beyond the personal and private: Modes of mobile phone sharing in urban India." In *The Reconstruction of Space and Time: Mobile Communication Practices*, edited by S.W Campbell and R Ling, 231–250. New Jersey: Transaction Publishers, 2009.

TRAI. Telecom Regulatory Authority of India. 2014. Telecom subscription data as on May 31, 2014. Accessed at http://www.trai.gov.in/WriteReadData/WhatsNew/Documents/PR-TSD-May,%2014.pdf.

UNCRC. 1989. United Nations Convention on the Rights of the Child, G.A. res. 44/25, annex, 44 U.N. GAOR Supp. (No. 49) at 167, U.N. Doc. A/44/49 (1989), entered into force September 2 1990. /C/93/Add.5 of 16 July 2003.

Walton, M, G. Marsden, S. Habreiter and S. Allen. "Degrees of sharing: promixate media sharing and messaging by young people in Khayeltsha." *Proceedings of the 14th international conference on human-computer integration with mobile devices and services*, Mobile HCI '12. New York, NY, 2012. Accessed at http://dl.acm.org/citation.cfm?id=2371636.

Wang, J. "Youth Culture, Music, and Cell phone Branding in China." *Global Media and Communication* 1, no.2 (2005): 185–201.

---

1   The NGO is a community based organization that has been operating in the slums for almost 20 years. The NGO is working towards various children's rights goals including equal opportunity education for girls, free primary schooling, and supporting children's nutrition and health programs.

2   Didi literally means "elder sister" in Urdu, Hindi and Bengali, but it is also widely used in courteous address to unrelated women, sometimes also emphasizing a difference in social status.

3   Pseudonyms for all youth participants have been used throughout the chapter, and all identifying markers have been removed.

4   "Look, look, the *tanawala* is using a mobile!"

5   "Hold the mobile correctly!"

List of Authors

Kabita Chakraborty is an Assistant Professor at York University in Toronto, Canada. Her key areas of research are youth culture in slum communities in South Asia; young people's experiences of migration in Asia-Pacific; young women's sexual and reproductive health in South and Southeast Asia; participatory methods with children and youth, and problematizing international children's rights discourses. She is an honorary research fellow at the Gender Studies Programme, University of Malaya in Kuala Lumpur, Malaysia. Her forthcoming book "Young Muslim Women in India: Bollywood, Identity and Changing Lives" will be published by Routledge.

Maitrayee Chaudhuri is with the Centre for the Study of Social Systems, Jawaharlal Nehru University (JNU), New Delhi, India. She is currently Chairperson of the Centre and was earlier the Director of the Centre for Women's Studies in JNU. She has written widely in the areas of gender, media and on disciplinary and pedagogic questions pertaining to sociology. Among her published works are: "The Indian Women's Movement: Reform and Revival" (1993); "Feminism in India" (2005); "The Practice of Sociology and Sociology in India: Intellectual and Institutional Practices" (2003). Her forthcoming book is "Recasting India: Gender, Media and Public Discourse".

Urmila Goel is a social and cultural anthropologist and author based in Berlin, Germany. Her research interests are migration, racism, heteronormativity and intersectionality. She conducts her research mostly among those marked as Indians in German-speaking Europe and has published extensively in this area. More information can be found on her website www.urmila.de.

Thomas K. Gugler graduated in South Asian Studies, Religious Studies and Psychology from Ludwig Maximilian University in Munich and did his Ph.D. in Islamic Studies at the University of Erfurt. He was a Research Fellow at the Zentrum Moderner Orient in Berlin (2006–2009) and at the Department for Near Eastern Studies, University of Vienna, Austria. He is currently working on "Plurality and Culture in Contemporary South Asia" within the Cluster of

Excellence "Religion & Politics" at the Centre for Islamic Theology, University of Muenster, Germany. He regularly contributes articles to "Gigi – Zeitschrift für sexuelle Emanzipation", his monographs include "Ozeanisches Gefühl der Unsterblichkeit" (2009) and "Mission Medina" (2011).

Jesna Jayachandran is currently associated with the Department of Sociology, Guru Nanak Dev University, India. She completed her doctoral research in Sociology from Jawaharlal Nehru University, New Delhi, India. She recently co-authored a chapter on "Theory and Methods in Sociology" with Maitrayee Chaudhuri (2013), in Yogendra Singh (ed.). ICSSR Research Surveys and Explorations: Indian Sociology, Vol I, New Delhi: Oxford University Press. Some of her chapters in print are on reflections from an exploration to unravel news making in the Arab Gulf and on intercepting religion in the Gulf news beat. Her areas of research interest are media-society interface, culture and pedagogy.

Nadja-Christina Schneider has a background in South Asian Studies, Islamic Studies and Modern History. At the Institute of Asian and African Studies at Humboldt University Berlin, she is currently responsible for the Cross-Sectional Department Mediality and Intermediality in Asian and African Societies. Her main area of research is in the interrelationship between processes of medialisation and sociocultural change in India. She has also worked and published extensively on debates about Religion, Gender and Personal Laws in India.

Fritzi-Marie Titzmann received her PhD from Humboldt University Berlin, with a dissertation on the Indian Online Matrimonial Market. Her research focuses on gender, new media and social change in India with particular interest in digital phenomena. Recent publications include "Changing Patterns of Matchmaking: The Indian Online Matrimonial Market" (2013), "Medialisation and Social Change. The Indian Online Matrimonial Market as a New Field of Research" (2011), and "Matchmaking 2.0: The Representation of Women and Female Agency in the Indian Online Matrimonial Market" (2011). She is a faculty member at the Institute of Indology and Central Asian Studies at Leipzig University, Germany.

Maren Wilger is an M.A. student of Modern South and Southeast Asian Studies at Humboldt University Berlin. She has been working as a Student Assistant for the Department for Southeast Asian History and Society since 2009 and is the co-editor of a working paper on Death in South- and Southeast Asia (B. Baumann, S. Hoffmann, M. Wilger [eds]. Der Tod im Kulturvergleich. Süd- und Südostasiatische Perpektiven (2013)). Her forthcoming publications include an article in a volume titled "Ghost Movies in Southeast Asia and Beyond", edited by Peter Bräunlein. Her research interests include South and Southeast Asian pop, film and queer culture; information technologies and media in cross-cultural comparison.

KOMMUNIKATIONSWISSENSCHAFT

Band 1 Karsten Weber: Das Recht auf Informationszugang. Begründungs-Muster der politischen Philosophie für informationelle Grundversorgung und Eingriffsfreiheit. 352 Seiten. ISBN 978-3-86596-011-5

Band 2 Joachim R. Höflich & Maren Hartmann (eds.): Mobile Communication in Everyday Life: Ethnographic Views, Observations and Reflections. 326 Seiten. ISBN 978-3-86596-041-2

Band 3 Christoph Gehrmann, Katharina Müller: (Nah)Sprechen – (Fern)Sehen: Kommunikativer Alltag in der DDR. Wandel dörflicher Gemeinschaften unter dem Einfluss technischer und gesellschaftlicher Veränderungen: Eine Studie zur Umgestaltung des kommunikativen Alltags am Beispiel eines Dorfes in Thüringen. 258 Seiten. ISBN 978-3-86596-099-3

Band 4 Maren Hartmann/Patrick Rössler/Joachim R. Höflich (eds.): After the Mobile Phone? Social Changes and the Development of Mobile Communication. 226 Seiten. ISBN 978-3-86596-167-9

Band 5 Selina Ingold: Showbühne der Selbstdarstellung. Social-Web-Nutzung von Musikschaffenden am Beispiel MySpace. 326 Seiten. ISBN 978-3-86596-455-7

Band 6 Nadja-Christina Schneider/Fritzi Titzmann (eds.): Studying Youth, Media and Gender in Post-Liberalisation India. Focus on and beyond the 'Delhi Gang Rape'. 218 Seiten. ISBN 978-3-86596-535-6

Frank & Timme

Verlag für wissenschaftliche Literatur